MRCGP PRACTICE PAPERS MCQs and EMQs Second edition

MRCGP
PRACTICE PAPERS
MCQs and EMQs
Second edition

Edited and compiled
by

PETER ELLIS
MA MMedEd MRCGP

Medical and Educational Advisor, London
Previously General Practitioner, Trainer,
Course Organizer and Examiner
Royal College of General Practitioners

PETER G ELLIOTT
BSc MBChB MRCGP DRCOG

Examiner, Royal College of General Practitioners
Course Organizer
Clwyd North Vocational Training Scheme

Knutsford
Cheshire
Telephone: 01565 752000

First edition 1993
Second edition 1999
Reprinted 2000

ISBN: 1 901198 29 4

A catalogue record for this book is available from the British Library.

Typeset by **EDITEXT**, Charlesworth, Derbyshire (01457 857622)
Printed by MFP Design and Print, Stretford, Manchester

CONTENTS

INTRODUCTION

The membership examination of the Royal College of General Practitioners is a constantly changing animal, and in the past it contained Multiple Choice Question papers, Modified Essay Question papers, Traditional Essay Questions and Practice Topic Questions.

The MRCGP Examination is now a modular examination consisting of four modules:

1. Paper 1 — the examiner-marked paper
2. Paper 2 — the machine-marked paper
3. An assessment of consulting skills
4. Oral examination.

To be successful in the MRCGP examination candidates must pass all four modules. There is a credit accumulation system and the modules can be taken together or at different sessions and can be taken in any order. This book is about the machine-marked written paper, Paper 2, available twice a year.

The machine-marked paper is designed to test the knowledge and application of that knowledge by candidates. The paper contains Multiple Choice Questions (MCQs) and Extended Matching Questions (EMQs). The MCQs are designed to assess knowledge and the EMQs are aimed at assessing the application of knowledge. The paper lasts for three hours. In that time candidates will usually be required to answer a maximum of 400 true/false items of the MCQ type and 100 questions of the problem-solving EMQ type. All answers are recorded by candidates on sheets that can be machine-marked.

There is no negative marking and so there is no point in leaving a question blank when you do not know the answer. It pays to guess! Questions are machine scored on a basis of +1 mark for a correct answer and 0 for a wrong or missed response.

This book contains five practice papers, each of 400 MCQ-type items and 100 EMQ-type items. The items are laid out in the same format as the MRCGP examination. We have, however, added check boxes alongside each item to facilitate a system of self-assessment for those who wish to evaluate their knowledge upon completion of each practice paper.

We wish to express thanks to PasTest for their help with this book.

P. Ellis, 1999

EXAM PREPARATION AND TECHNIQUE

In trying to pass any examination it helps to plan an effective revision programme that concentrates on the elements that are being examined and not the areas that the exam cannot or does not test.

There are certain basic principles that are relevant to each part of the MRCGP exam.

- **Read relevant literature**
  Remember that this is an examination of British general practice. You will gain far more from reading a book about the consultation than from reading about ENT or ophthalmology, etc. in a textbook.

- **Ask yourself WHY?**
  The exam asks you to appraise critically what you are doing. After every consultation ask yourself about the outcome: did you feel happy about it, do you think the patient was satisfied with your management? If not, why not, and how could you have managed the situation better. After every article you read, ask yourself why the article was written, whether it was relevant, what the main points were that the author was trying to get across, and were there better ways of achieving the same result? Be critical in a constructive way about your work and your reading.

- **Form an alliance with other candidates**
  By meeting on a regular basis you can stimulate one another to be more critical. You can also divide the onerous task of ploughing through journals between the group and become very much more knowledgeable very quickly. Finally, by talking to colleagues you will retain more factual knowledge and also be able to clarify your ideas and opinions more clearly.

There are also specific techniques that will help you to prepare for the machine-marked paper. It is often thought that you cannot improve your score in machine-marked examinations by repeatedly doing tests. We do not think that this is true. Candidates who do not improve their scores are using practice papers in the wrong way. What normally happens is that a candidate will spend a lot of time reading textbooks and then do a practice examination. It is far better to do an examination first, and then spend a lot of time reading around the answers and extending your knowledge in this way. Even with good teaching notes you still need to read around the topic.

There are only a limited number of areas relevant to general practice on which machine-marked questions can be set and by doing a number of practice examinations in this way you can substantially increase your knowledge base and thus increase your overall score.

On Examination Day

By the time the day of the examination arrives you will certainly have invested a good deal of money, and probably a lot of time and effort in the exam. It is important that you do not blow it all on the day by making silly mistakes. Again there are certain basic rules for approaching each part of the MRCGP.

- **Do not be tired**
  This may sound simple but if you have nights on call in the three to four days before the examination, then swap them. Try to keep your workload to a minimum. If you arrive tired you will not cope well with several hours of written work.

- **Arrive in time**
  Every year, for both the written and oral examinations, candidates under-estimate the time it will take them to get to the examination venue. They arrive distressed and anxious and under these circumstances can never do themselves justice.

- **Key into the task**
  By arriving in plenty of time, you have the chance to prepare mentally for the examination. Reading a current journal quietly just before going into the exam will start your brain thinking about general practice and current issues. When you sit down to start working on the papers you will already be in the right frame of mind and this will save you valuable time.

- **Read the instructions**
  No matter how well you think you know the rules, always read the instructions at the beginning. There should be no changes from previous years but just in case there are, this is time well spent.

The majority of candidates will not be short of time in the machine-marked paper, however the following special techniques should help.

- Read the whole paper before you answer anything. This allows a lot of subconscious recall to happen before you start to mark your answers.
- Read every word in the stem and in each item. It is very easy to make simple mistakes by thinking that you read something that was not actually there.
- Mark the answer sheet carefully. Do not get the answer responses out of sequence. If you do have to alter a response rub it out well and mark the new response clearly. The answer sheets are marked by machine and an inadequately rubbed out answer could be interpreted as your true response.
- Answer every item. Remember there is NO negative marking and thus marks may be gained by guessing.

Finally, enjoy your study using this book, and good luck with the examination!

The Royal College of General Practitioners

SURNAME (Use block capitals)

INITIALS

INSTRUCTIONS	HOW TO MARK
✎ Use black lead pencil only (HB) ✎ Do NOT use ink or ballpoint pen ✎ Make heavy black marks that fill the lozenge completely ✎ Erase cleanly any answer you wish to change ✎ Make no stray marks on this sheet	Not like these: But like this:

ENTER CANDIDATE NUMBER HERE ☞

NOW SHOW THE NUMBER BY MARKING THE GRID ☞

0	0	0	0
1	1	1	1
2	2	2	2
3	3	3	3
4	4	4	4
5	5	5	5
6	6	6	6
7	7	7	7
8	8	8	8
9	9	9	9

☞ Each of the items in the first part of the question paper is either true or false. If you believe that the answer is true, you should fill in the T lozenge; if you believe that it is false, fill in the F lozenge.

☞ Enter your answers to items 1 to 150 on this side, then turn over and continue entering your answers on the other side. Your question paper may contain fewer than the 400 items allowed for this sheet.

1	T	F	31	T	F	61	T	F	91	T	F	121	T	F
2	T	F	32	T	F	62	T	F	92	T	F	122	T	F
3	T	F	33	T	F	63	T	F	93	T	F	123	T	F
4	T	F	34	T	F	64	T	F	94	T	F	124	T	F
5	T	F	35	T	F	65	T	F	95	T	F	125	T	F
6	T	F	36	T	F	66	T	F	96	T	F	126	T	F
7	T	F	37	T	F	67	T	F	97	T	F	127	T	F
8	T	F	38	T	F	68	T	F	98	T	F	128	T	F
9	T	F	39	T	F	69	T	F	99	T	F	129	T	F
10	T	F	40	T	F	70	T	F	100	T	F	130	T	F
11	T	F	41	T	F	71	T	F	101	T	F	131	T	F
12	T	F	42	T	F	72	T	F	102	T	F	132	T	F
13	T	F	43	T	F	73	T	F	103	T	F	133	T	F
14	T	F	44	T	F	74	T	F	104	T	F	134	T	F
15	T	F	45	T	F	75	T	F	105	T	F	135	T	F
16	T	F	46	T	F	76	T	F	106	T	F	136	T	F
17	T	F	47	T	F	77	T	F	107	T	F	137	T	F
18	T	F	48	T	F	78	T	F	108	T	F	138	T	F
19	T	F	49	T	F	79	T	F	109	T	F	139	T	F
20	T	F	50	T	F	80	T	F	110	T	F	140	T	F
21	T	F	51	T	F	81	T	F	111	T	F	141	T	F
22	T	F	52	T	F	82	T	F	112	T	F	142	T	F
23	T	F	53	T	F	83	T	F	113	T	F	143	T	F
24	T	F	54	T	F	84	T	F	114	T	F	144	T	F
25	T	F	55	T	F	85	T	F	115	T	F	145	T	F
26	T	F	56	T	F	86	T	F	116	T	F	146	T	F
27	T	F	57	T	F	87	T	F	117	T	F	147	T	F
28	T	F	58	T	F	88	T	F	118	T	F	148	T	F
29	T	F	59	T	F	89	T	F	119	T	F	149	T	F
30	T	F	60	T	F	90	T	F	120	T	F	150	T	F

Designed and printed by The Test Agency Ltd., Cray House Henley RG9 4AE Tel +44 (0) 1491 413413

Sample computer sheet for MCQs, reproduced by kind permission of the Royal College of General Practitioners. The design of this sheet may change without notice.

The Royal College of General Practitioners

SURNAME (Use block capitals)

INITIALS

EXTENDED MATCHING QUESTIONS

☞ For each item, choose ONE and ONLY ONE option and complete the appropriate lozenge.

☞ Mark your answer following the instructions for marking on the answer sheet for the true-false items.

☞ The two answer sheets are processed separately; make sure you have entered your name and candidate number, and coded your number by marking the grid.

ENTER CANDIDATE NUMBER HERE ☞

NOW SHOW THE NUMBER BY MARKING THE GRID ☞

0	0	0	0
1	1	1	1
2	2	2	2
3	3	3	3
4	4	4	4
5	5	5	5
6	6	6	6
7	7	7	7
8	8	8	8
9	9	9	9

1	A	B	C	D	E	F	G	H	I	J	K	L	M	N	O	P	Q	R	S	T	U
2	A	B	C	D	E	F	G	H	I	J	K	L	M	N	O	P	Q	R	S	T	U
3	A	B	C	D	E	F	G	H	I	J	K	L	M	N	O	P	Q	R	S	T	U
4	A	B	C	D	E	F	G	H	I	J	K	L	M	N	O	P	Q	R	S	T	U
5	A	B	C	D	E	F	G	H	I	J	K	L	M	N	O	P	Q	R	S	T	U
6	A	B	C	D	E	F	G	H	I	J	K	L	M	N	O	P	Q	R	S	T	U
7	A	B	C	D	E	F	G	H	I	J	K	L	M	N	O	P	Q	R	S	T	U
8	A	B	C	D	E	F	G	H	I	J	K	L	M	N	O	P	Q	R	S	T	U
9	A	B	C	D	E	F	G	H	I	J	K	L	M	N	O	P	Q	R	S	T	U
10	A	B	C	D	E	F	G	H	I	J	K	L	M	N	O	P	Q	R	S	T	U
11	A	B	C	D	E	F	G	H	I	J	K	L	M	N	O	P	Q	R	S	T	U
12	A	B	C	D	E	F	G	H	I	J	K	L	M	N	O	P	Q	R	S	T	U
13	A	B	C	D	E	F	G	H	I	J	K	L	M	N	O	P	Q	R	S	T	U
14	A	B	C	D	E	F	G	H	I	J	K	L	M	N	O	P	Q	R	S	T	U
15	A	B	C	D	E	F	G	H	I	J	K	L	M	N	O	P	Q	R	S	T	U
16	A	B	C	D	E	F	G	H	I	J	K	L	M	N	O	P	Q	R	S	T	U
17	A	B	C	D	E	F	G	H	I	J	K	L	M	N	O	P	Q	R	S	T	U
18	A	B	C	D	E	F	G	H	I	J	K	L	M	N	O	P	Q	R	S	T	U
19	A	B	C	D	E	F	G	H	I	J	K	L	M	N	O	P	Q	R	S	T	U
20	A	B	C	D	E	F	G	H	I	J	K	L	M	N	O	P	Q	R	S	T	U
21	A	B	C	D	E	F	G	H	I	J	K	L	M	N	O	P	Q	R	S	T	U
22	A	B	C	D	E	F	G	H	I	J	K	L	M	N	O	P	Q	R	S	T	U
23	A	B	C	D	E	F	G	H	I	J	K	L	M	N	O	P	Q	R	S	T	U
24	A	B	C	D	E	F	G	H	I	J	K	L	M	N	O	P	Q	R	S	T	U
25	A	B	C	D	E	F	G	H	I	J	K	L	M	N	O	P	Q	R	S	T	U
26	A	B	C	D	E	F	G	H	I	J	K	L	M	N	O	P	Q	R	S	T	U
27	A	B	C	D	E	F	G	H	I	J	K	L	M	N	O	P	Q	R	S	T	U
28	A	B	C	D	E	F	G	H	I	J	K	L	M	N	O	P	Q	R	S	T	U
29	A	B	C	D	E	F	G	H	I	J	K	L	M	N	O	P	Q	R	S	T	U
30	A	B	C	D	E	F	G	H	I	J	K	L	M	N	O	P	Q	R	S	T	U
31	A	B	C	D	E	F	G	H	I	J	K	L	M	N	O	P	Q	R	S	T	U
32	A	B	C	D	E	F	G	H	I	J	K	L	M	N	O	P	Q	R	S	T	U
33	A	B	C	D	E	F	G	H	I	J	K	L	M	N	O	P	Q	R	S	T	U
34	A	B	C	D	E	F	G	H	I	J	K	L	M	N	O	P	Q	R	S	T	U
35	A	B	C	D	E	F	G	H	I	J	K	L	M	N	O	P	Q	R	S	T	U
36	A	B	C	D	E	F	G	H	I	J	K	L	M	N	O	P	Q	R	S	T	U
37	A	B	C	D	E	F	G	H	I	J	K	L	M	N	O	P	Q	R	S	T	U
38	A	B	C	D	E	F	G	H	I	J	K	L	M	N	O	P	Q	R	S	T	U
39	A	B	C	D	E	F	G	H	I	J	K	L	M	N	O	P	Q	R	S	T	U
40	A	B	C	D	E	F	G	H	I	J	K	L	M	N	O	P	Q	R	S	T	U

Designed and printed by The Test Agency Ltd., Cray House Henley RG9 4AE Tel +44 (0) 1491 413413

Sample computer sheet for EMQs, reproduced by kind permission of the Royal College of General Practitioners. The design of this sheet may change without notice.

PRACTICE PAPER 1 — SECTION 1: MCQs

Total time allowed for sections 1 and 2 is three hours. Section 1 has 400 items, section 2 has 100. Indicate your answers clearly by putting a tick or cross in the box alongside each answer or by writing the appropriate letter in Section 2.

The following are criteria to be fulfilled in a screening programme:

- ☐ 1 the condition must be important
- ☐ 2 clinical examination is not necessary
- ☐ 3 treatment at all stages of the disease is possible
- ☐ 4 there is a recognisable latent or early symptomatic stage
- ☐ 5 there must be an agreed policy on who should be screened and treated

The following are true of hyperthyroidism:

- ☐ 6 the majority of cases are due to Graves' disease
- ☐ 7 toxic multinodular goitre is accompanied by raised TSH levels
- ☐ 8 block-replacement regimes are the treatment of choice for toxic adenomata
- ☐ 9 Graves' ophthalmopathy is more prevalent in smokers
- ☐ 10 post-partum thyroiditis typically has a thyrotoxic phase followed by a hypothyroid phase

A practice leaflet must include the following information in order to comply with the 1990 contract:

- ☐ 11 the age or date of birth of the doctors
- ☐ 12 the date of first registration of the practice nurse
- ☐ 13 the fees the practice charges for reports and certificates
- ☐ 14 whether the practice is computerized
- ☐ 15 the means by which disabled patients may gain access to the building

The following drugs are associated with sexual dysfunction:

- ☐ 16 clomipramine
- ☐ 17 propranolol
- ☐ 18 indomethacin
- ☐ 19 chlorpromazine
- ☐ 20 prednisolone

Concerning basal cell carcinoma

☐ 21 it is the most common skin malignancy
☐ 22 it occurs at sites of maximum skin exposure
☐ 23 it typically starts as a small ulcer
☐ 24 crusting of the lesion indicates another diagnosis
☐ 25 it is more common in those with freckles

A 45-year-old male presents with a history of long term alcohol abuse, the following would be true if he had alcoholic cirrhosis:

☐ 26 absence of jaundice excludes the diagnosis
☐ 27 spider naevi are rare
☐ 28 pain over the liver is a frequent finding
☐ 29 testicular atrophy is common
☐ 30 prognosis is unaffected by cessation of alcohol once cirrhosis has developed

A patient presents at 32 weeks' gestation with a primary attack of genital herpes, the following are true:

☐ 31 transplacental spread of the virus is rare
☐ 32 acyclovir orally has been shown to be teratogenic
☐ 33 if herpes lesions are present at the onset of labour, caesarean section is indicated
☐ 34 pregnant women are more resistant to herpes than non-pregnant women
☐ 35 recurrent herpes carries the same risk to the fetus as a primary infection

Concerning the prescribing of antibiotics

☐ 36 in acute otitis media, most children are pain free within 24 hours only if given antibiotics
☐ 37 sinus pain is greatly reduced
☐ 38 it increases the patients' intention to consult on a future occasion
☐ 39 patients' expectations are important

Concerning Henoch–Schönlein purpura

☐ 40 there is typically a preceding upper respiratory tract infection
☐ 41 associated arthritis typically affects small joints of the hands and feet
☐ 42 arthritis lasts for an average of six weeks
☐ 43 haematuria occurs in the majority of cases
☐ 44 biopsy of skin lesions shows a characteristic appearance

The following treatments have been shown to be of benefit in the treatment of cyclical breast pain:

☐ 45 pyridoxine
☐ 46 diuretics
☐ 47 tamoxifen
☐ 48 gamolenic acid
☐ 49 hormone replacement therapy

A 23-year-old patient presents with disturbed behaviour, the following are diagnostic of schizophrenia:

☐ 50 paranoid delusions
☐ 51 thoughts being inserted into the patient's mind
☐ 52 voices in the third person commenting on the patient's actions
☐ 53 visual hallucinations
☐ 54 ideas of reference

The following diseases are notifiable to the district community physician:

☐ 55 malaria
☐ 56 rubella
☐ 57 chicken pox
☐ 58 AIDS
☐ 59 mumps

The differential diagnosis of a single ulcer occurring in the mouth should include

☐ 60 aphthous ulcer
☐ 61 lichen planus
☐ 62 primary syphilis
☐ 63 agranulocytosis
☐ 64 Behçet's disease

Concerning Section 47 of the National Assistance Act

☐ 65 it allows removal of a patient from his home for a maximum of three weeks
☐ 66 applications must be made to a magistrate
☐ 67 the applicant must be the patient's General Practitioner
☐ 68 if admitted to hospital the patient may be treated without consent
☐ 69 the majority of those detained are below 65 years of age

A 14-year-old girl presents with symptoms of an eating disorder, the following would support that diagnosis:

☐ 70 loss of pubic hair
☐ 71 primary amenorrhoea
☐ 72 raised LH levels
☐ 73 raised ESR
☐ 74 low cortisol levels

Concerning emergency contraception

☐ 75 an intrauterine contraceptive device must be inserted within three days of coitus to be effective
☐ 76 insertion of an intrauterine contraceptive device has been shown to be more effective than hormonal methods
☐ 77 failed hormonal contraception is an indication for termination of pregnancy on the grounds of teratogenic risk
☐ 78 established breast feeding is a contraindication to hormonal post-coital contraception
☐ 79 surveys have shown that approximately 50% of women are unaware of post-coital methods of contraception

In bowel obstruction

☐ 80 colicky abdominal pain is characteristically the earliest symptom
☐ 81 passing flatus after the onset of pain casts doubt on the diagnosis
☐ 82 if the site of obstruction is in the distal large bowel, vomiting is a late feature
☐ 83 visible peristalsis is diagnostic of obstruction
☐ 84 bowel sounds are typically described as borborygmi

A child attends for the third time with a five week history of cough without malaise which has not responded to symptomatic remedies

☐ 85 chest X-ray is mandatory
☐ 86 a trial of bronchodilators is indicated
☐ 87 this is a typical presentation of pertussis
☐ 88 inhaled foreign bodies present in this way
☐ 89 a trial of antibiotics is indicated

In the literature about general practice consultations

☐ 90 Balint looked at doctors' personalities
☐ 91 Pendleton suggests that most important information is given as the patient is leaving
☐ 92 Neighbour describes 'safety-netting' to deal with feelings left over by one consultation before starting another
☐ 93 patient satisfaction is improved by longer consultations
☐ 94 Eric Berne described 'doctor-centred' and 'patient-centred' consultations
☐ 95 Pendleton suggests a task of choosing appropriate action for each problem presented

Concerning osteoarthritis

☐ 96 it shows a familial tendency
☐ 97 it is more common in overweight people
☐ 98 the picture of radiological damage correlates closely with the clinical condition
☐ 99 if a diagnosis of early osteoarthritis is made, joint exercise should be severely restricted
☐ 100 it is most common in the hips

A 45-year-old man presents with hearing loss; the following would support a diagnosis of it being noise-induced:

☐ 101 a conductive deafness
☐ 102 predominantly low frequency loss
☐ 103 recruitment
☐ 104 no response to a hearing aid
☐ 105 acute onset of hearing loss in one ear

Your practice has a high proportion of shiftworkers, research has shown that

☐ 106 the majority of shiftworkers dislike nightwork
☐ 107 they have an increased incidence of industrial accidents
☐ 108 they have an increased cardiovascular mortality
☐ 109 they have an increased incidence of peptic ulceration
☐ 110 there is an increase in feelings of paranoia

Concerning solvent abuse

☐ 111 it is typically an activity of males rather than females
☐ 112 deaths are associated with the presence of aerosol propellants (freons)
☐ 113 persistent cerebellar signs are suggestive of prolonged use
☐ 114 the majority of abusers will stop within six months of starting the habit
☐ 115 the occurrence of visual hallucinations would suggest other psychopathology

The following are true of primary nocturnal enuresis in childhood:

☐ 116 the majority of children are dry throughout the night by the age of three years
☐ 117 if associated with daytime wetting is more likely to be associated with organic disease
☐ 118 pad and buzzer alarms become a more effective treatment in the child who is wet after the age of 10 years
☐ 119 persistence into adult life occurs in less than 1% of patients
☐ 120 repeatedly lifting a child during the night has been shown to be as effective as drug therapy

The following items are available on an FP10:

☐ 121 pen insulin injection devices
☐ 122 click count syringes for the visually impaired
☐ 123 finger pricking devices
☐ 124 glucose tablets
☐ 125 blood pricking lancets

Withdrawal of corticosteroids is typically associated with

☐ 126 conjunctivitis
☐ 127 hypertension
☐ 128 loss of weight
☐ 129 arthritis
☐ 130 painful itchy skin nodules

A higher rate night visit fee is paid for the following:

☐ 131 you have a rota with another single-handed General Practitioner and he performs a visit on your patient
☐ 132 if a visit is received at 0745 and made at 0805
☐ 133 a patient telephones you at 0700 and you meet them at your surgery at 0755
☐ 134 your local community hospital calls you to see one of your patients in the casualty department at 0300
☐ 135 a patient calls you to attend a threatened miscarriage at 0100

Concerning epidemiology of chronic bronchitis

☐ 136 Northern Ireland has the highest mortality rate for chronic bronchitis in the world
☐ 137 more than 15% of males between 40–60 years have been shown to have evidence of chronic bronchitis
☐ 138 chronic bronchitis accounts for more lost time from work than any other illness
☐ 139 the disease is more prevalent in urban than in rural areas

Concerning tinnitus

☐ 140 it is typically associated with conductive deafness
☐ 141 it is associated with gout
☐ 142 it has been shown to be due to a carotid bruit in some cases
☐ 143 treatment of associated depression is rarely helpful
☐ 144 cochlear nerve section is associated with a worsening of the noise

In questionnaire design

☐ 145 open and closed questions are best not combined in one questionnaire
☐ 146 if a questionnaire is valid, then patients generally give the same answers if they complete it a second time
☐ 147 comprehensibility indicates that almost all areas in a subject have been addressed
☐ 148 a Likert scale is often used to assess attitudes
☐ 149 open questions are easy to analyse

When considering gastric and duodenal ulceration

☐ 150 night pain is more common with duodenal ulcers
☐ 151 a gastric ulcer is more likely to bleed
☐ 152 *Helicobacter pylori* is found in over 90% of patients with duodenal ulcer
☐ 153 a positive family history is common for both sites
☐ 154 a recent survey has shown that of patients over 40 years of age presenting with dyspepsia for the first time the majority will have a malignancy

Carcinoma of the bladder

☐ 155 typically presents with haematuria
☐ 156 incidence is increasing in women
☐ 157 is associated with cigarette smoking
☐ 158 if superficial, the majority will not recur within five years if treated by cystodiathermy
☐ 159 is associated with previous abuse of alcohol

The following features would suggest a cerebral infarct rather than a cerebral haemorrhage:

- ☐ 160 bilateral extensor plantar responses
- ☐ 161 a previous transient ischaemic attack
- ☐ 162 co-existing cardiac disease
- ☐ 163 consciousness impaired 24 hours after the onset of the event
- ☐ 164 abrupt onset accompanied by vomiting

The following are at an increased risk of chronic open-angled glaucoma:

- ☐ 165 extremely long-sighted patients
- ☐ 166 diabetics
- ☐ 167 relatives of patients with glaucoma
- ☐ 168 patients over 65 years of age
- ☐ 169 those with astigmatism

An unexplained finding of thrombocytopenia on a routine full blood count would be explained by

- ☐ 170 inadequate mixing of the sample
- ☐ 171 polyarteritis nodosa
- ☐ 172 systemic lupus erythematosus (SLE)
- ☐ 173 intercurrent viral infection
- ☐ 174 treatment with dipyridamole

The following are risk factors for increased mortality in an elderly patient with a chest infection:

- ☐ 175 co-existing atrial fibrillation
- ☐ 176 a very low white cell count
- ☐ 177 hypotension
- ☐ 178 recent influenza vaccine
- ☐ 179 confusion

The following statements have been shown to be true of lipid-lowering drugs:

- ☐ 180 cholestyramine is allowed in pregnancy and breast feeding
- ☐ 181 simvastatin is associated with sleep disturbance
- ☐ 182 the flushing induced by nicotinic acid is typically improved by low-dose aspirin
- ☐ 183 regular monitoring of liver function tests is necessary on treatment with bezafibrate
- ☐ 184 none of the available agents is licensed for use in children

General Practitioners

- ☐ 185 are responsible for any errors made by their practice nurse
- ☐ 186 are responsible for care of their patients at all times
- ☐ 187 are obliged to order any drug (that does not appear on the black list) for the treatment of a patient on a NHS prescription form
- ☐ 188 are responsible for errors made by a spouse when answering the telephone
- ☐ 189 have complaints made against them most often because of failure to refer to hospital

Concerning a 25-year-old patient presenting with a history of heavy periods

- ☐ 190 approximately half the patients who complain of heavy periods have a measurably normal menstrual loss
- ☐ 191 dysfunctional uterine bleeding is usually caused by fibroids
- ☐ 192 mefenamic acid reduces bleeding by an average of 25%
- ☐ 193 dilatation and curettage is indicated in all patients
- ☐ 194 endometrial ablation can be performed using laser treatment

The following may be associated with a diagnosis of retinal detachment:

- ☐ 195 myopia
- ☐ 196 previous cataract surgery
- ☐ 197 normal distance vision
- ☐ 198 black spots in front of the eyes
- ☐ 199 co-existing diabetic retinopathy

Subarachnoid haemorrhage in the over 65-year-olds

- ☐ 200 only accounts for approximately 5% of all cases
- ☐ 201 is typically due to a ruptured atherosclerotic blood vessel
- ☐ 202 characteristically presents with headache
- ☐ 203 has a decreased mortality in comparison with younger patients
- ☐ 204 has a worse prognosis in hypertensive patients

The following drugs have been shown to decrease mortality after a myocardial infarction:

- ☐ 205 captopril
- ☐ 206 timolol
- ☐ 207 isosorbide mononitrate
- ☐ 208 nifedipine
- ☐ 209 streptokinase

A patient visiting this country from Australia is involved in a road traffic accident. Immediate and follow up care is necessary. Which of the following statements are true?

- ☐ 210 immediate and necessary care is provided by the NHS free of charge
- ☐ 211 all follow-up care is private
- ☐ 212 all prescriptions issued must be private
- ☐ 213 domiciliary nursing is provided on the same basis as to UK residents
- ☐ 214 a fee can be charged for attending the patient at the road traffic accident

Constitutional delay in puberty is associated with the following:

- ☐ 215 boys are more often affected than girls
- ☐ 216 bone age on X-ray examination corresponds to chronological age
- ☐ 217 gonadotrophins are typically raised
- ☐ 218 a family history of delayed puberty or menarche

When considering breast feeding

- ☐ 219 the duration of early feeds should be limited
- ☐ 220 both breasts must be used at each feed
- ☐ 221 poor positioning of the baby is the most common cause of nipple pain
- ☐ 222 terminating feeding prematurely from one breast will decrease the nutritional value of the feed
- ☐ 223 late onset sore nipples are typically due to thrush
- ☐ 224 breast feeding is associated with an increase in the incidence of breast cancer in later life

When considering statistical bias in a scientific paper

- ☐ 225 retrospective studies are generally more open to bias than prospective studies
- ☐ 226 subjective results are more prone to bias than objective studies
- ☐ 227 standardization decreases bias
- ☐ 228 stratified sampling causes more bias than random sampling
- ☐ 229 control groups are essential to decrease bias
- ☐ 230 random numbers are preferable to regular samples

The following factors would suggest an increased risk of suicide in depressed patients:

- ☐ 231 co-existing problems of alcohol abuse
- ☐ 232 history of aggressive behaviour
- ☐ 233 co-existing chronic physical illness
- ☐ 234 living in a rural environment
- ☐ 235 married status

Concerning patients with backache

- ☐ 236 a specific diagnosis is usually possible
- ☐ 237 10% of patients can be expected to have a recurrence of pain within the next 4 years
- ☐ 238 about 5 million days are lost from work each year because of back pain
- ☐ 239 about 1 in 5 of all new orthopaedic referrals from GPs are for patients with back pain
- ☐ 240 history and examination are more important than investigations in management decisions in back pain
- ☐ 241 about 90% of patients with mechanical back pain will recover within 6 weeks

An adult patient who is otherwise well complains of hair loss all over the scalp. The following are possible causes:

- ☐ 242 iron deficiency
- ☐ 243 scalp ringworm
- ☐ 244 anticoagulant therapy
- ☐ 245 alopecia areata
- ☐ 246 trichotillomania

Concerning ectopic pregnancy

- ☐ 247 the frequency is increasing in the UK
- ☐ 248 ectopic pregnancies secrete lower levels of HCG (human chorionic gonadotrophin) than a corresponding uterine gestation
- ☐ 249 ultrasound alone is diagnostic in the majority of cases
- ☐ 250 there is a positive association with the presence of an IUCD in the uterine cavity
- ☐ 251 the death rate is increasing in the UK

When treating an uncomplicated urinary tract infection in a pregnant patient the following drugs are considered to be free from any adverse affect on the pregnancy:

☐ 252 trimethoprim
☐ 253 nitrofurantoin
☐ 254 amoxycillin
☐ 255 ciprofloxacin
☐ 256 cephalexin

Pompholyx

☐ 257 is a contact dermatitis
☐ 258 characteristically occurs on the soles of the feet and the palms of the hands
☐ 259 is unresponsive to topical steroids
☐ 260 is associated with atopic conditions
☐ 261 is typically itchy

When considering ovarian cancer

☐ 262 it is more common in multiparous women
☐ 263 there is an increased incidence if a first degree relative has had the disease
☐ 264 the overall five-year survival is greater than 50%
☐ 265 the majority of patients present with abnormal vaginal bleeding
☐ 266 protection afforded by the combined oral contraceptive is proportional to the duration of usage

Cognitive behaviour therapy

☐ 267 concentrates on negative patterns of thinking
☐ 268 is suitable for marital and sexual problems
☐ 269 is of benefit in eating disorders
☐ 270 patients who abuse substances have been shown to benefit
☐ 271 chronic pain is unresponsive to treatment by this method

Plasma monitoring has been shown to be of value in the treatment of epilepsy with the following drugs:

☐ 272 primidone
☐ 273 ethosuximide
☐ 274 sodium valproate
☐ 275 vigabatrin
☐ 276 clonazepam

Concerning faecal occult blood testing

☐ 277 it fulfils Wilson's criteria for a screening test
☐ 278 in screening programmes the majority of positive stool samples are false positives
☐ 279 with a three-day test the sensitivity for colonic carcinoma is over 90%
☐ 280 the test is more sensitive for caecal tumours than for sigmoid tumours
☐ 281 banana ingestion has been shown to cause false positives

In diabetic retinopathy

☐ 282 it typically starts in the peripheral retina
☐ 283 it is the most common cause of blindness in those under 65 years of age
☐ 284 it typically responds to laser treatment
☐ 285 micro-aneurysms are a feature of background retinopathy
☐ 286 new vessel formation can occur on the conjunctiva

A one-year-old boy presents with an episode of unconsciousness during an episode of crying. The following would support a diagnosis of breath holding attack:

☐ 287 recovery within one minute
☐ 288 upturned eyes during the attack
☐ 289 drowsiness after the attack
☐ 290 extended tonic posture during the attack
☐ 291 cyanosis

Prolapsed intervertebral discs are associated with

- ☐ 292 a positive femoral stretch test with an L4–L5 lesion
- ☐ 293 pain in the muscles innervated by the damaged nerve root
- ☐ 294 an L2–L3 lesion, accompanied by an extensor plantar response
- ☐ 295 loss of bladder function
- ☐ 296 loss of ankle reflex if L5–S1 root is compressed

In pseudomembranous colitis

- ☐ 297 it is typically associated with previous antibiotic therapy
- ☐ 298 *Yersinia* is the most commonly isolated organism
- ☐ 299 treatment with metronidazole has been shown to be effective
- ☐ 300 the passing of fresh blood in the stools is a characteristic feature
- ☐ 301 it is associated with an eosinophilia in the peripheral blood film

A patient with Alzheimer's disease is recognised to have the following signs and symptoms:

- ☐ 302 a preference for routine
- ☐ 303 a loss of long term memory
- ☐ 304 a loss of speech in the later stages
- ☐ 305 spatial disorientation
- ☐ 306 ataxia

In the management of non-insulin-dependent diabetes mellitus

- ☐ 307 metformin is associated with weight gain
- ☐ 308 sulphonylureas become less effective with time
- ☐ 309 tight blood sugar control is the goal of treatment in the elderly
- ☐ 310 the majority of newly diagnosed patients will show clinical evidence of retinopathy
- ☐ 311 the diet for overweight patients should contain approximately half the total calories as carbohydrate

A three-year-old child presents with rhinitis, sneezing and conjunctivitis typical of hay fever. The following treatments are approved for use in this age group:

- ☐ 312 ipratropium bromide nasal spray (Rinatec)
- ☐ 313 xylometazoline nasal drops
- ☐ 314 terfenadine suspension (Triludan)
- ☐ 315 azelastine nasal spray (Rhinolast)
- ☐ 316 sodium cromoglycate eye drops (Opticrom)

When investigating a patient for ischaemic heart disease

- ☐ 317 ST segment changes on a resting ECG indicate myocardial ischaemia
- ☐ 318 on exercise, testing the degree of ST depression at a given workload is of diagnostic relevance
- ☐ 319 exercise testing associated with a fall in blood pressure is of good prognostic significance
- ☐ 320 24-hour ambulatory monitoring shows a ratio of painless to painful ischaemia of 4:1
- ☐ 321 coronary angiography has significant morbidity in 5% of patients

Dupuytren's contracture

- ☐ 322 is typically painful
- ☐ 323 most commonly affects the ring finger
- ☐ 324 is associated with epilepsy
- ☐ 325 is typically seen in white men
- ☐ 326 is characteristically unilateral

Risk factors which increase the likelihood of congenital dislocation of the hip include

- ☐ 327 delivery by caesarean section
- ☐ 328 being first born
- ☐ 329 being male
- ☐ 330 having a positive family history
- ☐ 331 the left hip

The following have been shown to respond to placebos in clinical trials:

☐ 332 hyperlipidaemia
☐ 333 hay fever
☐ 334 blood glucose levels
☐ 335 blood pressure levels
☐ 336 post-operative pain

The following are true of heartsink patients:

☐ 337 the majority are women
☐ 338 they typically present with a single problem
☐ 339 they have higher referral rates than the average population
☐ 340 the average General Practitioner is able to identify more than 50 such patients on his list
☐ 341 they have significantly more social problems than the average population

When considering a diagnosis of phimosis in childhood

☐ 342 by 6 months of age approximately 50% of boys have a retractable foreskin
☐ 343 circumcision is associated with a higher complication rate than other childhood operative procedures
☐ 344 the inability to clean under the foreskin is associated with the development of cancer of the penis in adulthood
☐ 345 if untreated has been shown to lead to problems with sexual function in later life

Studies have shown that people in social class 5 have an increased incidence of the following conditions when compared with those in social class 1:

☐ 346 motor vehicle accidents
☐ 347 pneumonia
☐ 348 lung cancer

Glue ear is associated with

☐ 349 a peak incidence at approximately 7 years of age
☐ 350 an increased incidence of tympanosclerosis after grommet insertion
☐ 351 an increased incidence in winter and spring
☐ 352 an increased incidence in the children of smokers
☐ 353 spontaneous resolution within 12 months in over 90% of children

Sickle cell disease is associated with

☐ 354 priapism
☐ 355 impaired fertility in women
☐ 356 an increased incidence of stroke
☐ 357 gallstones in the majority of patients
☐ 358 an enlarged spleen after the first decade of life

Psoriatic arthropathy is associated with the following features:

☐ 359 a preceding history of skin lesions in the majority of patients
☐ 360 non-involvement of the distal interphalangeal joints
☐ 361 subcutaneous nodules
☐ 362 the presence of eye lesions in the majority of patients
☐ 363 the development of some evidence of joint involvement in the majority of patients with psoriasis

The following statements are true about jaundiced patients:

☐ 364 non-A–non-B hepatitis can be transmitted by drinking contaminated water
☐ 365 hepatitis B is associated with the development of hepatocellular carcinoma
☐ 366 acute cholangitis carries a mortality rate of about 40%
☐ 367 hepatitis A typically produces a carrier state following the acute infection

In patients with anorexia

☐ 368 hypercalcaemia is often seen
☐ 369 downy hair on the face and trunk can be a clinical feature
☐ 370 there is an abnormal attitude to body weight
☐ 371 there is loss of libido in men

An 80-year-old male patient has been complaining of feeling tired all the time and you have found no abnormality on examination. Following a range of investigations you can safely conclude that the results below are purely due to the effects of ageing

☐ 372 a serum sodium of 125 mmol/l
☐ 373 a serum urea of 9.5 mmol/l
☐ 374 a serum bilirubin of 22 mmol/l
☐ 375 a serum calcium of 2.0 mmol/l
☐ 376 a drop of 30 mmHg in systolic blood pressure on standing

The following are true about the epidemiology of AIDS:

☐ 377 the UK has the highest incidence in Europe
☐ 378 in the USA, AIDS is one of the top five causes of death
☐ 379 approximately 10 million people world wide are HIV positive
☐ 380 20% of UK AIDS cases are intravenous drug addicts
☐ 381 over 50% of HIV positive patients in Scotland are intravenous drug abusers

When considering symptoms due to a carcinoma of the colon at the time of presentation

☐ 382 pain occurs in the majority of patients with a right-sided lesion
☐ 383 a palpable mass is present in the majority of those with a lesion in the left colon
☐ 384 change in bowel habit is present with the majority of rectal lesions
☐ 385 the majority of right-sided lesions bleed
☐ 386 the majority of rectal lesions bleed

Dithranol

- ☐ 387 is indicated for rapidly spreading psoriatic lesions
- ☐ 388 in prolonged usage is associated with an increase in the incidence of skin malignancies
- ☐ 389 'short contact' therapy has been shown to be less effective than conventional treatment
- ☐ 390 is contraindicated if potent steroids have been used in the previous 14 days

After bereavement

- ☐ 391 grieving is abnormal if it lasts for more than 6 weeks
- ☐ 392 morbidity and mortality are raised for 2–3 years
- ☐ 393 20% of widowers die within the first year of bereavement
- ☐ 394 women are affected by post-bereavement mortality more than men
- ☐ 395 shock and blunted emotion is commonly the initial reaction

Febrile convulsions

- ☐ 396 have a prevalence of 2–5%
- ☐ 397 are typically associated with fevers due to bacterial infections
- ☐ 398 post-ictally are typically associated with transient neurological deficits
- ☐ 399 in a 3-year-old child who fails to respond to 5 mg rectal diazepam, the dose cannot be repeated for one hour
- ☐ 400 have a stronger family history than idiopathic epilepsy

Visual loss

Causes of visual loss, presenting to General Practitioners, include

A migraine
B central retinal vein occlusion
C senile macular degeneration
D optic neuritis
E retinal detachment
F vitreous haemorrhage

Choose the most appropriate of these causes for the following scenarios:

☐ 1 a 55-year-old woman wakes with blurred vision and develops a visual loss over the next few hours; ophthalmoscopy shows extensive retinal haemorrhages throughout the fundus

☐ 2 a 71-year-old retired publican develops a progressive loss of central vision with difficulty reading, but he has relatively preserved vision in the peripheral fields

☐ 3 a 44-year-old laboratory technician, who is very myopic, develops a rapidly progressive visual loss in part of the visual field; she describes the progression of sight loss as 'like a curtain' across her visual field

☐ 4 a 25-year-old housewife developed gradual loss of vision with mostly intact peripheral vision; the visual loss recovers but she mentions fairly intense eye pain which she describes as between her eye and her ear

☐ 5 a 42-year-old doctor has a sudden loss of vision with nausea; she makes a complete recovery within hours but mentions visual distortion and headache before the vision was lost

Depression

Treatments used in depression include

A amitriptyline
B carbamazepine
C lofepramine
D lithium
E phenelzine
F fluvoxamine

Match the appropriate treatment to the following statements:

- ☐ 6 patients are instructed not to eat cheese, pickled herring or broad bean pods
- ☐ 7 used in bipolar disease and epilepsy
- ☐ 8 a selective serotonin re-uptake inhibitor
- ☐ 9 a tricyclic drug with sedative properties
- ☐ 10 thyroid function should be monitored during treatment
- ☐ 11 one of the less sedative tricyclic antidepressants
- ☐ 12 is usually given in a dose of 140 mg daily, in a split dose

Social class

The Registrar General has six divisions of social class

A 1
B 2
C 3N
D 3M
E 4
F 5

Which social class is appropriate for the following:

- ☐ 13 a teacher
- ☐ 14 a labourer
- ☐ 15 a secretary
- ☐ 16 an electrician
- ☐ 17 one-third of the population is in this social class
- ☐ 18 a junior hospital doctor

Mental Health Act

The following are some sections of the Mental Health Act 1983:

A 2
B 3
C 4
D 7
E 136

Which section applies to the following situations?

- ☐ 19 used for assessment of a patient for a maximum period of 28 days
- ☐ 20 used for compulsory treatment of a patient with an established diagnosis
- ☐ 21 used for a maximum period of six months
- ☐ 22 used in relation to guardianship
- ☐ 23 used only in an emergency
- ☐ 24 used by the police

Child development

A 6 months
B 9 months
C 12 months
D 18 months
E 24 months

Children are seen at all ages in general practice. Certain skills are acquired by definite ages and there may be concern if these skills are not present. From the above list of ages, select the most appropriate age to indicate when the skills listed below will be acquired.

- ☐ 25 the child can build a 3–4 cube tower
- ☐ 26 the child can join 3 words making a simple sentence
- ☐ 27 the child has developed definite person preference
- ☐ 28 the child walks with one hand held
- ☐ 29 the child says 10–12 words with meaning
- ☐ 30 the child tolerates children playing alongside

Benefits

Welfare benefits received by patients include

A Attendance Allowance
B Severe Disablement Allowance
C Disability Living Allowance
D Incapacity Benefit
E Industrial Injury Disablement Benefit
F Exceptionally Severe Disablement Allowance

Match the following statements with the appropriate benefit:

☐ 31 a benefit to someone who needs help washing and dressing and toileting during the day only

☐ 32 a tax-free, non-means tested benefit payable to people under the age of 65 years

☐ 33 a benefit payable to people who are 80% or more disabled and are incapable of any work

☐ 34 a benefit paid to people over 65 years of age who require personal care or supervision during both the day and the night

☐ 35 this benefit may be paid to people between 5 and 65 years of age who are unable to walk

Paraesthesia and weakness

Paraesthesia and weakness in the lower limbs may be caused by

A meralgia paraesthesiae
B lateral popliteal nerve lesion
C peripheral neuropathy
D lumbar disc lesion
E subacute combined degeneration of the cord
F tabes dorsalis
G multiple sclerosis

Match the most appropriate diagnosis to the following clinical scenarios:

☐ 36 a 39-year-old bricklayer notices numbness of the outer border of his left foot with 'weakness' of his foot; examination reveals foot drop

☐ 37 a 42-year-old gardener complains of pain and pins and needles down the back of his left thigh and the lateral aspect of his left leg and foot

☐ 38 a 58-year-old unemployed man complains of shooting, sudden pain in his legs; he has an unsteady gait; at examination it is noted that his pupils are not responsive to light

☐ 39 a 48-year-old teacher complains of tight bands around her limbs; at examination she feels an 'electric shock' sensation down her legs when her neck is flexed

☐ 40 a 49-year-old policewoman complains of tingling on the outside aspect of her thigh; this can occur on sitting but seems worse on standing, though it disappears when she lies down

☐ 41 a 54-year-old historian, who has little medical history other than a gastrectomy in his twenties, presents with a numbness in his legs; examination reveals a 'stocking' sensory loss with extensor plantar responses.

Dermatology

The following words are commonly used in the description of skin conditions:

A crust
B scale
C macule
D vesicle
E papule
F nodule
G bullae
H pustule
I urticaria

Match the descriptions below with one of these words

☐ 42 a blister filled with blood-stained fluid
☐ 43 a skin bleb filled with clear fluid
☐ 44 a lump set deeply in the skin
☐ 45 a raised spot on the skin surface
☐ 46 a flat spot differing in colour from surrounding skin
☐ 47 horny cells loosened from the skin surface

Hypertension

Important hypertension trials include

A MRC Mild Hypertension Trial
B European Working Party on Hypertension in the Elderly
C Veterans Administration Co-operative Study
D Hypertension Detection and Follow-up Program, USA
E Systolic Hypertension in Elderly Program (SHEP) Co-operative Group
F Australian National Board Hypertension Study

Match the following statements to the appropriate study:

☐ 48 double-blind trial using hydrochlorothiazide, triamterene and placebo; only 840 patients recruited

☐ 49 low-dose diuretics, beta blockers and reserpine

☐ 50 double-blind trial in a group of people who were selected for compliance with a treatment regime

☐ 51 single-blind trial between bendrofluazide, propranolol and placebo; showed 1 CVA saved per 850 patient treatment years

☐ 52 used bendrofluazide in doses much larger than now used; those doses may exacerbate other risk factors

Literature

The following books and papers have been written concerning general practice:

A *What Sort of Doctor?* by a working party of the RCGP
B *The Exceptional Potential in Each Primary Care Consultation* by Stott and Davis
C *Doctors Talking to Patients* by Byrne and Long
D *The Doctor, his Patient and the Illness* by Michael Balint
E *The Inner Consultation* by Roger Neighbour
F *The Consultation: An Approach to Learning and Teaching* by Pendleton et al.

Match the statements below to the most appropriate book or paper listed above

☐ 53 coined the phrase 'Drug Doctor' to show the therapeutic effect of doctors as people themselves

☐ 54 suggested that a sharing style can address patients' ideas about their illness so they will be satisfied and comply with treatment

☐ 55 discussed housekeeping, meaning dealing with feelings left by one consultation

☐ 56 looked at doctors' accessibility and premises

☐ 57 a study of audio-taped consultations

☐ 58 noted differing consultation styles varying from 'doctor-centred' to 'patient-centred'

Dyspepsia

Drugs used in patients with dyspepsia include

A omeprazole
B ranitidine
C misoprostol
D magnesium trisilicate
E aluminium hydroxide
F cisapride
G metoclopramide

Match the following statements to the most commonly responsible drug:

☐ 59 can cause diarrhoea
☐ 60 can cause post-menopausal bleeding
☐ 61 can cause constipation
☐ 62 can cause galactorrhoea and gynaecomastia
☐ 63 can cause confusional state
☐ 64 can be responsible for a photosensitivity reaction

Normal distribution

The words below relate to a set of values in a normal distribution

A mode
B median
C standard deviation
D mean

Match the appropriate word to the descriptions below

☐ 65 the middle number when the values are all placed in arithmetical order
☐ 66 the most frequently occurring value
☐ 67 the square root of the variance
☐ 68 a measure of the distribution of the values around the arithmetic average

Studies

Studies of populations and diseases can be

A descriptive
B clinical trial
C case control
D correlation
E meta analysis

Match the studies below to one of the above types of study

☐ 69 the use of thalidomide is compared between patients who have had abnormal babies and those who have had healthy babies

☐ 70 the occurrence of lung cancer in a group of patients is compared with smoking status in that group

☐ 71 the prevalence of ischaemic heart disease is studied in a population who are randomly assigned to receive anti-oxidants or an inert substance

☐ 72 a survey to find out the prevalence of migraine in a population

☐ 73 the results of several investigations of exposure to radiation and the risk of leukaemia are combined to reach a conclusion

Screening

A screening test carried out in a study in general practice on child development gave the following results:

	Screening Test Positive	**Screening Test Negative**
Problem present	**74**	**23**
Problem absent	**25**	**258**

Options available

A 74/99	D 23/281	G 258/281	J 23
B 74/97	E 25/283	H 258/283	K 25
C 23/97	F 25/283	I 74	L 258

Select the appropriate option

☐ 74 positive predictive value
☐ 75 negative predictive value
☐ 76 specificity
☐ 77 sensitivity
☐ 78 false negative

Infectious diseases

A scarlet fever
B chickenpox
C measles
D rubella
E infectious mononucleosis

Match the appropriate disease to the following:

☐ 79 has a very long incubation period of 4–6 weeks
☐ 80 has a very short incubation period, an interval of 1–2 days between disease onset and appearance of rash, but a long infectivity period
☐ 81 90% of adults are immune; however the disease can be serious in adults who smoke, and pregnant women in the first trimester and at delivery
☐ 82 notifiable on clinical diagnosis; the rash is accompanied by conjunctivitis and fever
☐ 83 all pregnant women with suspected disease should be investigated serologically. Seronegative health staff are immunized

Anaemia

On a blood film, anaemia can be divided into three types

A microcytic
B macrocytic
C normocytic

Match the conditions below with the appropriate type of anaemia

- ☐ 84 thalassaemia
- ☐ 85 chronic renal failure
- ☐ 86 pernicious anaemia
- ☐ 87 alcoholism
- ☐ 88 menorrhagia in a pre-menopausal woman
- ☐ 89 malignancy

Lipid-lowering drugs

Lipid-lowering drugs include

A cholestyramine
B simvastatin
C bezafibrate
D nicotinic acid
E clofibrate
F probucol

Match the statements below to one of these drugs

- ☐ 90 an HMG CoA reductase inhibitor
- ☐ 91 there has been considerable experience of its use in children
- ☐ 92 predisposes to gallstones by increasing biliary cholesterol excretion
- ☐ 93 can cause sleep disturbance
- ☐ 94 can cause flushing which may be severe
- ☐ 95 an anion exchange resin which acts by binding bile acids, preventing their reabsorption

Lesions in the mouth

Lesions in the mouth can be due to a number of causes, including

A lichen planus
B measles
C syphilis
D erythema multiforme
E hand, foot and mouth disease
F *Monilia*
G Behçet's disease

Match the following scenarios with the most appropriate cause:

☐ 96 erosive lesions are seen in the mouth. They have a hard base. A flat papule, purplish in colour but with white streaks, is seen at the left wrist

☐ 97 ulcers are seen in the mouth looking like 'snail tracks', which are painless

☐ 98 recurrent oral ulceration is accompanied by arthritis and iritis in a 22-year-old man

☐ 99 painful ulcers are seen in the mouth of a 23-year-old student. He mentions a sore throat and recent spots on his buttocks

☐ 100 Koplik's spots are diagnostic

PRACTICE PAPER 2 — SECTION 1: MCQs

Total time allowed for sections 1 and 2 is three hours. Section 1 has 400 items, section 2 has 100. Indicate your answers clearly by putting a tick or cross in the box alongside each answer or by writing the appropriate letter in Section 2.

In Kawasaki's disease

☐ 1 it is most often seen in children over 5 years old
☐ 2 there is an acute febrile illness
☐ 3 there is a fatality of about 0.5 per 100 cases
☐ 4 coronary artery aneurysms are a sequel in about 5–10% of cases
☐ 5 there is often reddening which spares the palms and soles
☐ 6 fever lasting more than 5 days and swelling of cervical lymph nodes is often seen

In terminal care

☐ 7 the majority of people die at home
☐ 8 the majority of patients with pain have more than one type of pain
☐ 9 over 90% of patient pain can be controlled with drugs
☐ 10 with severe pain, intramuscular analgesics are more effective than the equivalent dose administered by the oral route
☐ 11 portable syringe devices need to have the syringe changed at approximately 6-hour intervals

Babies who are small for their gestational age are at risk of the following:

☐ 12 intraventricular haemorrhage
☐ 13 convulsions in later life
☐ 14 remaining small
☐ 15 learning difficulties
☐ 16 diabetes in later life

Korsakoff's syndrome is associated with

☐ 17 denial of amnesia
☐ 18 obsession with time
☐ 19 confabulation
☐ 20 ritualistic behaviour
☐ 21 echopraxia

Viral pneumonia has been shown to be a consequence of infections with the following:

☐ 22 measles
☐ 23 mumps
☐ 24 varicella
☐ 25 rubella
☐ 26 cytomegalovirus

In Bell's palsy

☐ 27 the majority of patients will make a recovery within 3 weeks
☐ 28 brain stem lesions will cause loss of taste
☐ 29 oral steroids have been shown to be effective
☐ 30 lacrimation is unaffected
☐ 31 repeat attacks resolve more readily than the initial attack

Concerning episiotomy

☐ 32 studies have shown that a wait of 1 hour for stitching is associated with significant infection
☐ 33 episiotomy has been shown to prevent development of rectocele
☐ 34 episiotomy rates are higher for home confinements
☐ 35 tearing of the perineum does not occur once episiotomy has been performed
☐ 36 Apgar scores of babies born to mothers who have had an episiotomy have been shown to be higher than those without

In differentiating between migraine and tension headache, the following would support a diagnosis of the latter:

☐ 37 a hatband distribution of pain
☐ 38 tender spots on the scalp during the headache
☐ 39 flushing at the onset of the headache
☐ 40 a watery eye during the period of the headache
☐ 41 facial pain occurring during an attack of headache

Infantile pyloric stenosis

- ☐ 42 shows an increased familial incidence
- ☐ 43 typically presents between 2–3 months of age
- ☐ 44 babies tend to become acidotic
- ☐ 45 is more common in males
- ☐ 46 blood in the vomit would indicate other pathology

Population studies have shown that disability in old age can be reduced by

- ☐ 47 lowering the average diastolic blood pressure by 10 mmHg
- ☐ 48 30 minutes walking daily
- ☐ 49 two servings of oily fish per week
- ☐ 50 decreasing the average calcium intake
- ☐ 51 decreasing the average sodium intake

Acute pancreatitis is associated with

- ☐ 52 gallstones
- ☐ 53 raised cholesterol levels
- ☐ 54 mumps infection
- ☐ 55 first attacks that are less severe than subsequent episodes
- ☐ 56 hypocalcaemia

Common types of accidents in people over 65 years include

- ☐ 57 falls
- ☐ 58 poisoning
- ☐ 59 road traffic accidents
- ☐ 60 fire

Concerning warts

- ☐ 61 the majority of patients with warts develop immunity within 2 years
- ☐ 62 salicylic acid preparations should be applied for 3 months or more
- ☐ 63 topical podophyllum must be left on the wart without washing for 24 hours
- ☐ 64 cryotherapy with liquid nitrogen typically scars
- ☐ 65 podophyllum is teratogenic

You are consulted by the parents of an apparently healthy child who refuses to sleep at night. The following are true:

☐ 66 at 3 months the average child has approximately four episodes of nocturnal wakefulness
☐ 67 at 6 months the majority of children have 15 hours of sleep during the night
☐ 68 a regular night time routine has been shown to solve the majority of sleep problems
☐ 69 children with persistent sleep disturbance have an increased incidence of other behavioural problems
☐ 70 a child who persistently cries at night should be left no longer than 5 minutes

The following drugs used in the treatment of rheumatoid arthritis have the side-effects stated:

☐ 71 gold injections cause exfoliative dermatitis
☐ 72 penicillamine is associated with azoospermia
☐ 73 methotrexate has been implicated in hepatic fibrosis
☐ 74 sulphasalazine is associated with thrombocytopenia
☐ 75 chloroquine produces retinal damage

The following are true of hand, foot and mouth disease:

☐ 76 a sore throat is characteristic
☐ 77 typically the spots are itchy
☐ 78 spots appearing on the buttocks would exclude the diagnosis
☐ 79 it has an incubation period of approximately 21 days
☐ 80 it typically responds to oral penicillin

The majority of patients with Down's syndrome will

☐ 81 have an IQ of between 20 and 50
☐ 82 die before they reach 50 years of age
☐ 83 have a congenital heart disorder
☐ 84 have a behaviour disorder
☐ 85 develop hypothyroidism

A 30-year-old man presents with a knee effusion following a recent episode of urethral discharge. The following would support a diagnosis of Reiter's disease:

☐ 86 clear synovial fluid on aspiration
☐ 87 an ESR of 60 mm/h
☐ 88 stomatitis
☐ 89 lesions on the soles of the feet
☐ 90 conjunctivitis

Motor neurone disease is typically associated with

☐ 91 symptoms of dementia
☐ 92 painful muscle cramps in the early stages of the disease
☐ 93 a symmetrical distribution of weakness and wasting
☐ 94 a survival of more than 5 years from the time of onset
☐ 95 the preservation of sphincter function

In subarachnoid haemorrhage

☐ 96 the majority of patients will die without warning
☐ 97 the peak age range is in the under 35-year-olds
☐ 98 there is a familial tendency
☐ 99 the majority of patients who have surgery achieve their previous quality of life
☐ 100 the risk of epilepsy is increased following a haemorrhage

The following are associated with the second trimester of pregnancy:

☐ 101 a cardiac output which is about 40% above the non-pregnant state
☐ 102 enhanced absorption of dietary iron
☐ 103 increased gastric acid secretion
☐ 104 delay in gastric emptying
☐ 105 increased introversion

The following drugs have been shown to potentiate the effects of alcohol:

☐ 106 phenytoin
☐ 107 indomethacin
☐ 108 atenolol
☐ 109 chlorpheniramine
☐ 110 monoamine oxidase inhibitors

The following statements are about the Mental Health Act (England and Wales) 1983:

☐ 111 Section 3 is for a minimum period of 6 months
☐ 112 Section 4 requires one medical recommendation by a doctor who has seen the patient within 12 hours of application
☐ 113 detention under sections 2, 3 and 4 must be in the interests of the patient's own health or safety
☐ 114 Section 3 is renewable
☐ 115 the Mental Health Act forms can only be completed in the patient's home or in hospital

Laser is used for the treatment of the following ophthalmological conditions:

☐ 116 amaurosis fugax
☐ 117 acute glaucoma
☐ 118 senile macular degeneration
☐ 119 diabetic background retinopathy
☐ 120 myopia

Puerperal depressive illness

☐ 121 has been shown to occur in 10% of pregnancies
☐ 122 is more common in single parents
☐ 123 is associated with lack of 'bonding'
☐ 124 is associated with a previous psychiatric history
☐ 125 has been shown to be associated with a decreased level of progestogen 6 weeks post-delivery

In carcinoma of the cervix

☐ 126 it has an association with human papilloma virus infection
☐ 127 the majority of patients survive more than 5 years
☐ 128 smoking has been shown to increase the risks of contracting the disease
☐ 129 cytology has been shown to be reliable in identifying frank carcinoma
☐ 130 the peak incidence occurs between 40 and 55 years of age

Concerning hypoglycaemia

☐ 131 it is defined as a blood glucose level of <2.2 mmol/l
☐ 132 catecholamines decrease blood glucose concentrations
☐ 133 alcohol potentiates the effects of insulin
☐ 134 strict control of diabetes makes patients less sensitive to falls in blood glucose levels
☐ 135 the face typically flushes at the onset of a hypoglycaemic episode

When looking at lesions on the ear the following should be considered:

☐ 136 basal cell carcinoma typically appears on the helix
☐ 137 tophi appear on the earlobe
☐ 138 chilblains of the ear never itch
☐ 139 psoriasis typically occurs all over the ear
☐ 140 kerato-acanthoma do not appear on the ear

Pulmonary fibrosis may result following administration of the drugs named below

☐ 141 methotrexate
☐ 142 erythromycin
☐ 143 nitrofurantoin
☐ 144 amiodarone
☐ 145 busulphan

When considering flat feet (pes planus)

☐ 146 symptoms fail to correlate with the degree of structural alteration
☐ 147 the majority of children age 2 years have the condition
☐ 148 painful mobile flat feet are an indication for corrective surgery
☐ 149 they are typically associated with painful night cramps
☐ 150 if familial typically respond to corrective measures

The following expenses are directly reimbursed by the FHSA:

☐ 151 rent on premises
☐ 152 repairs to premises
☐ 153 lighting and heating costs
☐ 154 dressings and drugs for use in the surgery
☐ 155 insurance premium on the surgery premises

Polymyalgia rheumatica and temporal arteritis are related in the following respects:

☐ 156 the age/sex distribution is the same
☐ 157 Asians are more often affected
☐ 158 myalgia is a typical feature
☐ 159 biopsy findings are identical
☐ 160 typical changes in the plasma electrophoretic pattern

The following statements are true of eardrums with a central perforation:

☐ 161 they typically produce a mucoid discharge
☐ 162 they are associated with the production of cholesteatoma
☐ 163 repair is possible via a tympanoplasty
☐ 164 urgent referral to an ENT surgeon is indicated

Concerning weight

☐ 165 a patient with a Body Mass Index of just greater than 20 is only slightly overweight

☐ 166 Body Mass Index is measured by the weight in kilograms divided by the square of the height in centimetres

☐ 167 GPs are more successful than others in helping patients reduce weight

☐ 168 exercises increase the basal metabolic rate for several hours

☐ 169 weight-watching groups use strategies like fines, prizes and the example of others

Dyspepsia treatments are noted for the following side-effects:

☐ 170 aluminium salts cause diarrhoea

☐ 171 cisapride is typically associated with acute dyskinesia in young adults

☐ 172 misoprostol is associated with intermenstrual bleeding

☐ 173 metoclopramide is associated with elevated prolactin levels

☐ 174 H_2 receptor antagonists are associated with confusion in the elderly

☐ 175 omeprazole is associated with photosensitivity reactions

Avascular necrosis of the femoral head

☐ 176 is associated with slipped upper femoral epiphysis

☐ 177 is an occupational hazard of deep sea divers

☐ 178 is improved by the use of non-steroidal anti-inflammatory drugs

☐ 179 pain is typically of sudden onset

☐ 180 X-ray changes are apparent at an early stage

Amiodarone in the treatment of ventricular arrhythmias is

- ☐ 181 contraindicated in the presence of impaired left ventricular function
- ☐ 182 associated with the presence of corneal deposits
- ☐ 183 associated with biochemical abnormalities of the thyroid
- ☐ 184 associated with skin sensitivity that is resistant to treatment with sunblock creams
- ☐ 185 associated with a dose related incidence of side-effects

When advising patients about to undergo air travel a GP should be aware of the following facts:

- ☐ 186 people with a vital capacity less than 50% of the mean predicted for them, should not fly
- ☐ 187 there is no increase in fit frequency of epileptics
- ☐ 188 diabetics on oral hypoglycaemic agents will need to decrease their dosage if undertaking a prolonged eastbound flight
- ☐ 189 motion sickness on aircraft shows a tendency to increase with age
- ☐ 190 recent eye surgery is a contraindication to flying

Concerning indicative prescribing budgets

- ☐ 191 they are only allocated to fundholding practices
- ☐ 192 if a practice underspends its budget, amounts saved can be added to future years' budgets
- ☐ 193 practice formularies are compulsory
- ☐ 194 if a practice overspends, its budget remuneration can be withheld by the FHSA
- ☐ 195 patients on 'expensive' medication are not included in the budget

The following would support a diagnosis of irritable bowel syndrome:

- ☐ 196 nocturnal diarrhoea
- ☐ 197 absence of pain
- ☐ 198 associated menstrual disturbance
- ☐ 199 abdominal pain worsening on defaecation
- ☐ 200 onset associated with a proven gastrointestinal infection

Your practice is reviewing its protocol for antenatal care. Research has shown that

- ☐ 201 routine ultrasound reduces the incidence of induction for alleged post-maturity
- ☐ 202 anti-smoking education reduces the incidence of low birth weight babies
- ☐ 203 measuring fundal heights routinely decreases peri-natal mortality
- ☐ 204 routine antenatal care detects the majority of small for gestational age babies
- ☐ 205 routine kick charts have been shown to reduce the chances of perinatal death

Concerning breast lumps

- ☐ 206 cysts are more prevalent in post-menopausal women
- ☐ 207 cysts should not be aspirated by General Practitioners
- ☐ 208 the majority of solitary breast cysts will recur within 2 years of initial aspiration
- ☐ 209 patients with breast cysts have an increased risk of developing breast cancer
- ☐ 210 lumpy breasts which are cyclically painful have been shown to respond to oil of evening primrose

The following patients are not charged for an eye examination:

- ☐ 211 diabetics
- ☐ 212 those on income support
- ☐ 213 pregnant women
- ☐ 214 people over 65 years of age
- ☐ 215 those with a parent with glaucoma

Under the terms of service of a General Practitioner's contract, he is allowed to accept a fee from a patient on the practice list for the following:

- ☐ 216 ear piercing
- ☐ 217 initial treatment following a road traffic accident
- ☐ 218 seat belt exemption certificates
- ☐ 219 signing a form for the Disability Living Allowance
- ☐ 220 writing a letter in support of a patient's housing application

High-risk groups for diabetes include

☐ 221 women with gestational diabetes
☐ 222 women who have had low birth weight babies
☐ 223 men and women with a family history of late onset diabetes
☐ 224 people with a history of anorexia
☐ 225 people with repeated urinary tract infections

Atrial fibrillation typically is a presenting feature of the following:

☐ 226 rheumatic fever
☐ 227 sarcoidosis
☐ 228 thyrotoxicosis
☐ 229 alcoholic cardiomyopathy
☐ 230 Reiter's syndrome

The following are true of normal pressure hydrocephalus:

☐ 231 cognitive impairment occurs after the onset of gait disturbance
☐ 232 a Parkinsonian gait is the typical abnormality when walking
☐ 233 urinary incontinence can be present in the absence of disturbance of gait or mental function
☐ 234 lumbar puncture is contraindicated
☐ 235 less than 25% of patients improve after a ventricular shunt operation

Following an episode of deliberate self-harm:

☐ 236 the majority of patients will repeat one or more acts of non-fatal harm within one, year
☐ 237 provision of intensive psychiatric and social help has been shown to significantly reduce the rate of repetition
☐ 238 the provision of 'hotlines' (e.g. Samaritans) has significantly reduced the incidence of deliberate self-harm
☐ 239 the majority of patients admitted to a general hospital following an episode of self-harm require transfer to a psychiatric unit
☐ 240 the risk of a successful suicidal attempt within the next year is approximately 10%

In polycythaemia vera

- ☐ 241 splenomegaly is typical
- ☐ 242 it is associated with gout
- ☐ 243 intractable itching would cast doubt on the diagnosis
- ☐ 244 the majority eventually develop acute leukaemia
- ☐ 245 radiotherapy treatment decreases the chance of developing leukaemia

The differential diagnosis of sudden loss of vision should include the following:

- ☐ 246 migraine
- ☐ 247 central retinal vein occlusion
- ☐ 248 senile macular degeneration
- ☐ 249 optic neuritis
- ☐ 250 toxic optic neuropathy

When considering child surveillance in general practice

- ☐ 251 a child must register separately with a GP for child surveillance
- ☐ 252 child health clinics attract a health promotion clinic payment from the FHSA
- ☐ 253 child surveillance payments include an allowance for giving childhood immunisations
- ☐ 254 all GPs are eligible for inclusion in the Child Health Surveillance List
- ☐ 255 once a child is accepted onto the child surveillance list of a GP, that GP must perform all the developmental assessment

The following have been shown to be associated with an increased incidence of recurrent miscarriage:

- ☐ 256 systemic lupus erythematosus (SLE)
- ☐ 257 raised levels of luteinizing hormone
- ☐ 258 diabetes mellitus
- ☐ 259 thyroid disease
- ☐ 260 parental chromosomal abnormalities

Concerning acute bronchiolitis

☐ 261 respiratory syncytial virus (RSV) is the most commonly isolated organism
☐ 262 it typically affects infants in the first year of life
☐ 263 it typically causes stridor
☐ 264 it shows a seasonal pattern
☐ 265 complete laryngeal obstruction is possible on examination of the throat

After head injury there is an increased incidence of the following:

☐ 266 hypochondriasis
☐ 267 depressive illness
☐ 268 schizophrenia
☐ 269 suicide
☐ 270 personality disorder

When prescribing topical steroids

☐ 271 absorption is enhanced by inclusion of urea in the preparation
☐ 272 a single application to the arm of a 70 kg adult male will use approximately 4 g of preparation
☐ 273 if used continuously they increase hair growth
☐ 274 ointments are indicated for most steroid-responsive conditions
☐ 275 depigmentation has been shown to occur at the site of prolonged usage

In England and Wales, notifiable deaths include

☐ 276 when a doctor has not attended within 28 days
☐ 277 deaths arising from an industrial disease
☐ 278 when a baby dies and there is doubt about whether it was born alive
☐ 279 deaths in prison
☐ 280 deaths in patients with chronic alcoholism

Arterial leg ulceration is associated with the following:

☐ 281 pain
☐ 282 pigmentation
☐ 283 induration and oedema of the gaiter area
☐ 284 typically sited on the foot
☐ 285 punched out appearance

The following are true when considering periods:

☐ 286 the average age of onset in the UK is approximately 11 years of age
☐ 287 the average age at which patients have their last period is 50 years of age in the UK
☐ 288 the earlier periods start the later they finish
☐ 289 if the onset of periods is delayed beyond 16 years of age referral for investigation is indicated
☐ 290 estimation of LH and FSH levels is a reliable method of determining if a patient is post-menopausal

Dry eyes

☐ 291 are a cause of epiphora
☐ 292 are worse in warm weather
☐ 293 are associated with sarcoidosis
☐ 294 Sjögren's test is diagnostic
☐ 295 are associated with entropion

The following factors would suggest a need for referring a patient with a mole to a dermatologist in order to exclude malignant change:

☐ 296 size less than 1 cm diameter
☐ 297 an irregular outline
☐ 298 colour variation
☐ 299 erythema around the margin
☐ 300 scaling on the surface

Lithium carbonate

☐ 301 is effective in the control of schizophrenia
☐ 302 is available as a long-acting depot preparation
☐ 303 is associated with increased mortality due to renal damage
☐ 304 is associated with abnormalities of thyroid function
☐ 305 is an effective agent for rapid control of symptoms

Under the access to Medical Reports Act 1988

☐ 306 the doctor supplying the report must receive a copy of the patient's consent
☐ 307 the doctor has the right to refuse to amend a report even if requested to do so by the patient
☐ 308 the patient has the right to view the report for up to one year after it has been sent to the insurance company or employer
☐ 309 the doctor can charge a fee if the patient requests a copy of the report
☐ 310 the doctor has the right to refuse to divulge all or part of the report to a patient

Schizoid personality disorders are associated with

☐ 311 being ill at ease in company
☐ 312 self-sufficiency
☐ 313 obsessional behaviour
☐ 314 self-dramatisation
☐ 315 lack of warmth

When considering normal distribution

☐ 316 the mean uses all information available
☐ 317 the median is easier to calculate than the mean
☐ 318 the median is not affected by extreme values
☐ 319 the mode is the value that occurs most frequently
☐ 320 variation indicates the spread of the curve

When treating undescended testes

☐ 321 no testis descends spontaneously after 1 year of age
☐ 322 all testes should be in the scrotum by 5 years of age
☐ 323 a unilateral undescended testis found after 16 years of age should be excised
☐ 324 orchidopexy has been shown to increase the chances of fertility
☐ 325 hernial sacs are present in the majority of boys at the time of orchidopexy

An elderly patient presents with symptoms of dementia, the following would suggest a depressive cause rather than Alzheimer's disease:

☐ 326 recent onset of symptoms
☐ 327 the patient continually complaining of memory loss
☐ 328 mental ability worsening in the evening
☐ 329 'don't know' as a response to many questions
☐ 330 a previous history of depressive illness

Jet lag is

☐ 331 due to an upset in circadian rhythm
☐ 332 less marked when going towards USA from UK
☐ 333 helped by sleeping on the plane
☐ 334 helped by maintaining a good non-alcoholic fluid intake
☐ 335 of about 24 hours' duration

When following up patients with breast cancer

☐ 336 fixed regimes of long term follow up (5 year) by hospital have been shown to lead to a more favourable outcome
☐ 337 treatment with tamoxifen has been shown to improve prognosis in post-menopausal patients
☐ 338 the incidence of cancer in the opposite breast is no greater than the incidence of breast cancer for women as a whole
☐ 339 hormone manipulation has a greater response rate than chemotherapy in the management of advanced disease

A survey of adult females who have been the victims of child sexual abuse has shown that

☐ 340 the majority have some lasting psychiatric problems
☐ 341 the worst prognosis was when abuse took place repeatedly with an older man
☐ 342 they had difficulty in maintaining intimate relationships

Upon employing a new member of staff a General Practitioner should be aware that they immediately have the following statutory employment rights:

☐ 343 to receive an itemised pay statement
☐ 344 to have paid time off for antenatal care
☐ 345 to be given a minimum period of notice of termination of employment
☐ 346 to receive payment for absence due to pregnancy
☐ 347 to receive a written statement of reasons for dismissal

The following are true of the use of sumatriptan in the treatment of migraine:

☐ 348 after s.c. injection of a single dose, the majority of patients will have a recurrence of headache within 48 hours
☐ 349 s.c. administration is the treatment of choice in hemiplegic migraine
☐ 350 concurrent administration with ergotamine preparations is contraindicated
☐ 351 ventricular arrhythmias have been reported with recommended doses of the drug

When considering the organisation of care for those with gout

☐ 352 allopurinol is contraindicated in the presence of renal calculi
☐ 353 the majority of patients with gout will have co-existing hypertension
☐ 354 lipid levels are higher in those with gout than in the general population
☐ 355 alcohol decreases the renal urate clearance
☐ 356 the majority of those with gout will have a positive family history

The following may have oral manifestations:

☐ 357 systemic gold therapy
☐ 358 bulimia
☐ 359 erythema multiforme
☐ 360 pemphigus vulgaris
☐ 361 lichen planus

Department of Health recommendations for influenza vaccination include adults and children in the following groups:

☐ 362 health care workers
☐ 363 patients in residential homes
☐ 364 patients with diabetes mellitus
☐ 365 patients with leukaemia
☐ 366 patients in heart failure

Maternity medical services

☐ 367 must be provided by a doctor on the obstetric list
☐ 368 are payable as for a full term gestation, for a live delivery occurring before 28 weeks' gestation
☐ 369 are payable for a patient who requests and subsequently receives a therapeutic abortion from the outset of the pregnancy
☐ 370 the complete fee is only payable if the GP is present at the time of delivery
☐ 371 fee for post-natal visits is payable for visits done up to 28 days' post-confinement

When considering the management of upper gastrointestinal bleeding

☐ 372 the majority of patients will require surgery
☐ 373 H_2 antagonists have been shown to stop initial bleeds
☐ 374 the mortality rate is about 10%
☐ 375 gastric ulcers are more likely to bleed than duodenal ulcers
☐ 376 urgent endoscopic assessment at the time of hospital admission has been shown to decrease mortality

Significant interactions have been shown to occur between the following drugs if given concurrently:

- ☐ 377 terfenadine and erythromycin
- ☐ 378 ciprofloxacin and theophylline
- ☐ 379 cimetidine and warfarin
- ☐ 380 omeprazole and alginate preparations
- ☐ 381 allopurinol and captopril

When considering drug abuse the following are true:

- ☐ 382 the majority of opiate abusers will still be addicted 7 years after starting the habit
- ☐ 383 methadone liquid can be injected intravenously
- ☐ 384 10–20% of opiate users will die from drug-related causes
- ☐ 385 cocaine abuse is associated with underprivileged groups in society
- ☐ 386 amphetamine abuse is associated with paranoid psychosis
- ☐ 387 the majority of people who abuse cannabis progress to 'harder' drugs

Alcohol abuse

- ☐ 388 can be detected by CRATE questionnaire
- ☐ 389 can be detected by MAST questionnaire
- ☐ 390 gives increased risk of carcinoma of oesophagus
- ☐ 391 is a high risk in fishermen
- ☐ 392 is a high risk in single males over 40 years of age

***Candida albicans* has been implicated in the development of the following oral conditions:**

- ☐ 393 angular cheilitis
- ☐ 394 ranula
- ☐ 395 denture stomatitis
- ☐ 396 Sjögren's syndrome

The following would suggest a diagnosis of non-ulcer dyspepsia:

- ☐ 397 morning retching
- ☐ 398 night pain
- ☐ 399 antacid relief
- ☐ 400 inconsistent relationship between symptoms and food ingestion

PRACTICE PAPER 2 — SECTION 2: EMQs

Shoulder pain

Causes of shoulder pain seen in general practice include

A rheumatoid arthritis
B osteoarthritis
C pyogenic arthritis
D trauma
E polymyalgia rheumatica
F shoulder–hand syndrome
G Herpes zoster
H referred pain from the neck and back
I lesions in musculo-tendon cuff

Which of these would be the most likely cause of shoulder pain in the following patients?

☐ 1 a 43-year-old taxi driver has 'nagging' pains in the right shoulder, worse on turning his head to reverse

☐ 2 a 61-year-old man, who made a good recovery from a myocardial infarct 3 months ago, now has a painful stiff right shoulder with a slightly swollen right hand

☐ 3 a 39-year-old man has 'concerning' shoulder pain that occurs only in a particular range of movements; it interferes with putting on his shirt; deep tenderness is noted at examination

☐ 4 a 69-year-old lady has morning stiffness and aching in neck, shoulders and arms; she appears vaguely unwell but has no inflammation of any joints although she has had some headaches recently

☐ 5 a 23-year-old gardener has developed a hot, red, swollen left shoulder joint; he also has cellulitis of his left hand following a scratch at work

☐ 6 a 49-year-old lady has a painful stiff left shoulder worse in the mornings; she has had gradually worsening stiffness of both hands over the preceding 6 months

Epilepsy

The following drugs are used in the control of epilepsy:

A primidone
B sodium valproate
C vigabatrin
D phenytoin
E carbamazepine
F clonazepam

Match the statements to the appropriate drugs

☐ 7 is converted to phenobarbitone
☐ 8 also used increasingly in recurrent depressive illness
☐ 9 highly protein bound, making interpretation of blood tests difficult
☐ 10 may give false positive urine test for ketones
☐ 11 can cause gingival hypertrophy and tenderness, and may lower plasma calcium

Mental Health Act

In the Mental Health Act 1983 the following sections are of importance:

A Section 2
B Section 3
C Section 4
D Section 7
E Section 12
F Section 136

Match the statements below with the appropriate section from those above

☐ 12 appropriate for detention of a patient who is acting in a bizarre way and warrants compulsory assessment
☐ 13 appropriate for emergency detention of a patient by a single medical practitioner
☐ 14 can be used by police when they need to detain someone who they believe is suffering from mental illness
☐ 15 appropriate for guardianship
☐ 16 appropriate for detention of a schizophrenic patient who refuses treatment and is a danger to other people
☐ 17 is used to approve doctors recognised as having special expertise in mental health

Statistics

The following terms are used in medical statistics:

A correlation
B predictive value
C incidence
D confounding
E confidence

Match the statements below with the most appropriate term

☐ 18 depends on the prevalence of disease in the population studied
☐ 19 occurrence of new cases in a population in a period of time
☐ 20 needs to be eliminated in a good study
☐ 21 depends on sensitivity and specificity of the test
☐ 22 occurs when a variable changes in a direct way with another variable

Coronary heart disease

The following look at the risk of coronary heart disease:

A British Regional Heart Study
B Framingham Heart Study
C North Karalia Project
D WHO European Collaborative Trial
E Dundee Risk Score
F Shaper Score
G Seven Countries Study

Which of these is appropriate to the following?

☐ 23 looks at relative risk of having a heart attack over the next 5 years
☐ 24 showed that the mean serum total cholesterol is the most important factor in determining population risk for coronary heart disease

☐ 25 looks at the absolute risk of having a heart attack over the next 5 years

☐ 26 assessed risk factors in a middle-aged group in the USA and studied fatal and non-fatal coronary events

☐ 27 looked at a group of men in USA with a high risk of a coronary event and studied interventions to reduce the risk factors

☐ 28 was set up because of high mortality rate from coronary events in Finland

☐ 29 recruited patients from British General Practices and linked risk factors with fatal and non-fatal coronary events

Prescribing

Various schemes and bodies exist to improve prescribing in general practice, such as

A The PACT Scheme
B Medical Audit Advisory Group
C National Medicines Resource Centre
D Prescribing Unit, Leeds University General Practice Department
E Prescribing Adviser
F Prescribing Allocation Group

Match the following statements with one of the above:

☐ 30 investigates the range of prescribing

☐ 31 produces quarterly prescribing reports for GPs

☐ 32 centrally funded; produces monthly bulletins

☐ 33 monitors indicative prescribing

☐ 34 advises NHS Executive on allocation of drug budgets to regions and practices

Professions

People professionally associated with general practice include

A Health Visitors
B Practice Managers
C Community Nurses
D Practice Nurses
E Social Workers

Match these statements to the most appropriate person

☐ 35 is usually employed by the Health Authority, gives practical and psychological support to patients and families, spending most time in practical tasks
☐ 36 is employed usually by the Health Authority and has some statutory duties
☐ 37 are usually employed by General Practice Principals, are often experienced nurses and may have family planning training
☐ 38 often have a large role in the hiring and training of staff

Lipid trials

In trials on lipids the following are well-known:

A WOSCOPS
B Scandinavian Simvastatin Survival Study (4S)
C ASPIRE Steering Group
D Cholesterol and Recurrent Events Study (CARE)

Which comments relate to which study?

☐ 39 many survivors of myocardial infarcts have not had their blood lipids measured
☐ 40 patients without known coronary disease have their risk of cardiovascular disease reduced by statins if the cholesterol level is above 6 mmol/l
☐ 41 studied survivors of myocardial infarcts with mildly elevated cholesterol levels and used pravastatin therapy
☐ 42 studied patients with known coronary disease and showed that treatment with a statin produced a 30% drop in total mortality

Misuse of drugs

The Misuse of Drugs Regulations 1985 categorises five groups of drugs

A Schedule 1
B Schedule 2
C Schedule 3
D Schedule 4
E Schedule 5

To which schedule do the following drugs belong?

☐ 43 diamorphine
☐ 44 diethylpropion
☐ 45 diazepam
☐ 46 amylobarbitone
☐ 47 cannabis

Benefits

Welfare Benefits include

A Family Credit
B Child Benefit
C Income Support
D Invalid Care Allowance
E Social Fund Benefits
F Widow's payment

Which of the above relate to the following:

☐ 48 means tested benefit payable to someone working less than 16 hours per week on low income
☐ 49 means tested benefit payable to someone with children who is working more than 16 hours per week on low income
☐ 50 payable to someone who is unable to work because they are looking after a disabled person
☐ 51 payable to meet exceptional expenses such as funeral expenses
☐ 52 a tax-free payment to someone with a child under 16 years of age

Developmental milestones

Children reach significant developmental milestones at certain ages

A 6 months
B 9 months
C 12 months
D 18 months
E 24 months

At what age would most children be able to do the following:

☐ 53 walk with one hand held or unsupported
☐ 54 jump using both feet
☐ 55 build a tower of 6–7 blocks
☐ 56 transfer cube from one hand to another
☐ 57 crawl on tummy
☐ 58 say at least one word with meaning
☐ 59 usually ask for potty

Immunisations

The following immunisations are given for foreign travel:

A yellow fever
B tetanus
C polio
D hepatitis A
E typhoid

Match the following statements with the immunisations:

☐ 60 given 3 yearly; adverse reactions more common after repeated injections and more marked over 35 years of age
☐ 61 given 10 yearly but not given under 9 months of age
☐ 62 given 5–10 yearly and would be suitable for travellers to Northern Europe
☐ 63 a live vaccine which can rarely cause paralysis in recipients or contacts
☐ 64 testing for antibodies may be worthwhile in travellers over 50 years of age

Screening

The results of a screening test in general practice looking for asthma were as follows:

	Screening test positive	Screening test negative
Asthma present	**221**	**49**
Asthma not present	**74**	**156**

Options available

A	49/270	G	156/205
B	49/205	H	156/230
C	221/270	I	221
D	221/295	J	49
E	74/230	K	74
F	74/295	L	156

Select the appropriate option

☐ 65 specificity
☐ 66 sensitivity
☐ 67 positive predictive value
☐ 68 negative predictive value
☐ 69 false negative

Swellings in the neck area

Swellings in the neck may be due to

A enlarged salivary gland
B branchial cyst
C dermoid cyst
D thyroglossal cyst
E sebaceous cyst

Match one of these to the following statements:

☐ 70 may contain hair; arise along the lines of embryological development
☐ 71 filled with keratin; has a punctum

- ☐ 72 occurs in midline; moves on swallowing
- ☐ 73 remnant of second pharyngeal pouch
- ☐ 74 can occur with a notifiable infectious disease
- ☐ 75 a swelling in the neck that moves with the protrusion of the tongue

Paraesthesia

Causes of numbness and paraesthesia in the upper limbs include

A carpal tunnel syndrome
B ulnar nerve lesion
C peripheral neuropathy
D cervical spondylosis
E multiple sclerosis
F syringomyelia
G cortical lesions

Match the following clinical scenarios to the most appropriate diagnosis:

- ☐ 76 a 43-year-old teacher has pain and tingling in her right hand; she describes this as mainly affecting her index and middle fingers and it is worse at night
- ☐ 77 a 46-year-old electrician has numbness of his right hand and lower arm; examination reveals a 'glove' type sensory loss with distal weakness and some wasting
- ☐ 78 a 44-year-old plumber has tingling in his right hand and arm; some neck stiffness is noted on examination
- ☐ 79 a 39-year-old housewife complains of 'electric shock' type feeling worse on neck movements, especially flexion; she also mentions 'tight bands' around the upper limbs and ribs
- ☐ 80 a 41-year-old accountant has tingling in his left little finger; examination reveals slight wasting of the small muscles of the left hand
- ☐ 81 a 38-year-old carpenter has noticed that he injured his left hand under his little finger but did not feel the injury; examination reveals loss of pain and temperature sensation in the hand and arm, with slight weakness

Studies

Studies in general practice include those which are either

A cohort study
B case control

Choose the appropriate type for the following descriptions:

☐ 82 population-based
☐ 83 more potential for bias
☐ 84 long term follow-up is usually required
☐ 85 the incidence rate of a disease can be calculated
☐ 86 relatively easy to conduct
☐ 87 relatively inexpensive to conduct
☐ 88 relatively time-consuming to conduct

Literature

The following books have been written about general practice:

A *Games People Play* by Eric Berne
B *Six Minutes for the Patient* by Balint and Norell
C *Culture, Health and Illness* by Cecil Helmen
D *The Consultation: An Approach to Learning and Teaching* by Pendleton et al.
E *The Inner Consultation* by Roger Neighbour
F *The Doctor, His Patient and The Illness* by Michael Balint

Match the following statements to the most appropriate book listed above:

☐ 89 describes a consultation model with five check points, including connecting
☐ 90 describes 'apostolic function'
☐ 91 looked at parent, adult and child behaviour
☐ 92 defined seven communication tasks, including defining the reasons for the patient's attendance
☐ 93 discusses illness behaviour with patients trying to answer questions like 'why me, why now?'
☐ 94 describes the 'flash'

Ear problems

Lesions on the ear include

A chilblains
B squamous cell carcinoma
C tophi
D psoriasis
E eczema
F kerato-acanthoma

Match the following descriptions to one of the above:

☐ 95 rapidly grow on the helix
☐ 96 affects the entire ear
☐ 97 affects behind and below the ears, and elsewhere on the body
☐ 98 appears on antihelix usually
☐ 99 appears on helix and may need biopsy for diagnosis
☐ 100 painful and itchy

PRACTICE PAPER 3 — SECTION 1: MCQs

Total time allowed for sections 1 and 2 is three hours. Section 1 has 400 items, section 2 has 100. Indicate your answers clearly by putting a tick or cross in the box alongside each answer or by writing the appropriate letter in Section 2.

Statistics about accidents show that

☐ 1 road traffic accidents are the most common cause of accidents in young children
☐ 2 falls are the most common cause of accidents in people over 65 years
☐ 3 seat belt legislation resulted in little reduction in death or serious accidents for drivers
☐ 4 drowning is an unusual cause of accidents in children under 14 years
☐ 5 alcohol is a significant factor in accidents occurring in young people and the elderly

An incidental finding of a raised prolactin level could be explained by

☐ 6 hypothyroidism
☐ 7 metoclopramide
☐ 8 pregnancy
☐ 9 bromocriptine
☐ 10 acromegaly

The following have been shown to be ototoxic:

☐ 11 quinine
☐ 12 frusemide
☐ 13 erythromycin
☐ 14 ciprofloxacin
☐ 15 nifedipine

A 54-year-old patient presents with her periods 'restarting' after an absence of one year

☐ 16 an investigation is mandatory
☐ 17 topical oestrogens are a probable cause
☐ 18 cervical polyps do not cause symptoms at this age
☐ 19 urethral caruncles do not bleed
☐ 20 if accompanied by discharge this increases the likelihood of carcinoma of the cervix

Concerning coronary artery bypass grafting

☐ 21 it does not improve the survival of those with persisting anginal pain at rest
☐ 22 operative mortality is approximately 10% in the UK
☐ 23 females have a higher operative risk than males
☐ 24 if angina is absent at one year, recurrence risk is minimal
☐ 25 internal mammary artery conduits produce better results than saphenous vein grafts

When diagnosing hysteria

☐ 26 patients have high levels of depression
☐ 27 amnesia occurs in the majority of people with the diagnosis
☐ 28 'Belle indifference' typically occurs
☐ 29 it characteristically occurs in later life
☐ 30 symptoms are associated with a psychological advantage to the patient

Mumps, measles and rubella (MMR) vaccine

☐ 31 more than 85% of 2-year-old children have been vaccinated in the UK
☐ 32 the incidence of confirmed rubella in pregnancy has more than halved since introduction of the vaccine
☐ 33 it is contraindicated in children who are HIV positive
☐ 34 meningoencephalitis has been reported following exposure to the vaccine
☐ 35 should be used within one hour of reconstitution

Epidemiology of smoking and alcohol use in the UK

☐ 36 more women smoke than men
☐ 37 the average male smoker consumes approximately 20 cigarettes per day
☐ 38 cigarette smoking in children aged 11–15 years is falling
☐ 39 patients with alcohol problems consult their GPs twice as often as the average patient
☐ 40 heavy drinkers who do not smoke have an increased incidence of cancers

When considering post-viral fatigue syndrome

☐ 41 fatigue is the second most common reason to consult the doctor by the general population
☐ 42 delayed fatigue developing after exertion would suggest a different diagnosis
☐ 43 the majority of patients have no psychopathology
☐ 44 depression is the most common psychiatric disorder
☐ 45 prolonged rest is the treatment of choice

A patient presents with acute onset of a painful, photophobic red eye with impairment of vision. The following are possible diagnoses:

☐ 46 episcleritis
☐ 47 iritis
☐ 48 keratitis
☐ 49 sub-conjunctival haemorrhage
☐ 50 glaucoma

The differential diagnosis of a pustular rash occurring on the palms of the hands should include

☐ 51 infected eczema
☐ 52 scabies
☐ 53 pustular psoriasis
☐ 54 ichthyosis
☐ 55 erythema multiforme

In schizophrenia

☐ 56 the onset is usually between 15 and 45 years of age
☐ 57 the age of onset is earlier in females
☐ 58 paranoid delusions are usually diagnostic
☐ 59 a long duration of untreated psychosis predicts a chronic disease pattern
☐ 60 apathy is common in chronic schizophrenia

A 1-year-old child without diarrhoea attends the surgery, the following would suggest significant dehydration:

☐ 61 crying with few tears
☐ 62 visible weight loss
☐ 63 bradycardia
☐ 64 dry mouth
☐ 65 irritability

A 20-year-old patient with asthma rapidly becomes more dyspnoeic

☐ 66 the extent of rhonchi predicts the severity of the attack
☐ 67 pneumothorax typically occurs in this age group
☐ 68 tachycardia is a reliable predictor of severity
☐ 69 peak flow levels are unreliable in judging severe disease
☐ 70 the majority of acute attacks develop within 24 hours of the first symptom

Obesity is associated with the following conditions:

☐ 71 hiatus hernia
☐ 72 endometrial carcinoma
☐ 73 hyperlipidaemia
☐ 74 infertility
☐ 75 hypertension

The following additional factors would indicate significant pathology with the presentation of headaches around the eye:

☐ 76 haloes around lights
☐ 77 sleep disturbances due to the headache
☐ 78 a red eye
☐ 79 amblyopia
☐ 80 a pale optic disc

In alcohol withdrawal syndrome

☐ 81 the risk of developing symptoms is related to the amount of intake
☐ 82 seizures typically occur within the first 12 hours after stopping drinking
☐ 83 delirium tremens has a mortality in excess of 20%
☐ 84 auditory hallucinations occurring after 72 hours of the last alcohol intake would signify that there was some other pathology
☐ 85 withdrawal symptoms typically commence within 3–6 hours of the last drink

Sudden infant death syndrome (SIDS) is associated with the following:

☐ 86 a difficult delivery in labour
☐ 87 a mother addicted to narcotic agents
☐ 88 a decreasing risk with greater parity
☐ 89 sleeping in a prone position
☐ 90 being a twin

When treating scabies with gamma benzene hexachloride (Quellada)

☐ 91 the application should be preceded by a hot bath
☐ 92 it is contraindicated in pregnant women
☐ 93 itching that fails to resolve 2 weeks after treatment is an indication for a further application
☐ 94 a single application left in contact with the skin has been shown to be adequate treatment
☐ 95 treatment of the face is essential if all the mites are to be eradicated

Concerning Hodgkin's disease

☐ 96 it most commonly presents with a fever
☐ 97 cervical lymph nodes are most commonly involved
☐ 98 hepatomegaly is a typical finding at presentation
☐ 99 chemotherapy is the most appropriate treatment for localised disease
☐ 100 the majority of patients can be cured

Agoraphobic patients

☐ 101 are typically female
☐ 102 have a higher incidence of marital problems than the general population
☐ 103 typically have a fear of fainting
☐ 104 if they report depersonalisation this would indicate other pathology
☐ 105 show a good response to aversion therapy

Fixed drug eruptions

☐ 106 always occur at the same site with a specific drug
☐ 107 appear within 5–10 minutes of administration
☐ 108 discoloration of the skin remains for several months
☐ 109 have blistering in the lesions which makes the diagnosis unlikely
☐ 110 have well-defined borders

These statements are about personality types

☐ 111 Type A personalities have twice the risk of stroke compared to Type B
☐ 112 Type A personalities show impatience and competitiveness
☐ 113 cyclothymic personality is linked to bipolar affective disorder
☐ 114 for treatment to be effective, it usually has to be given as an in-patient
☐ 115 a pre-morbid schizoid personality is a predictive factor of chronicity in a schizophrenic

You decide that your present premises are inadequate and wish to move to a new property

☐ 116 improvement grants can be used to help towards the construction of new premises
☐ 117 if you are a training practice a separate room must be provided for the trainee
☐ 118 the cost rent scheme limits the size of the consultation rooms
☐ 119 notional rent is paid by the FHSA to reimburse existing GPs for capital tied up in their own surgery
☐ 120 once a practice undertakes a cost rent scheme it is unable to change back to notional rent reimbursement

Concerning paracetamol overdosage

- ☐ 121 ingestion of 10 g is associated with the development of liver damage
- ☐ 122 chronic alcohol ingestion protects against liver damage
- ☐ 123 antidote therapy is ineffective if given more than 15 hours after the overdose
- ☐ 124 patients on carbamazepine are at greater risk of toxic effects
- ☐ 125 mortality has significantly decreased in the last 10 years

The Access to Health Records Act 1990

- ☐ 126 provides rights of access to computer held records only
- ☐ 127 health visitor records are exempt
- ☐ 128 there is no right of access to notes made before November 1991
- ☐ 129 a doctor has 21 days to respond to a request for access
- ☐ 130 a fee may be charged for allowing a patient access

The following statements are true of cardiac valve disease in the elderly:

- ☐ 131 aortic stenosis is the commonest valve lesion
- ☐ 132 a soft murmur excludes aortic stenosis
- ☐ 133 rheumatic heart disease is the cause of the majority of cases of mitral stenosis
- ☐ 134 prolapsed mitral valve is the main cause of mitral regurgitation
- ☐ 135 the majority of patients over 70 years of age have a murmur

The following are high risk factors for osteoporosis:

- ☐ 136 late menarche
- ☐ 137 early menopause
- ☐ 138 nulliparity
- ☐ 139 alcoholism
- ☐ 140 high salt consumption

In mental retardation due to fragile X syndrome

☐ 141 the majority of mothers are mildly mentally handicapped
☐ 142 bat ears are associated
☐ 143 it can be detected antenatally
☐ 144 infantile autism is associated
☐ 145 there is a male predominance

The regulations governing the availability of General Practitioners under the terms of service, include the following:

☐ 146 full time unrestricted GPs must be available to patients for a minimum of 26 hours per week
☐ 147 GPs must be available for 45 weeks per year
☐ 148 the times of availability must be approved by the FHSA
☐ 149 job sharing GPs must still be available for 5 days per week
☐ 150 the hours of availability to patients include travelling time

The following drugs undergo significant first-pass metabolism:

☐ 151 salbutamol
☐ 152 paracetamol
☐ 153 codeine
☐ 154 metoclopramide
☐ 155 acyclovir

During the normal ovulatory cycle

☐ 156 after ovulation, cervical mucus is a watery, stretchy, transparent secretion
☐ 157 during ovulation the os will admit the tip of a finger
☐ 158 basal body temperature is higher in the luteal phase
☐ 159 after ovulation the cervix remains soft to the touch
☐ 160 ovulation predictor tests measure oestrogenic surge

Concerning Parkinson's disease

☐ 161 tremor is the most prominent feature of Parkinsonism in the elderly
☐ 162 it has a prevalence of approximately 1 in 1000 in the elderly
☐ 163 prolonged use of levodopa is associated with 'freezing' episodes
☐ 164 selegiline is only suitable for patients who no longer respond to levodopa
☐ 165 it does not cause cognitive impairment

The following advice is given to patients about driving ordinary cars:

☐ 166 patients who have a pacemaker fitted should not drive
☐ 167 after a heart attack, patients should avoid driving for 3 months
☐ 168 an epileptic can only drive when he has been fit-free for 2 years
☐ 169 patients experiencing a migraine headache should not drive
☐ 170 patients should not drive for 4 weeks following coronary angioplasty
☐ 171 patients should not drive for 12 hours following minor out-patient surgery requiring a general anaesthetic

When considering fibroids

☐ 172 spontaneous shrinkage takes place at the menopause
☐ 173 hormone replacement therapy has been shown to stimulate growth of fibroids
☐ 174 gonadotrophin releasing hormone analogues cause significant decrease in the size of fibroids
☐ 175 gonadotrophin releasing hormone analogues cause increased bone loss
☐ 176 surgery is indicated for fibroids that have a size over that of a 14–16 week gestation

The following have been shown to trigger anxiety states:

☐ 177 monoamine oxidase inhibitors
☐ 178 hypoglycaemia
☐ 179 severe angina
☐ 180 caffeine
☐ 181 paroxysmal atrial tachycardia

Teratogenicity has been shown to occur as follows with the drugs listed:

☐ 182 sodium valproate, has been shown to be associated with an increased risk of spina bifida
☐ 183 phenytoin is associated with congenital heart disease
☐ 184 carbamazepine is associated with bone marrow depression
☐ 185 lithium carbonate is associated with congenital heart disease
☐ 186 heparin is associated with central nervous system defects

Acute suppurative otitis media

☐ 187 has a peak incidence at 2–3 years of age
☐ 188 is more common in smoking households
☐ 189 is more common in atopic individuals
☐ 190 the majority are bacterial in origin
☐ 191 approximately 5% will develop mastoiditis

Concerning pulmonary embolism in pregnancy

☐ 192 the majority of cases occur antenatally
☐ 193 primigravidae are more at risk than belle multigravidae
☐ 194 patients with a previous history of thromboembolism should have prophylactic treatment throughout the pregnancy
☐ 195 it is the commonest cause of maternal death in the UK
☐ 196 those who have an instrumental delivery are at greater risk of a post-natal embolism than those who deliver normally

In acute appendicitis

☐ 197 increasing dietary fibre has been shown to decrease the incidence of the condition
☐ 198 it occurs in more than 10% of the population
☐ 199 the majority of elderly patients have perforated by the time they reach surgery
☐ 200 the majority of children have perforated by the time they reach surgery
☐ 201 retrocaecal appendices are associated with classic symptoms

Concerning consent in the United Kingdom

☐ 202 all material risks to a patient must be given
☐ 203 information about a risk can only be withheld if it would pose a serious threat of psychological detriment to the patient
☐ 204 consent must be given in writing
☐ 205 patients under 16 years of age are able to give consent
☐ 206 for taking intimate samples under the Police and Criminal Evidence Act, parental consent is needed for those under 17 years of age

Under the terms of the 1990 contract a General Practitioner will be reimbursed for the following minor surgical procedures:

☐ 207 insertion of a hormonal implant
☐ 208 colposcopy
☐ 209 injection of a frozen shoulder with depot steroids
☐ 210 removal of a nasal foreign body
☐ 211 liquid nitrogen applied to a verruca

Concerning leukaemia in childhood

☐ 212 the peak incidence is at 7–12 years of age
☐ 213 the majority are acute myeloblastic leukaemia
☐ 214 the majority of patients with acute lymphoblastic leukaemia will survive 5 years after cessation of therapy
☐ 215 maintenance cytotoxics are usually needed for about 3 years
☐ 216 the average GP will see one new case every 200 years

When prescribing hormone replacement therapy the following are true:

☐ 217 diabetes is an absolute contraindication to treatment
☐ 218 oestradiol implants have been shown not to improve atrophic vaginitis
☐ 219 breakthrough bleeding whilst on treatment can be safely ignored
☐ 220 unopposed oestrogen therapy has an adverse effect on lipid levels
☐ 221 to be effective in the treatment of osteoporosis, it should be given for approximately 10 years

In cancer of the colon

☐ 222 a diet high in animal fat and low in fibre appears to be a risk factor
☐ 223 familial adenomatous polyposis coli always leads to cancer of the colon if the patient lives to normal life span
☐ 224 hereditary non-polyposis colorectal cancer accounts for about 15% of cases of colonic cancer
☐ 225 familial adenomatous polyposis presents in early teenage years with loose stools and mucus
☐ 226 faecal occult blood testing is a sensitive test for colonic cancer

Concerning impotence in men

☐ 227 if of sudden onset is more likely to be organic
☐ 228 is more common in those with peripheral arterial disease
☐ 229 when treated with papaverine, it is given into the dorsal vein of the penis
☐ 230 an erection produced by papaverine typically lasts 12 hours
☐ 231 vacuum condoms are available on NHS prescription

The senile squalor syndrome (Diogenes syndrome)

☐ 232 typically affects married couples
☐ 233 the majority have significant psychiatric illness
☐ 234 is significantly associated with heavy alcohol intake
☐ 235 rapidly improves on admission to hospital
☐ 236 patients are of above average intelligence

Pulled elbow

- ☐ 237 affects children of pre-school age
- ☐ 238 is caused by a fall on the outstretched hand
- ☐ 239 requires operative reduction
- ☐ 240 X-rays show a characteristic appearance
- ☐ 241 is more common on the left than the right

When differentiating between ulcerative colitis and Crohn's disease, the following are true:

- ☐ 242 rectal bleeding is more common in Crohn's disease
- ☐ 243 rectal involvement is present in the majority of patients with ulcerative colitis
- ☐ 244 strictures are a frequent occurrence in ulcerative colitis
- ☐ 245 abdominal pain is typical of Crohn's disease
- ☐ 246 the majority of patients with Crohn's disease present with diarrhoea

Concerning squint

- ☐ 247 it is a typical presentation of retinoblastoma
- ☐ 248 paralytic squints are more common in children than in adults
- ☐ 249 operative treatment will correct amblyopia at the age of 8 years
- ☐ 250 patching can lead to amblyopia in the 'good' eye
- ☐ 251 co-operation of the child is necessary before considering referral

Oral contraceptives confer the following gynaecological benefits:

- ☐ 252 decreased incidence of cervical erosion
- ☐ 253 suppression of benign breast disease
- ☐ 254 decrease in ovarian cancer
- ☐ 255 decrease in endometrial cancer
- ☐ 256 decreased risk of carcinoma *in situ* of the cervix

A 30-year-old female patient presents with episodes of vomiting, the following would suggest a diagnosis of Addison's disease:

☐ 257 abdominal pain
☐ 258 weight loss
☐ 259 hypokalaemia
☐ 260 very low blood urea
☐ 261 hypertension

The incidence of dementia has been shown to be reduced by

☐ 262 social support of the bereaved
☐ 263 a well-balanced diet
☐ 264 avoidance of beef
☐ 265 treatment of hypertension
☐ 266 over 75 screening by General Practitioners

Restless legs

☐ 267 are a familial complaint
☐ 268 show a tendency to worsen in the evening
☐ 269 are worsened by benzodiazepine hypnotics
☐ 270 an association with systemic disease has not been shown
☐ 271 is associated with excessive coffee ingestion

In milestones of childhood development

☐ 272 by 9 months, most children are standing with support
☐ 273 at 6 weeks, most children are smiling and their eyes follow in the horizontal plane
☐ 274 at 9 months, most children can walk with one hand held
☐ 275 at 1 year, most children can use about 20 words with meaning
☐ 276 by the age of 3 years, most children are dry by day
☐ 277 at 3 years, children can usually walk up and down stairs alone

Audit

☐ 278 is prescriptive
☐ 279 is a passive process
☐ 280 is looking for mistakes
☐ 281 is solely concerned with problem solving
☐ 282 the boundaries between audit and research are clear-cut

The following drugs are available without a doctor's prescription:

☐ 283 terfenadine tablets
☐ 284 glyceryl trinitrate tablets
☐ 285 chloroquine tablets
☐ 286 miconazole cream
☐ 287 pyridoxine 50 mg tablets

Acute pyelonephritis in pregnancy

☐ 288 typically presents in the first trimester
☐ 289 reoccurs in approximately one-quarter of cases
☐ 290 is associated with an increased chance of pre-term labour
☐ 291 is associated with fetal growth retardation
☐ 292 ciprofloxacin is indicated for treatment

A 23-year-old male presents with low back pain, the following would support a diagnosis of ankylosing spondylitis:

☐ 293 early morning stiffness in the back
☐ 294 raised ESR
☐ 295 an associated peripheral arthritis
☐ 296 a recent history of painful red eye
☐ 297 a positive family history

The following conditions cause skin rashes that are intensely itchy:

☐ 298 dermatitis artefacta
☐ 299 polymorphic eruption of pregnancy
☐ 300 nodular
☐ 301 dermatitis herpetiformis
☐ 302 lichen simplex

Puerperal psychosis

☐ 303 typically presents by the 10th day following delivery
☐ 304 typically presents with mania, eventually becoming depressive
☐ 305 is associated with an increased risk of infanticide
☐ 306 ECT has been shown to be of no value in treatment
☐ 307 typically remits within 2–3 months

Adult gastrointestinal infections have been shown to have the following characteristics:

☐ 308 *Campylobacter* typically produces a febrile illness
☐ 309 *Shigella* is associated with blood in the stools
☐ 310 *Giardia* produces severe colicky pain
☐ 311 *Salmonella* without blood stream invasion lasts 3–4 days
☐ 312 *Salmonella* with blood stream invasion typically lasts 7–10 days

When considering fibrinolytic drugs in myocardial infarction

☐ 313 streptokinase is given by i.v. bolus injection
☐ 314 the use of aspirin is contraindicated for 12 months after use of streptokinase
☐ 315 fibrinolytic drugs are contraindicated in patients over 80 years of age
☐ 316 streptokinase can be repeated 3 months after initial use if a second infarct develops at that time
☐ 317 a recently diagnosed duodenal ulcer is a contraindication to the use of a fibrinolytic

The following are true of developmental milestones in a normal child:

☐ 318 at 6 weeks the Moro reflex is still retained
☐ 319 at 7 months the majority can stand without support
☐ 320 at 12 months they can say 3 words with meaning
☐ 321 at 30 months the majority will be dry at night
☐ 322 at 54 months the majority can dress themselves

Hypertrophic cardiomyopathy

☐ 323 is an inherited disorder
☐ 324 is typically a disease of old age
☐ 325 characteristically presents with shortness of breath
☐ 326 is the most common cause of sudden death in athletes
☐ 327 electrocardiographic changes are typical

Poor predictive factors for chronic schizophrenia include

☐ 328 history of perinatal trauma
☐ 329 insidious onset
☐ 330 late onset
☐ 331 higher socio-economic class
☐ 332 schizoid personality trait
☐ 333 family history of schizophrenia
☐ 334 living in a Third World country

A 32-year-old female patient presents with acute onset of neck pains of musculo-skeletal origin. It has been shown that at this age

☐ 335 the majority of patients are pain free after one month
☐ 336 the majority of patients will have recurrence of pain within 2 years
☐ 337 soft cervical collars are of proven benefit in reducing the duration of symptoms
☐ 338 non-steroidal anti-inflammatory drugs have been shown to be of benefit in reducing the duration of symptoms
☐ 339 manipulative techniques (e.g. Cyriax) have been shown to be of no additional benefit

Corneal ulcers due to *Herpes simplex* infection

☐ 340 recur in the majority of cases
☐ 341 if associated with anterior uveitis may lead to secondary glaucoma
☐ 342 typically need treatment with acyclovir for more than 2 weeks
☐ 343 decreases visual acuity in the majority of patients
☐ 344 have a characteristic appearance on staining the cornea with fluorescein
☐ 345 are typically painless

Chlamydial infection

☐ 346 typically causes a vaginitis
☐ 347 is asymptomatic in the majority of women
☐ 348 is the most common cause of chronic prostatitis
☐ 349 if discovered in pregnancy is best left untreated until after delivery
☐ 350 associated urethritis is typically associated with a dysuria and a negative midstream urine culture

Epidemiology of backache in the United Kingdom

☐ 351 more than 10 million working days are lost per year
☐ 352 the average General Practitioner sees less than 30 acute backs per year
☐ 353 the majority recover within one month without treatment
☐ 354 less than 1 in 200 undergo surgery
☐ 355 rest in the initial stages of treatment has been shown to reduce the overall time away from work

The following have been shown to trigger attacks of irritable bowel syndrome:

☐ 356 metronidazole
☐ 357 wheat bran
☐ 358 milk
☐ 359 nystatin
☐ 360 stress

Nocturnal cramps have been shown to be caused by

☐ 361 cirrhosis of the liver
☐ 362 venous obstruction
☐ 363 peripheral arterial disease
☐ 364 L5/S1 disc compression
☐ 365 salbutamol administration

Concerning breast-feeding

☐ 366 UK government health targets for the year 2000 include one that 75% of babies are to be breast-fed
☐ 367 mastitis is typically caused by *Streptococcus*
☐ 368 it typically takes longer than bottle feeding
☐ 369 it causes babies to be obese with the same frequency as bottle feeding
☐ 370 weaning onto cows' milk should take place at 6 months of age

When considering the drug treatment of asthma with inhaler devices

☐ 371 the incidence of oral candidiasis is increased by the use of spacer devices
☐ 372 salmeterol is indicated for p.r.n. usage
☐ 373 intermittent terbutaline has been shown to lead to long term worsening of asthma
☐ 374 steroid dosage of 600 mg daily has been shown to be associated with adrenal suppression in adults
☐ 375 sodium cromoglycate is of no proven value in treating acute asthmatic attacks

Basic practice allowance

☐ 376 is not paid to partners who work less than full time
☐ 377 must be claimed annually
☐ 378 is paid in full to a single-handed GP with a list of 1000 patients
☐ 379 in a group practice the total list size is used to calculate the eligibility for the allowance

Active management of the third stage of labour by use of controlled cord traction and oxytocic drugs has been shown to be associated with

☐ 380 a shorter third stage of labour
☐ 381 a decreased incidence of post-partum haemorrhage
☐ 382 an increased incidence of retained placenta
☐ 383 an increased incidence of post-partum hypertension
☐ 384 an increased incidence of post-partum vomiting

Hypercalcaemia can result from

- ☐ 385 malignancy
- ☐ 386 hypothyroidism
- ☐ 387 use of thiazide diuretics
- ☐ 388 immobilisation
- ☐ 389 vitamin D deficiency
- ☐ 390 renal dialysis

Amitriptyline has been shown to be of benefit in the treatment of

- ☐ 391 post-viral fatigue syndrome
- ☐ 392 Bell's palsy
- ☐ 393 post-herpetic neuralgia
- ☐ 394 irritable bowel syndrome
- ☐ 395 migraine

A baby is diagnosed as having a patent ductus arteriosus at 7 days of age. The following are true:

- ☐ 396 closure typically takes place within 48 hours of birth
- ☐ 397 prematurity is associated with delay in closure
- ☐ 398 indomethacin has been shown to promote closure
- ☐ 399 without treatment the majority of patients will die before 30 years of age
- ☐ 400 infective endocarditis rarely complicates the condition

Chest pain

Causes of chest pain seen in general practice include

A	pulmonary embolism	E	oesophageal reflux
B	myocardial infarction	F	related to spinal cord
C	pericarditis	G	aortic aneurysm
D	pneumothorax	H	cardiac neurosis

Which would be the most likely diagnosis in the following patients?

☐ 1 a tall man of 22 years who experiences a tight pain and becomes very short of breath suddenly

☐ 2 a rather obese 43-year-old lady experiences repeated burning pain especially on bending to put on her shoes and in the evening after dinner

☐ 3 a 24-year-old female has sudden central chest pain; friends say she went 'blue' and she starts spitting up specks of blood

☐ 4 a 52-year-old man has aching upper chest pain and shoulder pain which he has noticed since changing office one week ago

☐ 5 a 68-year-old man describes a dull ache which suddenly became a 'tearing' feeling; this pain goes into his back and he feels cold and clammy

☐ 6 a 64-year-old man experiences severe chest pain with sudden onset of sweating and difficulty breathing; he told his work colleagues he had pain in his right arm and they noticed he was very pale

☐ 7 a 44-year-old man describes pain under his left nipple, and is unable to take a deep breath; he is tender in the area of pain and around the heart apex beat area

Headaches

Types of headache include

A tension headache
B cervical nerve root irritation
C migraine
D cluster headaches
E sinusitis
F depression

Match the following statements with the most appropriate type of headache:

☐ 8 a 35-year-old woman with patches of tenderness in the scalp during headaches
☐ 9 a 40-year-old man with episodes of severe headaches and a watery eye
☐ 10 a 32-year-old woman who describes her headache as a weight on the top of the head
☐ 11 a 54-year-old woman with aches and pains, poor appetite and a persistent headache
☐ 12 a 42-year-old teacher who gets flushing and pallor at the onset of her headache
☐ 13 a 46-year-old secretary who describes a throbbing headache associated with difficulty in focusing on her shorthand work

Stroke management

The following are sometimes used in the management of stroke:

A warfarin
B aspirin
C CT scan
D MRI scan
E carotid endarterectomy

Match the following with the most appropriate from the above list:

☐ 14 used in the primary prevention of strokes when the risk appears relatively low
☐ 15 used in the primary prevention of strokes in a patient over 65 years who has had a transient ischaemic attack
☐ 16 useful when needing to separate infarction from haemorrhage
☐ 17 useful when a carotid bruit is heard on clinical examination
☐ 18 used in high-risk patients
☐ 19 useful in a 60-year-old man with atrial fibrillation but no family or personal history of stroke

Childhood milestones

Children's ages

A 12 months
B 18 months
C 2 years
D 3 years
E 4 years
F 5 years

At what age would most children be able to perform the following tasks?

☐ 20 can state age and sex
☐ 21 can state first and last name
☐ 22 can say 2–3 words with meaning
☐ 23 can build a 3–4 cube tower
☐ 24 can hop on one foot
☐ 25 can copy a circle

Breast cancer screening

The following are important reports and trials about breast cancer screening:

A Health Insurance Plan
B Malmo Mammographic Screening Trial
C The Nijmegen Project
D UK Trial of Early Detection of Breast Cancer Group
E The Forrest Report

Match the following with one of the above:

☐ 26 invited some women to learn breast self-examination
☐ 27 an early randomly controlled control trial, with a one yearly screening interval, showed a 30% reduction in mortality in woman aged 40–60 years
☐ 28 a randomly controlled trial involving women older than 45 years showing no significant difference in mortality between screened and controlled group survival
☐ 29 was used as the basis for the introduction of the UK National Breast Screening Programme
☐ 30 a case control trial using one view mammography of women 35 years and older showed greater than 50% reduction of mortality

Diabetes

The following studies concern diabetic retinopathy:

A The Oslo Study
B The Pima Indians of Arizona
C The Bedford Study
D The Stena Study

Match the following statements to the most appropriate study:

☐ 31 the most marked worsening was seen in those with worst and best control
☐ 32 studied a group of whom 50% are diabetic
☐ 33 patients showed slowed deterioration with subcutaneous insulin infusion
☐ 34 these studies showed that retinopathy only developed in those with high fasting sugars or high 2 hour sugar after a glucose tolerance test.

Income

General practice income is derived from various sources, including

A non-medical income
B private medical work
C practice allowances
D capitation fees
E item-of-service payments
F reimbursements

Match the following with the appropriate source:

☐ 35 solicitors' reports
☐ 36 work as a school medical officer
☐ 37 child health surveillance
☐ 38 night visit payments
☐ 39 computer systems payment
☐ 40 rural practice payment
☐ 41 lecturing on an MRCGP course

Thrombolytic trials

Thrombolytic treatment trials and groups include

A GREAT group survey
B ISIS-2
C European Myocardial Infarct Project
D British Heart Foundation Working Group
E GISSI

For which of these is the following true?

☐ 42 suggests that GPs who give thrombolytics at home should have a defibrillator available
☐ 43 double-blind trial of anistreplase against placebo in home or hospital; it showed mortality was almost 50% lower in the early treatment group in this rural study
☐ 44 compared anistreplase against placebo in different situations – showed cardiac deaths were about 15% less in pre-hospital treatment
☐ 45 compared streptokinase and aspirin usage

Mental Health Act

The following are some sections of the 1983 Mental Health Act:

A 2
B 3
C 5
D 135
E 136

Which section applies to the following situations?

☐ 46 gives the police right of entry into premises to remove a patient to a place of safety
☐ 47 used in an emergency situation in hospital
☐ 48 used for a maximum of 28 days
☐ 49 hospital managers must appeal on behalf of the patient on renewal if the patient does not appeal
☐ 50 allows police to remove a patient from a public place to a place of safety

Benefits

The following are some of the many welfare benefits:

A Severe Disablement Allowance
B Attendance Allowance
C Disability Living Allowance
D Incapacity Benefit
E Statutory Sick Pay

Which benefit relates to the following?

☐ 51 paid to a person who requires help with mobility and is virtually unable to walk
☐ 52 paid by employers to employees for 28 weeks
☐ 53 for someone incapable of any work, who has not paid any National Insurance Contributions and is at least 80% disabled
☐ 54 paid to someone over 65 who requires substantial personal care or supervision
☐ 55 paid to a person under 65 who requires help with personal care day and night
☐ 56 paid at three rates to someone who continues to be unfit for any work

Infectious diseases

There is usually an interval between the onset of disease and the appearance of a rash in the following infectious diseases:

A rubella
B chickenpox
C scarlet fever
D measles
E typhoid

Match the following with the appropriate disease:

☐ 57 a longish period of 7–14 days between disease onset and rash
☐ 58 usually 3–5 days between onset and appearance of rash

☐ 59 a very short interval or none at all between onset and rash; the rash is characteristic with lesions of different stages

☐ 60 a short interval of 1–2 days; a very long infectivity period which can be dramatically shortened by appropriate treatment

☐ 61 a very short or no interval between disease onset and rash; the rash is often transient and clinical diagnosis unreliable

Statistics

In statistics the following are commonly used:

A standard deviation
B mode
C median
D mean
E correlation coefficient

Match the following statements with the appropriate term:

☐ 62 the most commonly occurring value
☐ 63 if +1, this indicates a complete direct association
☐ 64 measures the dispersion around the average value
☐ 65 the middle figure when all are put in order
☐ 66 the arithmetic average

Screening

The results of a screening test looking for diabetes in a general practice study were as follows:

	Screening test positive	**Screening test negative**
Diabetes present	**164**	**57**
Diabetes not present	**31**	**98**

Options available:

A	164	G	31/129
B	57	H	31/195
C	31	I	57/155
D	98	J	57/122
E	164/195	K	98/129
F	164/221	L	98/155

Select the appropriate option

- ☐ 67 sensitivity
- ☐ 68 specificity
- ☐ 69 positive predictive value
- ☐ 70 negative predictive value
- ☐ 71 false positive

Scrotal swellings

Some causes of lumps found in the scrotum include

A inguinal hernia
B epididymal cyst
C hydrocoele
D TB of epididymis
E testicular tumour

Choose the most appropriate of these in the following circumstances:

- ☐ 72 in a 32-year-old man there is a lump in the scrotum which appears hard; the testis cannot be felt but the lump transilluminates very well
- ☐ 73 in a 38-year-old man there is a small swelling in the scrotum; on examination the upper end of the swelling cannot be found
- ☐ 74 a 34-year-old presents with a swelling in his scrotum; the testes appear normal clinically but there is a lump in the scrotum which transilluminates slightly
- ☐ 75 a 41-year-old has noticed on self-examination a lump on one side of the scrotum; this is confirmed as being a hard thickening just separate from the testis

Rheumatoid arthritis

Drugs used in the treatment of rheumatoid arthritis include

A methotrexate
B chloroquine
C gold
D penicillamine
E sulphasalazine

Match the following statements with the most appropriate of these drugs:

☐ 76 can cause exfoliative dermatitis
☐ 77 can cause retinal damage
☐ 78 can cause hepatic and pulmonary fibrosis
☐ 79 oral pigmentation, similar to that in Addison's disease, may be seen
☐ 80 can be used in severe uncontrolled psoriasis
☐ 81 monthly Amsler testing by the patient may be used in long-term therapy
☐ 82 can be associated with azoospermia
☐ 83 loss of taste may occur but returns whether or not treatment is stopped

Mouth ulcers

The causes of mouth ulcers include

A Reiter's syndrome
B primary syphilis
C trauma
D lichen planus
E aphthous ulcers
F hand, foot and mouth disease

Match the descriptions below with one of the above causes

☐ 84 associated with arthritis, iritis and genital ulcers
☐ 85 has a painless, hard base
☐ 86 small round ulcers with a red margin, often painful
☐ 87 lesions are 'cotton wool' patches or erosive
☐ 88 sore throat is an early feature. There are often spots on the buttocks
☐ 89 lesions on soles and palms, vesicular in nature, may be seen

Diabetes

Oral anti-diabetic drugs include the following:

A chlorpropamide
B glibenclamide
C metformin
D acarbose

Match the following statements with the most appropriate of the above drugs:

- ☐ 90 delays the digestion of starch and sucrose and so delays increase in blood glucose levels after meals
- ☐ 91 a short-acting sulphonylurea
- ☐ 92 a biguanide
- ☐ 93 used especially in overweight patients either first or when diet and other treatment has failed
- ☐ 94 may cause hypoglycaemia especially in the elderly
- ☐ 95 may cause lactic acidosis in patients with renal failure

Bodies allied to general practice

Local and national bodies allied to general practice and having a close impact on it include

A HEC
B MAAG
C GMC
D PPA
E GPC

Match the following statements with the appropriate body:

- ☐ 96 an authority of regional status accountable to the Secretary of State; promotes training schemes for workers in the field
- ☐ 97 has status of Special Health Authority and has one of the biggest computer systems within the NHS
- ☐ 98 provides guidelines on expected standards of care and conduct
- ☐ 99 formerly known as GMSC; it is a committee of the BMA
- ☐ 100 a local body established in co-operation by FHSAs and LMCs

PRACTICE PAPER 4 — SECTION 1: MCQs

Total time allowed for sections 1 and 2 is three hours. Section 1 has 400 items, section 2 has 100. Indicate your answers clearly by putting a tick or cross in the box alongside each answer or by writing the appropriate letter in Section 2.

The following statements are about cancer of the cervix uteri:

☐ 1 it is a major cause of death in women
☐ 2 it is almost certainly caused by human papilloma virus (HPV) type 13
☐ 3 the time taken to progress from CIN I to invasive carcinoma is about 10 years
☐ 4 high-risk groups include early age of first pregnancy
☐ 5 people in a high socio-economic class are at high risk
☐ 6 the cervical screening programme has resulted in a decreasing death rate in young women

The following factors have been shown to have adverse prognostic significance in the acute stage of stroke:

☐ 7 pre-existing treated hypertension
☐ 8 bilateral extensor plantar responses
☐ 9 impaired level of consciousness
☐ 10 previous myocardial infarction
☐ 11 inability to walk

Polycystic ovary syndrome

☐ 12 is detectable by ultrasound
☐ 13 is associated with oligomenorrhoea
☐ 14 has an increased risk of early miscarriage
☐ 15 has a raised LH/FSH ratio
☐ 16 associated hirsutism responds to cyproterone acetate

Concerning head lice

☐ 17 the overall incidence is declining in the UK
☐ 18 resistance to standard preparations has not emerged
☐ 19 shampoos are more effective than lotions
☐ 20 treatment with carbaryl confers a residual protective effect
☐ 21 malathion is inactivated by swimming in chlorinated water
☐ 22 nit combing is essential if the disease is to be eradicated

Recent weight loss of over 5% in a patient over 65 has been shown to be associated with

☐ 23 physical illness in the majority of cases
☐ 24 malignancy in approximately 20%
☐ 25 the reason for the weight loss being usually apparent at the initial examination
☐ 26 follow-up being indicated in those with no apparent pathology
☐ 27 the majority of those without obvious pathology increasing their weight within one year

You have a 68-year-old woman in the practice with a diagnosis of 'pernicious anaemia'. She is maintained on monthly injections of hydroxocobalamin. On reviewing her case the following are true:

☐ 28 a Schilling test cannot be performed now that B12 stores are replete
☐ 29 dietary deficiency is more common than autoimmune gastric atrophy
☐ 30 dependency upon B12 is unknown
☐ 31 hydroxocobalamin is usually given every 3 months
☐ 32 excessive administration of B12 causes harmful side-effects

Wood's light

☐ 33 is a source of infra-red light
☐ 34 causes eczematous skin to fluoresce pink
☐ 35 causes scalp ringworm to fluoresce green
☐ 36 will detect complete loss of pigment in vitiligo
☐ 37 will help differentiate common warts from seborrhoeic warts

Depression in the elderly has been shown to be associated with

☐ 38 delusions of poverty
☐ 39 pseudodementia
☐ 40 a closer association with bereavement than in younger patients
☐ 41 agitation
☐ 42 retardation

Concerning cryotherapy

☐ 43 the majority of children of 5 years of age can tolerate cryotherapy
☐ 44 basal cell carcinomas are unsuitable for treatment
☐ 45 if a 'triple response' occurs the treatment should not be used again
☐ 46 local swelling means the length of application was excessive
☐ 47 liquid nitrogen destroys viruses

Prescriptions are issued free to patients with the following conditions:

☐ 48 rheumatoid arthritis
☐ 49 chronic glaucoma
☐ 50 asthma
☐ 51 myxoedema
☐ 52 hyperthyroidism

Concerning accidents in children

☐ 53 they are the most common cause of death in the 1–15 age group
☐ 54 the majority of accidental deaths occur in the home
☐ 55 every year 1:10 children will attend the doctor with an accidental injury
☐ 56 preventative education has been shown to save lives
☐ 57 5% of accidental poisonings are fatal

For people who have blind registration

☐ 58 a TV licence fee is not payable
☐ 59 parking concessions are available
☐ 60 Severe Disablement Allowance (SDA) is available for those of working age
☐ 61 free postage is available only on items relating to the incapacity

Hypertensive retinopathy has the following features:

☐ 62 cotton wool spots are a feature of grade III retinopathy
☐ 63 the changes associated with grade II retinopathy are reversible with good hypertensive control
☐ 64 retinal haemorrhages associated with retinopathy typically interfere with vision
☐ 65 papilloedema due to hypertension is indistinguishable from that due to raised intracranial pressure
☐ 66 arterio-venous crossing changes indicate arteriosclerosis

Pacemakers are associated with

☐ 67 a restriction in activity
☐ 68 the majority being implanted for the treatment of complete heart block
☐ 69 unreliable ECG appearances in the event of a myocardial infarction
☐ 70 the most common cause of death post-implant being primary pacemaker failure
☐ 71 a lifespan of at least 5 years

The following would suggest an atypical grief reaction:

☐ 72 onset of distress delayed until 4 weeks after the death
☐ 73 open hostility to relatives
☐ 74 extreme social isolation
☐ 75 absence from work for 6 weeks
☐ 76 non-specific suicidal ideas

You are consulted by the parents of a 5-year-old boy recently diagnosed as having cystic fibrosis

☐ 77 late diagnosis implies medical neglect
☐ 78 there is a 1:2 chance of subsequent children being affected
☐ 79 the majority of patients with this condition will die by late teenage
☐ 80 affected boys are usually azoospermic
☐ 81 affected adolescents have an increased incidence of glucose intolerance

In carpal tunnel syndrome

☐ 82 pain radiating to the shoulder excludes the diagnosis
☐ 83 the dominant hand is typically affected
☐ 84 local steroid injections typically worsen the pain
☐ 85 it is associated with hypothyroidism
☐ 86 thenar wasting is a characteristic feature

A 63-year-old man has a high ESR; the following would support a diagnosis of myeloma:

☐ 87 hypercalcaemia
☐ 88 osteosclerotic lesions on X-ray
☐ 89 rouleaux on a peripheral blood film
☐ 90 peripheral neuropathy
☐ 91 unexplained bruising

Concerning endometriosis

☐ 92 ectopic endometrium is found in the majority of patients who have a laparoscopy for infertility
☐ 93 medical treatment of endometriosis has been shown to improve future fertility
☐ 94 pain is proportional to the extent of the disease
☐ 95 cyclical pain casts doubt on the diagnosis
☐ 96 medical treatment rarely causes an improvement within 6 months

When considering multiple sclerosis

☐ 97 the peak age of onset is about 30 years of age
☐ 98 there is no hereditary disposition
☐ 99 the majority of patients have full remission after the first attack
☐ 100 specific diagnostic tests are now available
☐ 101 the mean life expectancy is over 30 years after the presenting complaint

The Children's Act 1989 states that

- ☐ 102 Emergency Protection orders have a maximum duration of 8 days
- ☐ 103 only social workers can apply for an Emergency Protection order on a child
- ☐ 104 parental access is precluded during an Emergency Protection order
- ☐ 105 care orders and supervision orders are mutually exclusive
- ☐ 106 police protection provisions allow parental responsibility to be transferred to the police

In acute torticollis

- ☐ 107 it typically occurs in the over 40 year age group
- ☐ 108 it indicates underlying cervical arthritic changes
- ☐ 109 only active movements are limited
- ☐ 110 pain typically increases in intensity throughout the day
- ☐ 111 the neck is typically flexed towards the painful side

Legislation on wearing seatbelts requires drivers to wear seatbelts with the following exceptions:

- ☐ 112 after recent surgery on the abdomen
- ☐ 113 when in an advanced stage of pregnancy
- ☐ 114 whilst the driver is reversing
- ☐ 115 after recent thoracic surgery

When considering inhaled corticosteroids

- ☐ 116 nebulised steroids are more efficient than metered dose inhalers
- ☐ 117 adrenal suppression in adults has been shown to occur with a total daily dose of 1000 micrograms
- ☐ 118 larger volume spacer devices increase oropharyngeal deposition
- ☐ 119 inhibition of growth in children using 800 micrograms daily has been reported

Concerning urinary tract infections in children

- ☐ 120 the majority have no structural abnormality
- ☐ 121 10% of children will have had an infection by the time they are 10 years of age
- ☐ 122 the commonest abnormal finding is vesico-ureteric reflux
- ☐ 123 approximately half will present with non-specific symptoms under the age of 2 years
- ☐ 124 they may present as a diarrhoeal illness

The following are true of infective endocarditis:

- ☐ 125 mitral valve prolapse is a risk factor
- ☐ 126 the route of the infecting organism is obvious in the majority of cases
- ☐ 127 the mortality is minimal once treatment commences
- ☐ 128 anaemia is an atypical finding
- ☐ 129 the plasma viscosity is typically elevated

When looking at nails which are discoloured the following are true:

- ☐ 130 penicillamine stains nails yellow
- ☐ 131 an irregular yellow area associated with a thickened nail plate is typically due to tinea infection
- ☐ 132 familial leuconychia causes small white streaks on the nails
- ☐ 133 yellow nail syndrome is associated with lymphoedema elsewhere in the body
- ☐ 134 chloroquine stains nails green

Concerning research in general practice

- ☐ 135 research protocols typically contain the curriculum vitae, of the researcher
- ☐ 136 ethical committees have no interest in the source of finance for a research project
- ☐ 137 all risks must be made known to the participating patients
- ☐ 138 retrospective studies from patients' records require consent from the patient concerned
- ☐ 139 structured interviews have been shown to need specialist interviewers to obtain accurate results

When considering meningococcal meningitis

- ☐ 140 vaccine is effective against all strains
- ☐ 141 prevalence is decreasing
- ☐ 142 resistance of strains to penicillin has emerged
- ☐ 143 chloramphenicol is the chemoprophylactic agent of choice
- ☐ 144 immediate family members have a minimally increased risk of contracting the disease from an infected house member

In bulimia nervosa

- ☐ 145 the majority of patients with this condition are underweight
- ☐ 146 drug treatment has been shown to be less effective than intensive psychological treatments
- ☐ 147 fetal abnormalities have been shown to be more common in those patients who have bulimia
- ☐ 148 if associated with anorexia it carries a worse prognosis
- ☐ 149 it is associated with diuretic abuse

Your practice is unsure whether to give iron supplements routinely in pregnancy. In discussing the matter the following are true:

- ☐ 150 plasma ferritin levels accurately reflect maternal iron stores
- ☐ 151 neonatal iron stores are acquired in the last trimester
- ☐ 152 iron supplementation has been shown to reduce iron depletion
- ☐ 153 iron requirements are greatest in the first trimester
- ☐ 154 ferrous salts have a higher incidence of side-effects than the other iron salts

Opiate analgesics have been shown to interact with the following:

- ☐ 155 paracetamol
- ☐ 156 chlorpromazine
- ☐ 157 phenytoin
- ☐ 158 cimetidine
- ☐ 159 lactulose

Contraceptive fees are payable

☐ 160 if a practice nurse fits a diaphragm
☐ 161 if a temporary resident requesting emergency contraception signs an Immediate and Necessary treatment form
☐ 162 if the doctor gives the patient advice only
☐ 163 if a female patient seeks advice about her partner having a vasectomy
☐ 164 if a GP performs a vasectomy

Concerning Sudden Infant Death Syndrome (SIDS)

☐ 165 first-born children are at particular risk
☐ 166 the risk in twins is greater than in singletons
☐ 167 most occur between 6 and 12 months of age
☐ 168 most occur between October and March
☐ 169 the risk is reduced by placing the baby in a supine position to sleep
☐ 170 babies born by breech delivery are at particular risk

The following are true of general practice in the United Kingdom:

☐ 171 the average list size of a GP is less than 2000 patients
☐ 172 the majority of GPs practice in partnerships of four or more doctors
☐ 173 approximately 25% of UK practices are recognised for vocational training
☐ 174 the majority of GPs practice from Health Centres
☐ 175 the average GP sees more than 150 patients per week in the surgery

In Gilbert's syndrome

☐ 176 it occurs in more than 2% of the population
☐ 177 a liver biopsy shows abnormal histology
☐ 178 jaundice is worsened after a large meal
☐ 179 it is associated with development of gallstones
☐ 180 it is associated with a decreased life expectancy

Depressive disorders are typically associated with

- ☐ 181 feeling worse in the evening
- ☐ 182 an abnormal dexamethasone suppression test
- ☐ 183 delusions of poverty
- ☐ 184 amenorrhoea
- ☐ 185 difficulty in falling asleep

Normal adolescence is characterised by the following:

- ☐ 186 the first sign of puberty in boys is testicular growth
- ☐ 187 the first sign of puberty in girls is the appearance of pubic hair
- ☐ 188 the major part of weight gain is due to deposition of fat
- ☐ 189 girls are ahead of boys in all aspects of pubertal development
- ☐ 190 full stature is achieved approximately 4 years after the peak growth spurt

A 30-year-old female patient presents with a febrile illness and tender red nodular lesions on the lower legs. The following are probable diagnoses:

- ☐ 191 Lyme disease
- ☐ 192 erysipelas
- ☐ 193 erythema nodosum
- ☐ 194 acanthosis nigricans
- ☐ 195 Kaposi's sarcoma

In hypothermia

- ☐ 196 immersion in water as a cause of hypothermia increases the probability of death
- ☐ 197 cardiac arrhythmias do not occur until the body temperature is 33°C
- ☐ 198 unconsciousness typically occurs below a temperature of 33°C
- ☐ 199 confusion is a feature of a core temperature of 34°C
- ☐ 200 rewarming should occur at the same rate at which a patient becomes cold

When considering cataract surgery

- ☐ 201 it is more successful if performed at a later stage
- ☐ 202 it increases the risk of retinal detachment
- ☐ 203 thickening of the posterior capsule is a complication of intracapsular extraction
- ☐ 204 bed rest is required for 24 hours post-operatively
- ☐ 205 intra-ocular implants are only suitable for myopic patients

The following are true of angiotensin-converting enzyme inhibitors:

- ☐ 206 drug-induced cough typically resolves if treatment is continued
- ☐ 207 they are associated with intra-uterine death
- ☐ 208 lithium carbonate toxicity is potentiated
- ☐ 209 hyponatraemia only occurs if they are given concurrently with diuretics
- ☐ 210 skin rashes occur in less than 1% of patients

A 15-year-old girl presents with anterior knee pain, a diagnosis of chondromalacia patella would be supported by

- ☐ 211 pain on pressing the patella
- ☐ 212 pain worse on ascending stairs rather than on descending
- ☐ 213 palpable crepitus on passive movements
- ☐ 214 a normal 'skyline' knee X-ray
- ☐ 215 hyperextension of the knee joint by 10° or more

The practice annual report must contain the following information before submission to the FHSA:

- ☐ 216 the numbers of patients who referred themselves to the local casualty department
- ☐ 217 a list of courses attended by the GPs
- ☐ 218 the names of all staff employed
- ☐ 219 the changes planned during the next year
- ☐ 220 the number of referrals made to the genito-urinary clinic
- ☐ 221 the arrangements by which patients may comment on the service available

Statements about miscarriage

- ☐ 222 only 25% of women who have had three recurrent miscarriages will have a baby without any medical intervention
- ☐ 223 bacterial vaginosis is a risk factor for mid-trimester miscarriage
- ☐ 224 a Rhesus-negative woman should be given anti-D within 72 hours of bleeding in any stage of the pregnancy
- ☐ 225 40–50% of first miscarriages are due to chromosomal abnormalities
- ☐ 226 between about 5% and 15% of all pregnancies end in miscarriage

Delusions

- ☐ 227 are diagnostic of schizophrenia
- ☐ 228 can be modified by contrary experience
- ☐ 229 are obsessions
- ☐ 230 are false ideas
- ☐ 231 can be secondary to hallucinations

Hypothyroidism is associated with

- ☐ 232 a gruff voice
- ☐ 233 pre-tibial myxoedema
- ☐ 234 anaemia
- ☐ 235 muscle cramp
- ☐ 236 a malar flush

Concerning opiate addiction

- ☐ 237 doctors not licensed may prescribe methadone to a drug addict
- ☐ 238 a central register of opiate addicts is maintained
- ☐ 239 withdrawal symptoms commence 12 hours after the last dose of methadone
- ☐ 240 convulsions are associated with rapid withdrawal

A patient requests a home confinement. In responding to her the following are true:

- ☐ 241 fetal monitoring of low risk cases decreases morbidity in the baby
- ☐ 242 a doctor must be present at a home confinement
- ☐ 243 an abnormal delivery is more common in lower social classes
- ☐ 244 the majority of babies require some form of specialised assistance at or shortly after birth
- ☐ 245 a General Practitioner is under a contractual obligation to provide home care if the patient insists on a domiciliary confinement

Snoring has been shown to be associated with

- ☐ 246 enlarged tonsils
- ☐ 247 hypothyroidism
- ☐ 248 excessive daytime sleepiness
- ☐ 249 morning headaches
- ☐ 250 systemic hypertension

A patient of another practice in your town decides to register with you

- ☐ 251 responsibility for this patient does not commence until the 10th day after signing the initial registration form
- ☐ 252 the patient must be offered a health check in writing
- ☐ 253 new patient health checks attract an item of service payment
- ☐ 254 you must complete the health check at the time of registration
- ☐ 255 a separate fee is claimable for immunisations given at the time of registration

Concerning ciprofloxacin

- ☐ 256 aluminium-containing antacids interfere with absorption
- ☐ 257 theophylline levels are elevated if the two drugs are given concurrently
- ☐ 258 it is ineffective against *Pseudomonas aeroginosa*
- ☐ 259 it has been shown to be less active in acid urine
- ☐ 260 it has been shown to be more effective than doxycycline in the treatment of *Chlamydia*

In laparoscopic cholecystectomy

- ☐ 261 it is only suitable for a minority of patients with gallstones
- ☐ 262 the operative time is longer
- ☐ 263 return to work is earlier
- ☐ 264 post-operative complications are more frequent
- ☐ 265 a nasogastric tube needs to be passed pre-operatively

The following are true of pre-eclampsia:

- ☐ 266 proteinuria is an early feature
- ☐ 267 circadian rhythm of blood pressure is reversed
- ☐ 268 90% of normal pregnant women have oedema at term
- ☐ 269 early control of blood pressure has been shown to retard its progression
- ☐ 270 it is associated with placental abruption

Seborrhoeic eczema in infancy

- ☐ 271 has a peak age of onset under 3 months of age
- ☐ 272 is typically itchy
- ☐ 273 resolves spontaneously in the majority of children
- ☐ 274 typically fails to respond to emollients
- ☐ 275 characteristically involves the flexures

Concerning rubella

- ☐ 276 the incubation period is 2–3 days
- ☐ 277 it is contagious
- ☐ 278 prodromal symptoms of fever and conjunctivitis are usually present
- ☐ 279 the rash is vesicular in nature and covers the trunk
- ☐ 280 infection in pregnancy is serious and usually involves a florid rash

The following would support a diagnosis of maxillary sinusitis:

- ☐ 281 swelling of the cheek
- ☐ 282 pain in the teeth
- ☐ 283 pain worse on bending
- ☐ 284 clear nasal discharge
- ☐ 285 tenderness over the maxillary antrum

Health visitors

☐ 286 must have a post-basic training in paediatric nursing
☐ 287 must have a post-basic training in obstetrics
☐ 288 the majority conduct over-75 screening on behalf of General Practitioners
☐ 289 have a statutory obligation to visit post-natally on the first day after discharge from hospital
☐ 290 have self-employed status

The following statements are true of eye disease:

☐ 291 recurrent chalazia are associated with acne rosacea
☐ 292 blepharitis is common in patients with psoriasis
☐ 293 correction of entropion requires an operation under general anaesthetic
☐ 294 alkalis are less damaging than acids if accidentally splashed into the eye
☐ 295 Kaposi's sarcoma can affect the conjunctiva

The following drugs have been shown to cause an increase in the level of the serum alkaline phosphatase:

☐ 296 nitrofurantoin
☐ 297 phenytoin
☐ 298 erythromycin
☐ 299 tetracycline
☐ 300 disulfiram

Concerning atrophic vaginitis

☐ 301 it is the main reason that healthy retired couples refrain from intercourse
☐ 302 *Candida* infection is the most common cause of associated itching
☐ 303 local oestrogen therapy initially burns on application
☐ 304 prolonged local oestrogen therapy needs to be supplemented with progestogen
☐ 305 oestrogenic effects on the sexual partner have been reported when the spouse uses topical oestrogens

Folic acid

☐ 306 is found in green vegetables
☐ 307 is absorbed in the upper small bowel
☐ 308 is degraded by cooking
☐ 309 will reverse the macrocytosis associated with alcoholism
☐ 310 body stores are usually adequate for 3 years

When identifying patients with psychological problems in a consultation, research has shown General Practitioners

☐ 311 miss many disorders
☐ 312 vary nine-fold in their diagnosis of psychological problems
☐ 313 who show more empathy detect more problems
☐ 314 who make eye contact detect more problems
☐ 315 who are good at dealing with interruptions to the consultation detect less problems

Absorption of the following drugs has been shown to be increased if they are given on an empty stomach:

☐ 316 digoxin
☐ 317 allopurinol
☐ 318 co-trimoxazole
☐ 319 theophylline
☐ 320 penicillin

When considering treatment for prostatic carcinoma

☐ 321 gonadotrophin-releasing analogues have been shown to be as effective as bilateral orchidectomy
☐ 322 asymptomatic, microscopically detected disease has been shown not to need treatment
☐ 323 stilboestrol administration is associated with an increase in deaths from cardiovascular disease
☐ 324 androgen receptor blockers are associated with an increase in metastatic bone pain in the first week of treatment
☐ 325 gonadotrophin releasing analogues are associated with gynaecomastia

Concerning jaundice in the neonate

☐ 326 approximately half of all children are visibly icteric in the first week of life
☐ 327 physiological jaundice typically reaches peak levels at the fourth day
☐ 328 occurring on the first day of life is typically physiological
☐ 329 it is associated with hypothyroidism
☐ 330 it is associated with urinary tract infection

In haemorrhagic disease of the newborn

☐ 331 formula milk fed babies are at particular risk
☐ 332 vitamin D is implicated
☐ 333 the risk is increased if the baby's mother has been on medication for epilepsy
☐ 334 a single dose of oral vitamin supplement is usually sufficient to prevent the disease
☐ 335 prematurity is a high risk

A recently born baby has been diagnosed as having a hemiplegia due to cerebral palsy. When counselling the parents subsequently the doctor should be aware that

☐ 336 the mean IQ is about 80
☐ 337 the majority of children have speech problems
☐ 338 the incidence of specific learning defects has been shown to be greater than for the general population
☐ 339 those with persistent hypotonia have a better prognosis than those who develop spasticity
☐ 340 for children with an IQ greater than 70, education should be in the normal system

In stress polycythaemia

☐ 341 the PCV is typically greater than 0.55
☐ 342 the total body red cell mass is raised
☐ 343 it is more common in females
☐ 344 it is associated with obesity
☐ 345 it is associated with excessive alcohol consumption

When counselling a couple with involuntary infertility, the following are true:

☐ 346 the most common reason for the problem is an abnormality of the Fallopian tubes
☐ 347 the majority of couples not using contraceptives will conceive within 12 months
☐ 348 reconstructive tubal surgery carries an increased risk of ectopic pregnancy
☐ 349 the majority of women receiving clomiphene for anovulation will still not ovulate
☐ 350 *in vitro* fertilisation is associated with an increased incidence of fetal abnormalities

Psychogenic hyperventilation is associated with

☐ 351 alkalosis
☐ 352 a decreased peak expiratory flow rate
☐ 353 paraesthesia of the hands
☐ 354 cyanosis

When updating practice premises under the Cost Rent Scheme

☐ 355 the final amount paid depends upon the district valuer's assessment of the overall value of the completed project
☐ 356 the practice has to pay the capital
☐ 357 the FHSA will reimburse interest on the loan
☐ 358 payment begins as soon as the building work has commenced
☐ 359 it is only available for building new premises

Following a bereavement it has been shown that:

☐ 360 approximately 20% of widowers die in the first year
☐ 361 mortality is greater for men than for women
☐ 362 mortality is still greater than expected at 2 years post bereavement

A 42-year-old man presents with a depressive illness, the following factors would support an unfavourable prognosis:

- ☐ 363 loss of mother prior to 12 years of age
- ☐ 364 previous depressive illness
- ☐ 365 involvement with local charitable organisations
- ☐ 366 obsessional personality
- ☐ 367 a wife housebound with multiple sclerosis

When initiating treatment with a progestogen-only contraceptive, the following points are true:

- ☐ 368 extra contraceptive precautions should be used if started on day 1 of the cycle
- ☐ 369 they should not be taken for 4 weeks prior to surgery
- ☐ 370 if switching from a combined oral contraceptive, they should be commenced after the 7-day break
- ☐ 371 post-abortion they should be started on the day after the operation
- ☐ 372 they are secreted in significant amounts in breast milk

A 13-year-old boy attends the surgery without an adult accompanying him, he has a sore throat. Legally a General Practitioner must

- ☐ 373 examine and prescribe as appropriate
- ☐ 374 refuse to see him unless a responsible adult is present
- ☐ 375 write to the parent asking them to come to the surgery
- ☐ 376 examine but not prescribe

Concerning postgraduate education allowance (PGEA)

- ☐ 377 part-time principals are not allowed to claim the allowance
- ☐ 378 more than 10 days' education in any one year cannot be counted
- ☐ 379 distance learning courses are not eligible
- ☐ 380 vocational training in the previous 1–2 months qualifies a newly registered principal for the full allowance

When considering whether to give a patient with a sore throat antibiotics, the following are true:

☐ 381 approximately 30% of throat swabs grow beta-haemolytic streptococcus
☐ 382 about 20% of throat swabs grow *Haemophilus influenzae*
☐ 383 the decrease in the incidence of rheumatic fever commenced at the time of the introduction of antibiotics
☐ 384 tonsillar exudate in an under 15-year-old is typically associated with glandular fever
☐ 385 enlarged tonsillar glands are typically associated with bacterial infection

In screening tests

☐ 386 a highly sensitive test will have a high false-negative rate
☐ 387 a highly specific test will have a low false-positive rate
☐ 388 the prevalence of a disease indicates the total number of cases that present in a population each year
☐ 389 the prevalence of a disease influences the predictive value of a test
☐ 390 the negative predictive value indicates those patients who refuse to have the screening test

When advising patients about exposure to sun, the following are true:

☐ 391 solar keratoses never progress to malignancy
☐ 392 solar keratoses are more common in fair-skinned people
☐ 393 chronic sun exposure leads to loss of skin elasticity
☐ 394 basal cell carcinoma never metastasize
☐ 395 sunburn typically develops within 2 hours of exposure

Owning dogs has been shown to be associated with

☐ 396 a decrease in presentation of minor health problems to the General Practitioner
☐ 397 an increase in one-year survival following a myocardial infarction
☐ 398 a lower blood pressure when matched with the average population
☐ 399 lower lipid levels when matched with the average population
☐ 400 increase in gastrointestinal infections

PRACTICE PAPER 4 — SECTION 2: EMQs

Child development

At the following ages, children have developed certain important skills:

A 6 months
B 12 months
C 18 months
D 24 months
E 3 years
F 4 years
G 5 years

Match the following with the appropriate age option:

☐ 1 plays with other children; able to stand on one leg briefly
☐ 2 plays imaginatively; able to copy a circle and a cross
☐ 3 able to count 12 objects
☐ 4 able to give first and last name and age; able to catch a ball
☐ 5 says 10–12 words with meaning
☐ 6 builds a 3–4 cube tower
☐ 7 walks whilst holding onto furniture

Polyarthritis

Types of polyarthritis include

A rheumatoid arthritis
B osteoarthritis
C ankylosing spondylitis
D rheumatic fever
E systemic lupus erythematosus
F Reiter's syndrome
G psoriatic arthropathy

Match the following to the most appropriate type of arthritis:

☐ 8 a 45-year-old lady has morning stiffness and symmetrical involvement of the joints in the hands and feet, which have been inflamed
☐ 9 a 30-year-old man presents with arthritis which moves from joint to joint
☐ 10 a 55-year-old man has pain in the hands, worse on movement; there are enlargements in the hands related to the distal interphalangeal joints

☐ 11 a 32-year-old man with non-symmetrical swelling of the distal interphalangeal joints; he mentions pitting of his nails

☐ 12 a 25-year-old man with painful, swollen knees and feet; he mentions continual back stiffness and recent pain in the eye

☐ 13 a 29-year-old lady with an abrupt onset of swelling of joints in hands and feet; she thinks this is associated with exposure to the sun, which has also caused a facial rash

☐ 14 a 22-year-old man who has a sudden onset of pain in knee, associated with a feeling of grit in the eyes; vesicles are noted on the soles of his feet and on the palms

Mental Health Act

The following sections of the Mental Health Act (1983) can be of importance:

A Section 2
B Section 3
C Section 4
D Section 5
E Section 7
F Section 12

Match the appropriate section to the following statements:

☐ 15 used to 'approve' doctors as having special expertise in psychiatric conditions

☐ 16 used in guardianship

☐ 17 used in emergency situations only, when the patient needs to be taken to hospital

☐ 18 used in emergency situations only, when the patient needs to be kept in a hospital, from where he wishes to leave

☐ 19 used to admit a patient with bipolar affective disorder, who is not taking medication and refuses any intervention; he is acting in a dangerous manner, and requires treatment

Numbness and paraesthesia

Numbness and feelings of paraesthesia are commonly encountered in general practice. The following are possible causes:

A meralgia paraesthetica
B carpal tunnel syndrome
C ulnar nerve lesion
D lateral popliteal nerve lesion
E peripheral neuropathy
F lumbar disc lesion
G multiple sclerosis

Choose the most appropriate cause for the following clinical scenarios:

☐ 20 a 36-year-old lecturer has intermittent recurrent symptoms in arms and legs, and describes 'shocks' when bending his neck

☐ 21 a 52-year-old rather obese man has noticed sensory loss in his lower legs; examination reveals distal weakness with 'stocking' type sensory loss

☐ 22 a 47-year-old lady notices tingling in her left hand which is worse at night; her index finger seems particularly affected by the tingling feeling

☐ 23 a 51-year-old obese man notices tingling in the outer aspect of his thighs

☐ 24 a 35-year-old man complains of back and leg pain with numbness down his left thigh

Benefits

The following welfare benefits are of importance:

A Statutory Sick Pay
B Severe Disablement Allowance
C Invalid Care Allowance
D Disability Living Allowance
E Incapacity Benefit
F Attendance Allowance

Match the following with the appropriate benefit:

☐ 25 paid to people incapable of work for at least 28 weeks who are at least 80% disabled

☐ 26 paid to people over 65 years who require considerable supervision or care during the day or night

☐ 27 paid to employees when unable to work because of a short term illness

☐ 28 paid to people who are incapable of work on medical grounds for more than 28 weeks and who have paid sufficient National Insurance Contributions

☐ 29 paid to people over 5 and under 65 years who are unable to walk because of a physical illness

Acts

The following Acts are of importance to General Practitioners:

A NHS and Community Care Act 1990
B Access to Health Records Act 1990
C Access to Medical Report Act 1988
D Data Protection Act 1984

Match the following statements with the appropriate Act:

☐ 30 allows General Practitioners to control a budget funding primary care services

☐ 31 allows patients to see reports prepared about them for insurance companies or employers

☐ 32 allows patients to see medical records about them

☐ 33 allows information to be held for a specific lawful purpose

Hypertension trials

The following are important trials in hypertension:

A Veterans Administration Co-operative Study
B Multiple Risk Factor Intervention Trial
C MRC Mild Hypertension Trial
D European Working Party on Hypertension in the Elderly
E SYST-EUR-Trial

For which of these trials is the following true:

☐ 34 showed that one CVA was prevented by 850 patient years of treatment

☐ 35 was carried out in a group who were highly compliant with a drug regime

☐ 36 recruited very few patients per centre and showed that deaths from CVA were not reduced in this group over 60 years of age

☐ 37 showed no reduction in CVAs in the treated group, but had a low incidence of CVAs in the control group

☐ 38 used a much larger dose of bendrofluazide than would be used now

Immunisations

Immunisations given to children include

A MMR
B DTP
C DT
D BCG
E polio

Which of the above apply to the following statements?

☐ 39 usually given at 12–15 months

☐ 40 often given at 2, 3 or 4 months, and then not given again

☐ 41 given usually over the age of 10 years

☐ 42 given between 3 and 5 years and then not given again

☐ 43 given only if tuberculin-negative

Statistics

The following are words and descriptions commonly used in statistics:

A mode
B bimodal
C single normal distribution
D positively skewed
E Equal variance, different means
F median
G mean
H equal means, different variance

Match the following to one of these words or descriptions:

☐ 44

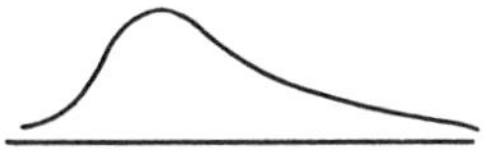

☐ 45

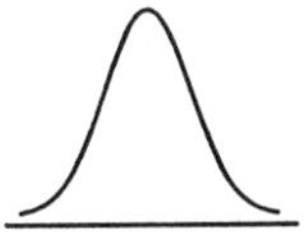

☐ 46

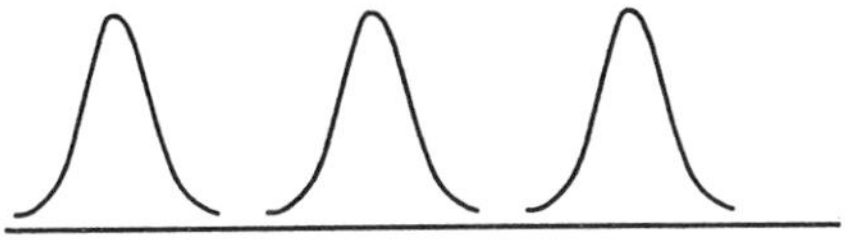

☐ 47

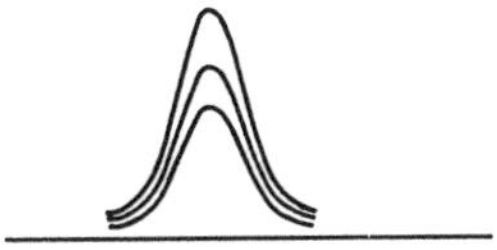

Studies

Statistical data in studies can be

A quantitative
B discrete
C continuous
D qualitative

Match the following statements with the type of data (use each type of data once only):

☐ 48 like blood pressure readings, can have any value
☐ 49 like the number of people seen in a surgery, has a definite value
☐ 50 data that can be given an exact number
☐ 51 data that can be described but not counted

Screening

The results of a screening test for a cancer are as follows:

	Disease present	Disease absent
Screening test positive	70	30
Screening test negative	10	90

Options available

A	70	G	30/100
B	30	H	70/80
C	10	I	90/100
D	90	J	30/120
E	70/100	K	90/120

Select the appropriate option

☐ 52 sensitivity
☐ 53 specificity
☐ 54 positive predictive value
☐ 55 negative predictive value
☐ 56 false positive
☐ 57 false negative

Eye problems

Causes of red eye seen in general practice include

A acute conjunctivitis
B acute iritis
C acute glaucoma
D episcleritis
E keratitis

Match the appropriate diagnosis to the clinical scenarios below

☐ 58 a 55-year-old woman with severe pain in one eye which is red; there is visual disturbance and the pupil is noted to be dilated

☐ 59 a 57-year-old lady with a painful red right eye; there is visual disturbance; the pupil appears normal but there is diffuse inflammation of the conjunctiva

☐ 60 a 49-year-old man has a sticky discharge from both eyes which are both red

☐ 61 a 48-year-old has intense pain in his left eye with redness of the eye especially around the cornea; the pupil is seen to be constricted

☐ 62 a 42-year-old man has a gritty feeling in the left eye and the lids feel sticky to him; there is slight inflammation of the left eye

Abdominal pain

The following causes of abdominal pain are sometimes seen in general practice:

A biliary colic
B peptic ulcer
C appendicitis
D renal colic
E pancreatitis
F diverticulitis

Match the following scenarios with one of these causes:

☐ 63 a 35-year-old accountant describes 'pain and wind' which sometimes wakes him at night, and has been intermittently present for about 3 months

☐ 64 a 48-year-old man describes severe abdominal pain which appears to radiate into his back

☐ 65 a 28-year-old has a 2-day history of abdominal pain with recent vomiting and raised temperature; there is tenderness in the right lower abdomen on examination

☐ 66 a 51-year-old lady describes intermittent abdominal pain which she finds hard to place; her abdomen is generally tender but especially in the right upper abdomen

☐ 67 a 43-year-old woman has intermittent abdominal and right-sided back pain, and has been vomiting; examination shows tenderness in the right abdomen but especially so in the right side of the back laterally

☐ 68 a 66-year-old retired banker described abdominal pain over the last few months, and complains of long term constipation; examination reveals tenderness especially in the left lower abdomen

Leg ulcers

Leg ulcers are usually either: (A) ischaemic or (B) venous

Match the following statements with the appropriate type of ulcer:

☐ 69 typically painful
☐ 70 typically pigmented
☐ 71 often in those patients over 70 years of age
☐ 72 often 'punched out' in appearance
☐ 73 surrounding skin is often affected

Thyroid disease

Thyroid cancers can be

A anaplastic
B papillary
C follicular

Match the following statements to the type of cancer:

☐ 74 most common thyroid cancer in the elderly
☐ 75 most commonest thyroid cancer in the young
☐ 76 particularly metastasises to bone
☐ 77 best prognosis

Heart problems

Tachycardia may be caused by a variety of conditions which include

A anxiety
B anaemia
C fever
D thyrotoxicosis
E phaeochromocytoma
F carcinoid syndrome

Match the following clinical scenarios with the most appropriate cause from the above list:

☐ 78 a 39-year-old female with diarrhoea and a racing regular heart beat; she is concerned about episodes of flushing and wheezing and wonders if this might be the menopause

☐ 79 a 41-year-old female has a regular fast heart beat; she is tall and thin and friends say her facial appearance has altered over the last few months

☐ 80 a 38-year-old female complains of palpitations along with a dull ache in the chest; she describes the need to take deep breaths as she can no longer breathe in satisfactorily

☐ 81 a 32-year-old female has palpitations and notices attacks of sudden sweating; her husband says she is often pale at that time and seems to have headaches.

Literature

The following literature discusses consultations:

A *The Doctor, his Patient and the Illness* by M Balint
B *Meetings Between Experts: An Approach to Sharing Ideas in Medical Consultations* by Tuckett et al.
C *The Consultation: An Approach to Learning and Teaching* by Pendleton et al.
D *The Inner Consultation* by R Neighbour
E *Doctors Talking to Patients* by Byrne & Long
F *The Doctor–Patient Relationship* by Freeling & Harris
G *Culture, Health and Illness* by C Helman
H *Games People Play* by E Berne

Match the following with the appropriate literature from the list above:

☐ 82 coined the phrase ‘drug doctor’

☐ 83 described consulting styles varying from ‘doctor-centred’ to ‘patient-centred’

☐ 84 devised consultation mapping

☐ 85 discussed management plans and outcomes being given different priorities by different people depending on their roles and values

☐ 86 described complex transactions between people in terms of their ego status

☐ 87 described the ‘apostolic function’ of a doctor

☐ 88 described seven communication tests, starting with defining the reason for the patient’s attendance

Cancers

A typical GP with an average list size sees new cases of cancers at varying intervals depending on the type of cancer. From the list of time intervals below, select the appropriate interval for each type of malignant tumour described.

Time intervals:

A 6 months
B 12 months
C 2 years
D 5–6 years
E 10 years
F 25 years

Types of malignant tumour

☐ 89 stomach
☐ 90 breast
☐ 91 brain
☐ 92 thyroid
☐ 93 bronchus
☐ 94 ovary

Social class

The Registrar General has six divisions of Social Class, with one division subdivided

A 1
B 2
C 3N
D 3M
E 4
F 5

Place the following in the correct division as above:

☐ 95 shopkeeper
☐ 96 lawyer
☐ 97 managing director
☐ 98 labourer
☐ 99 clerical office worker
☐ 100 teacher

PRACTICE PAPER 5 — SECTION 1: MCQs

Total time allowed for sections 1 and 2 is three hours. Section 1 has 400 items, section 2 has 100. Indicate your answers clearly by putting a tick or cross in the box alongside each answer or by writing the appropriate letter in Section 2.

Advice about driving heavy goods vehicles

☐ 1 an HGV driver should avoid driving for at least 6 months following a myocardial infarct and then may be allowed to continue if certain criteria are met
☐ 2 an HGV driver can drive if fit-free for 3 years
☐ 3 an HGV driver who develops insulin-dependent diabetes cannot continue to drive
☐ 4 an HGV driver should stop the vehicle if he has the beginning of a migraine attack
☐ 5 an HGV driver has minor trauma and has an abdominal X-ray at casualty which shows an aortic aneurysm; he should be advised to avoid driving because of the aneurysm

Allergic conjunctivitis is associated with

☐ 6 a mucopurulent ocular discharge
☐ 7 a reduction in visual acuity
☐ 8 photophobia
☐ 9 epiphora
☐ 10 a need to avoid contact lenses

When considering alcohol dependency in women, the following are true:

☐ 11 alcohol-dependent women are more prone to cerebral damage than men
☐ 12 alcoholic cirrhosis has a greater prevalence in women
☐ 13 affective disorders have been shown to be more common in male rather than female alcoholics
☐ 14 vulnerability to intoxication is dependent on the stage of the menstrual cycle
☐ 15 typically women begin drinking heavily earlier than their male counterparts

A prescription issued for a controlled drug must comply with the following:

☐ 16 it cannot be issued on a computer-generated script
☐ 17 the address of the doctor must be handwritten
☐ 18 the script must be marked with C.D. by the issuing doctor
☐ 19 the total quantity of the drugs must be given in words and figures
☐ 20 the frequency with which the drug is to be taken must be given in words and figures

When considering a diagnosis of diabetes mellitus

☐ 21 blood glucose progressively rises with age
☐ 22 the majority of people with glycosuria have diabetes
☐ 23 routine urine testing detects the majority of previously undiagnosed diabetics
☐ 24 a fasting blood glucose of greater than 7.2 mmol/l is diagnostic of diabetes
☐ 25 the majority of diabetics will have retinal changes at diagnosis

A 50-year-old man presents with pain in the left ear, on examination the ear appears to be normal. The following could account for the pain:

☐ 26 arthritis of C2–C3 level of the cervical spine
☐ 27 carcinoma of the pyriform fossa
☐ 28 impacted wisdom teeth
☐ 29 trigeminal neuralgia
☐ 30 tonsillitis

Chronic schizophrenia is characterised by the following:

☐ 31 apathy
☐ 32 slowness
☐ 33 somatic hallucinations
☐ 34 social withdrawal
☐ 35 depressive symptoms

Under the theoretical model of the consultation proposed by Stott and Davies the following aspects of a consultation are considered:

- ☐ 36 prevention
- ☐ 37 patients' expectations
- ☐ 38 management of continuing problems
- ☐ 39 modification of health seeking behaviour
- ☐ 40 sharing of the problem with the patient

A 45-year-old patient presents with chest pain, the following are more typically associated with a non-cardiac origin of the pain:

- ☐ 41 breathlessness on trivial effort
- ☐ 42 palpitations
- ☐ 43 exhaustion persisting during rest
- ☐ 44 lightheadedness
- ☐ 45 headache

When considering a diagnosis of dermatofibroma, the lesions

- ☐ 46 are more common in women
- ☐ 47 are typically pigmented
- ☐ 48 have malignant potential
- ☐ 49 typically ulcerate centrally
- ☐ 50 have an irregular edge

Concerning hepatitis B vaccine

- ☐ 51 seroconversion is age dependent
- ☐ 52 the preferred site of injection for maximal absorption is the buttock
- ☐ 53 hypersensitivity reactions occur in more than 5% of patients
- ☐ 54 local soreness occurs in less than 10% of injections
- ☐ 55 the genetic recombinant vaccine also protects against hepatitis C

In cervical smears

☐ 56 the sensitivity is about 50%
☐ 57 the specificity is very high at about 99%
☐ 58 the transformation zone moves into the cervical os in older women
☐ 59 CIN is a histological diagnosis
☐ 60 the false-negative rate may be dependent on the taker of the smear
☐ 61 false positives rarely occur

Psoriasis

☐ 62 will affect approximately 2 in every 100 patients
☐ 63 tends to leave scars
☐ 64 typically is itchy
☐ 65 on the face can be treated safely with dithranol
☐ 66 is typically symmetrical
☐ 67 usually begins between the ages of 15–25 years

When considering a protocol for the management of epilepsy within your practice

☐ 68 patients should be referred to a neurologist only after a second fit
☐ 69 if a first fit occurs after 30 years of age, idiopathic epilepsy is the probable diagnosis
☐ 70 the majority of epileptics have an inherited condition
☐ 71 the majority of GPs will be aware of all the epileptics on their lists
☐ 72 the majority of epileptics receive an annual check from either their GP or consultant

Concerning prescription analysis and cost reports (PACT)

☐ 73 they are only available on request
☐ 74 level 3 reports can be requested for an individual therapeutic group
☐ 75 an allowance is made for the increased prescribing needs of patients over 65 years of age
☐ 76 the prescription pricing authority data has an accepted inherent inaccuracy of about 5%
☐ 77 data is based on what the GP prescribes rather than what the chemist dispenses

Pregnant women should be advised to avoid

☐ 78 prepacked salad and coleslaw
☐ 79 paté
☐ 80 unwashed fruit
☐ 81 aerobics
☐ 82 emptying cat litter trays

A 19-year-old student presents with bloody diarrhoea 2 weeks after completing a backpacking holiday in east Africa. The following should be included in a differential diagnosis:

☐ 83 typhoid fever
☐ 84 amoebic dysentery
☐ 85 schistosomiasis
☐ 86 Lassa fever
☐ 87 malaria

When considering a diagnosis of post-traumatic stress disorder

☐ 88 it typically commences within 1 week of the event
☐ 89 the majority of those exposed to a disaster will suffer chronic symptoms
☐ 90 feelings of unreality occur
☐ 91 guilt feelings are typical
☐ 92 recovery is hindered by being pressed to talk about the event in the early stages

Urgent referral to an ophthalmologist is indicated for the following:

☐ 93 episcleritis
☐ 94 *Herpes zoster* with visual disturbance
☐ 95 blocked naso-lacrimal duct at 6 months of age
☐ 96 a dendritic ulcer
☐ 97 a corneal abrasion

A 2-year-old child becomes acutely ill. The following would support a diagnosis of Reye's syndrome:

☐ 98 chickenpox 10 days previously
☐ 99 behaviour changes
☐ 100 profuse vomiting
☐ 101 normal liver function tests
☐ 102 recent administration of aspirin

When considering the care of patients in community hospitals

☐ 103 the majority of GPs have access to such hospitals
☐ 104 the average age of patients in these hospitals is over 70 years
☐ 105 the average cost of an inpatient admission is greater than for a general hospital
☐ 106 the workload of GPs with access to community hospitals is greater
☐ 107 the majority of patients are discharged to their own homes

Synergism has been shown between the following pairs of drugs:

☐ 108 propranolol and nifedipine
☐ 109 bendrofluazide and glibenclamide
☐ 110 spironolactone and frusemide
☐ 111 ibuprofen and warfarin
☐ 112 ethanol and chlorpheniramine

In rheumatoid arthritis

☐ 113 if the rheumatoid factor is present, this is diagnostic in the elderly
☐ 114 morning stiffness wears off after about 10 minutes
☐ 115 the metacarpophalangeal joints are rarely involved
☐ 116 someone with a negative rheumatoid factor test can be reassured they do not have rheumatoid arthritis
☐ 117 regular use of NSAIDs can prevent disease progression
☐ 118 patients describe 'walking on pebbles'

When advising a patient about hysteroscopic endometrial ablation the following are true:

☐ 119 danazol is given pre-operatively
☐ 120 it is unsuitable in patients with previously treated CIN
☐ 121 the healing process takes 3 months
☐ 122 it is suitable for day case surgery
☐ 123 subsequent scanty bleeding would be an indication of treatment failure

When considering lesions of the Achilles tendon

☐ 124 tendonitis is associated with a raised heel tab on the shoe
☐ 125 local steroid injections are associated with rupture of the tendon
☐ 126 complete rupture is best treated by surgery
☐ 127 shoe raise typically leads to shortening of the tendon if used to treat Achilles tendonitis
☐ 128 ultrasound treatment leads to a worsening of the pain

The following would suggest that a patient who is HIV positive has developed 'full blown' AIDS:

☐ 129 persistent generalised lymphadenopathy
☐ 130 night sweats
☐ 131 non-Hodgkin's lymphoma
☐ 132 fatigue
☐ 133 weight loss

A 4-year-old boy is noted to have a cardiac murmur on routine examination, the following would indicate its innocent nature:

☐ 134 diastolic in timing
☐ 135 murmur louder on deep inspiration
☐ 136 short duration
☐ 137 soft murmur
☐ 138 a normal chest X-ray

Central features of manic disorders are

☐ 139 decreased libido
☐ 140 expansive ideas
☐ 141 decreased appetite
☐ 142 reduced sleep
☐ 143 retained insight

Carcinoma of the bronchus is associated with exposure to the following:

☐ 144 asbestos
☐ 145 silica dust
☐ 146 sulphur dioxide
☐ 147 aniline dyes
☐ 148 radon gas

The following would support a diagnosis of Ménière's disease:

☐ 149 tinnitus
☐ 150 a feeling of fullness in the ear
☐ 151 fluctuating sensorineural hearing loss
☐ 152 a positive Romberg's test
☐ 153 nystagmus occurring between acute attacks

An incidental finding of an easily palpable firm spleen is most likely due to

☐ 154 glandular fever
☐ 155 carcinomatosis
☐ 156 chronic myeloid leukaemia
☐ 157 lymphoma
☐ 158 myelosclerosis

Under the Abortion Act 1967, when a termination of pregnancy is to be performed, the following should be considered:

- ☐ 159 if the patient is married the consent of the husband is necessary
- ☐ 160 those under 16 years of age must have the consent of a parent
- ☐ 161 in an emergency situation only one practitioner need sign a recommendation
- ☐ 162 all operations are notified to the Department of Health
- ☐ 163 the Act does not apply in Northern Ireland

Concerning skin lesions on soles of feet

- ☐ 164 pompholyx affecting the soles is non-irritant
- ☐ 165 specific lesions on the soles occur in some cases of Reiter's syndrome
- ☐ 166 pustular psoriasis may occur
- ☐ 167 lichen planus lesions are characteristically seen

A elderly patient with previously stable anticoagulation treatment suddenly becomes unstable, the following causes should be considered:

- ☐ 168 alcoholism
- ☐ 169 cardiac failure
- ☐ 170 concurrent administration of cimetidine
- ☐ 171 malnutrition
- ☐ 172 concurrent administration of allopurinol

Statistically it has been shown that cigarette smoking decreases the incidence of the following diseases:

- ☐ 173 Farmer's lung
- ☐ 174 Parkinson's disease
- ☐ 175 endometrial cancer
- ☐ 176 ulcerative colitis
- ☐ 177 Alzheimer's disease

Concerning carcinoma of the oesophagus

- ☐ 178 the incidence is decreasing
- ☐ 179 adenocarcinoma has a better prognosis than squamous carcinoma
- ☐ 180 it is associated with coeliac disease
- ☐ 181 it typically presents with weight loss
- ☐ 182 it is a complication of achalasia

When considering the psychological aspects of pain

- ☐ 183 approximately 25% of patients with chronic pain will show significant response to a placebo
- ☐ 184 introverts seek pain relief sooner than extroverts
- ☐ 185 complaints of pain are more common in the elderly
- ☐ 186 pain perception is increased by social isolation

The following drugs can be successfully administered via a nebuliser:

- ☐ 187 terbutaline
- ☐ 188 sodium cromoglycate
- ☐ 189 theophylline
- ☐ 190 ipratropium bromide
- ☐ 191 beclomethasone

When considering diverticular disease

- ☐ 192 diverticula are seen more frequently in the distal colon
- ☐ 193 non-fermentable fibre is more effective than fermentable fibre in treatment
- ☐ 194 it has an increased incidence of carcinoma of the colon
- ☐ 195 bleeding is indicative of developing malignancy
- ☐ 196 pneumaturia is a rare complication

When applying for an order under the Mental Health Act

☐ 197 the nearest relative must be a first-degree relative
☐ 198 the majority of admissions under the Act from general practitioners are made under Section 4
☐ 199 doctors are at greater legal risk from failing to use the Act than from over-zealous use
☐ 200 psychiatric community nurses can make an application for admission
☐ 201 sexual deviancy, in itself, is a justification for compulsory admission

Concerning nitrate tolerance

☐ 202 tolerance to the adverse effects, such as headache, indicate tolerance to the therapeutic effects
☐ 203 it typically takes at least one month to develop
☐ 204 topical nitrates have been shown not to produce tolerance
☐ 205 isosorbide mononitrate has been shown not to produce tolerance
☐ 206 once tolerance has developed it is permanent

In epididymitis

☐ 207 it has a peak incidence at 12–18 years of age
☐ 208 iliac fossa pain is typical
☐ 209 the scrotal contents remain normal in size
☐ 210 ultrasound scanning is diagnostic
☐ 211 it is associated with chlamydial infection

A 78-year-old resident of a residential home becomes increasingly agitated. The following may account for this:

☐ 212 recent introduction of digoxin
☐ 213 paracetamol being given for osteoarthritis
☐ 214 temazepam. as a hypnotic that has been given for the last 5 years
☐ 215 a silent myocardial infarction
☐ 216 dehydration

In immunisations

- ☐ 217 cholera immunisation is important for several Third World countries
- ☐ 218 yellow fever vaccination is needed yearly for repeated travel
- ☐ 219 rabies immunisation is usually given into the gluteal muscle
- ☐ 220 gamma globulin should be given first in any course of immunisations before travel
- ☐ 221 live typhoid vaccine should be avoided if antibiotics are being taken
- ☐ 222 typhoid immunisation is not recommended after the age of 35 years

The following are true of a 'frozen shoulder':

- ☐ 223 recovery is usually complete
- ☐ 224 painful arc is typical of rotator cuff lesions
- ☐ 225 local tenderness bears no relationship to the site of the lesion
- ☐ 226 immobilisation is the treatment of choice
- ☐ 227 the pain is typically worse during the night

A young adult patient presents with dyspnoea, a chest X-ray shows hilar lymphadenopathy, the following are possible causes:

- ☐ 228 streptococcal pneumonia
- ☐ 229 sarcoidosis
- ☐ 230 lymphoma
- ☐ 231 tuberculosis
- ☐ 232 pulmonary rheumatoid disease

Concerning cervical smears

- ☐ 233 atypia on a single occasion correlates well with the presence of CIN
- ☐ 234 the majority of carcinomas of the cervix are diagnosed from cervical smears
- ☐ 235 if there is a history of genital warts a smear should be undertaken annually
- ☐ 236 cervical erosions typically produce an abnormal cervical smear
- ☐ 237 once fixed a cervical smear must reach the laboratory within 48 hours to allow accurate interpretation

The following would support a diagnosis of irritant contact dermatitis:

- ☐ 238 severity that varies with the amount of exposure to the irritant
- ☐ 239 rash developing 2 days after exposure
- ☐ 240 reactivation of a rash in other sites
- ☐ 241 positive patch tests
- ☐ 242 no previous exposure to the suspected irritant

Concerning Paget's disease

- ☐ 243 patients have been shown to become refractory to calcitonin therapy
- ☐ 244 deafness is a complication
- ☐ 245 cardiac failure is a complication
- ☐ 246 hypercalcaemia is typical
- ☐ 247 a normal alkaline phosphatase excludes the diagnosis

Toddler diarrhoea is characterised by the following:

- ☐ 248 typically occurs after an acute infection
- ☐ 249 is associated with failure to thrive
- ☐ 250 trial of a milk free diet has been shown to be beneficial
- ☐ 251 presence of undigested food in the stools
- ☐ 252 response to loperamide

Concerning benzodiazepine dependence

- ☐ 253 the majority of patients taking a benzodiazepine regularly for 6 months or more will suffer a withdrawal reaction on stopping the drug
- ☐ 254 dependence has been shown to occur after 3 weeks of treatment
- ☐ 255 a characteristic feature of withdrawal is loss of appetite
- ☐ 256 auditory hallucinations would indicate other psychopathology
- ☐ 257 beta-blockers have been shown to attenuate the withdrawal symptoms

When reading scientific papers

☐ 258 significance levels are greater the higher the value of p
☐ 259 accepting the Null hypothesis means that there is significant difference
☐ 260 Student's '*t*' test is used for significance testing on large samples
☐ 261 Spearman's rank correlation applies to results in a single group
☐ 262 standard deviation measures the variation about the mean

The following are true of vaginal contraceptive diaphragms:

☐ 263 they should be removed within 2 hours of intercourse
☐ 264 the size may need to be changed if the patients weight varies by more than 7 lb
☐ 265 they can be used if utero-vaginal prolapse is present
☐ 266 they need to be renewed annually
☐ 267 they can be used if the patient is allergic to rubber

When treating vomiting symptomatically

☐ 268 hyoscine is available as a skin patch
☐ 269 domperidone is licensed as an injection
☐ 270 cinnarizine is available without a prescription
☐ 271 prochlorperazine is associated with postural hypotension
☐ 272 chlorpromazine is as effective as prochlorperazine

Disability Living Allowance

☐ 273 is taxable but not means tested
☐ 274 is only for people with care or mobility problems
☐ 275 is payable if the person has only night-time needs
☐ 276 is usually based on self-assessment
☐ 277 requires an accurate medical diagnosis to have been made

Febrile convulsions

☐ 278 typically occur in the second year of life
☐ 279 are commoner in social class V
☐ 280 are more common in boys rather than girls
☐ 281 with complex fits lasting longer than 15 minutes have been shown to be associated with epilepsy in later life
☐ 282 show a familial incidence

Concerning varicose veins

☐ 283 sclerotherapy cures less than 10% over a 5-year period
☐ 284 ligation of the long saphenous vein is more complex than the short saphenous vein
☐ 285 after multiple avulsions compression is necessary for an average of 1 month
☐ 286 walking distances should be delayed until 1 week after surgery
☐ 287 the average patient with uncomplicated surgery for veins in one leg will require 6 weeks away from work

During pregnancy the following chronic diseases typically deteriorate:

☐ 288 epilepsy
☐ 289 migraine
☐ 290 multiple sclerosis
☐ 291 asthma
☐ 292 sickle cell disease

The following statements are true about eye drops:

☐ 293 fluorescein stains soft contact lenses
☐ 294 pilocarpine causes pupillary dilatation
☐ 295 oxybuprocaine causes stinging when installed into a normal eye
☐ 296 tropicamide anaesthetises the cornea
☐ 297 adrenaline produces local irritation

In Guillain–Barré syndrome

- ☐ 298 there is typically an antecedent 'viral' infection
- ☐ 299 sensory symptoms predominate over motor symptoms
- ☐ 300 it typically develops insidiously
- ☐ 301 the majority of cases recover
- ☐ 302 the central nervous system is typically spared

Concerning diabetic pregnancies

- ☐ 303 congenital abnormalities are more common
- ☐ 304 pre-term labour is increased in frequency
- ☐ 305 uncomplicated pregnancies are usually induced at 40 weeks' gestation
- ☐ 306 neonatal jaundice is increased in the offspring
- ☐ 307 epidural analgesia is contraindicated in diabetics

A 6-year-old boy presents with a limp and pain in the hip, the following differential diagnoses should be considered:

- ☐ 308 tuberculosis of the hip
- ☐ 309 Perthes' disease
- ☐ 310 slipped upper femoral epiphysis
- ☐ 311 septic arthritis
- ☐ 312 non-accidental injury

In considering the diagnosis of erythema multiforme

- ☐ 313 it typically occurs without any discernible precipitating cause
- ☐ 314 the rash is not characteristic
- ☐ 315 if mucous membranes are involved, carries a worse prognosis
- ☐ 316 recurrent episodes are extremely rare
- ☐ 317 it typically resolves after approximately 10 days

The following are true about cholesterol:

- ☐ 318 a raised cholesterol has been shown to be a risk factor for coronary artery disease
- ☐ 319 decreasing cholesterol has been shown to decrease overall mortality
- ☐ 320 a low cholesterol has a significant association with carcinoma
- ☐ 321 good dietary control will reduce cholesterol levels by about 30%
- ☐ 322 those who smoke should not be screened

Aspirin

- ☐ 323 has been shown to reduce the incidence of cataracts
- ☐ 324 reduces the mortality if given after a myocardial infarction
- ☐ 325 in low dose is associated with a risk of retinal haemorrhage
- ☐ 326 is effective in the treatment of venous thromboembolism
- ☐ 327 has been shown to have a role in the primary prevention of cerebrovascular disease

Proton pump inhibitors

- ☐ 328 can cause severe headaches
- ☐ 329 cause gynaecomastia more commonly than H_2-antagonists
- ☐ 330 are the treatment of choice for stricturing and erosive oesophagitis
- ☐ 331 can be used with antibiotics to eradicate *H. pylori*
- ☐ 332 are safe to use in breast feeding
- ☐ 333 can cause severe diarrhoea

Child physical abuse is associated with an increased incidence in

- ☐ 334 females
- ☐ 335 illegitimate children
- ☐ 336 those of low birthweight
- ☐ 337 those under 3 years of age

Excessive hair loss is associated with

- ☐ 338 seborrhoeic eczema
- ☐ 339 tinea capitis
- ☐ 340 minoxidil treatment
- ☐ 341 hormone replacement therapy
- ☐ 342 hirsutism

The following would indicate a diagnosis of stress incontinence in female patients:

- ☐ 343 nocturia occurring three times nightly
- ☐ 344 dribbling after passing water
- ☐ 345 leaking small amounts of urine
- ☐ 346 having to 'rush' to get to the toilet on time

The 'Red Book' (Statement of fees and allowances)

- ☐ 347 is a legally binding document
- ☐ 348 can only be amended by legislative change
- ☐ 349 is negotiated by the LMC on behalf of all general practitioners

Disability Living Allowance

- ☐ 350 is only available to people whose disability arises after the age of 65 years of age
- ☐ 351 is paid in addition to the mobility allowance if eligible
- ☐ 352 is paid after a qualifying period of 3 months
- ☐ 353 is a tax-free benefit

The following are true of pre-menstrual syndrome:

- ☐ 354 caffeine restriction has been shown to decrease symptoms
- ☐ 355 fertility is decreased in those who suffer from severe symptoms
- ☐ 356 the majority of women seek help from their doctor with symptoms related to the condition
- ☐ 357 suppression of ovulation typically relieves symptoms

Immediate hospital referral is indicated in a 3-year-old child who ingests one of the following:

- ☐ 358 10 tablets of penicillin V 250 mg
- ☐ 359 10 tablets of the combined oral contraceptive
- ☐ 360 10 quinine sulphate tablets
- ☐ 361 mercury from a thermometer
- ☐ 362 20 ml of houseplant food

When considering the nutritional values of equivalent amounts of foods, the following are true:

- ☐ 363 grapefruit contains more fibre than a banana
- ☐ 364 cornflakes contain more iron than spinach
- ☐ 365 rye crispbread is more calorific than wholemeal bread
- ☐ 366 green peppers are a rich source of vitamin C
- ☐ 367 dry red wine contains significantly more calories than dry white wine
- ☐ 368 beer is a good source of vitamin B

Accidental carbon monoxide poisoning

- ☐ 369 is the most common cause of death by poisoning in children
- ☐ 370 initial symptoms are characterised by headache
- ☐ 371 mental lethargy is typical
- ☐ 372 effects are typically reversed within 24 hours upon removal from the source
- ☐ 373 cyanosis occurs in the later stages

You are investigating a couple for involuntary infertility and the sperm count of the husband is returned showing azoospermia. The following are true:

- ☐ 374 the condition is strongly related to mumps orchitis
- ☐ 375 if due to Klinefelter's syndrome, FSH levels will be raised
- ☐ 376 in the majority of cases there is no pathological cause detected despite full investigation
- ☐ 377 endocrine treatment will achieve a viable sperm count in more than 29% of cases
- ☐ 378 intercourse the night prior to collecting the sample has been shown to produce a temporary azoospermia

Oral decongestants used for the treatment of common colds, are contraindicated in a patient

- ☐ 379 taking beta-blockers
- ☐ 380 who discontinued mono amine oxidase inhibitors 1 week previously
- ☐ 381 who is hypothyroid
- ☐ 382 who is diabetic
- ☐ 383 who is taking non-steroidal anti-inflammatory drugs

In Down's syndrome

- ☐ 384 there is an increased incidence of ischaemic heart disease
- ☐ 385 there is a deletion in chromosome 21
- ☐ 386 atrioventricular canal defects are common
- ☐ 387 patent ductus arteriosus is rarely seen
- ☐ 388 IQ is usually in the range 80–100
- ☐ 389 there is a higher incidence of hypothyroidism than in matched control subjects
- ☐ 390 there is a higher incidence of glue ear than in matched control subjcts

When considering tuberculosis in the United Kingdom

- ☐ 391 notifications of the disease are increasing
- ☐ 392 the majority of isolates are now resistant to isoniazid
- ☐ 393 trials conducted in the British Isles have failed to show the effectiveness of BCG vaccination
- ☐ 394 is significantly associated with the homeless population
- ☐ 395 about 30% of patients with AIDS will develop tuberculosis

Studies published in the United Kingdom have shown a significant association between low blood pressure and

- ☐ 396 tiredness
- ☐ 397 minor psychological symptoms
- ☐ 398 dizziness
- ☐ 399 raised serum cholesterol levels
- ☐ 400 a decrease in the patient's perceived feeling of well-being

Income

GPs derive their income from sources including

A non-medical income
B private medical work
C practice allowance
D capitation fees
E reimbursements
F item of service payments

Match the following with the appropriate source of income:

☐ 1 rural practice payment
☐ 2 temporary resident fee
☐ 3 emergency treatment
☐ 4 immediately necessary treatment
☐ 5 child health surveillance
☐ 6 immunisations
☐ 7 insurance report completion
☐ 8 cremation fee

Childhood development

Developmental milestones are looked for at various ages in children by parents and health professionals. Consider the following ages and match them with the developmental milestones shown:

A 6 weeks
B 12 weeks
C 6 months
D 12 months
E 18 months
F 2 years
G 3 years
H 4 years
I 5 years

☐ 9 chooses own friends; names 3–4 colours
☐ 10 feeds with spoon; scribbles
☐ 11 feeds with biscuit
☐ 12 turns head to sounds on level with ear
☐ 13 builds tower with 6–7 cubes
☐ 14 knows two colours; goes up stairs one foot per step, down stairs 2 feet per step
☐ 15 builds tower of 3–4 cubes

Statistics

A brief study of the numbers of phone calls received by different people in a general practice gave the following results.

Number received: 1, 1, 3, 5, 7, 8, 17

Calculate

- ☐ 16 the mean
- ☐ 17 the mode
- ☐ 18 the median

Benefits

Some important welfare benefits are

A	Income Support	E	Invalid Care Allowance
B	Family Credit	F	Severe Disablement Allowance
C	Incapacity Benefit	G	Disability Living Allowance
D	Child Benefit	H	Attendance Allowance

Match the following with one of the above:

- ☐ 19 tax-free non-means-tested payment for anyone with a child under 16 years
- ☐ 20 tax-free non-means-tested payment for people over 65 years who need help with personal care because of a physical or mental problem
- ☐ 21 tax-free payment for people working more than 16 hours/week and bringing up children on low wages
- ☐ 22 means-tested benefit for people working less than 16 hours/week on low income
- ☐ 23 payable to people incapable of any work who have paid National Insurance contributions
- ☐ 24 payable to people who have given up work to look after a disabled person

Screening

A study was carried out in a general practice setting on a screening tool. The study gave the following results:

	Problem present	Problem absent
Screening tool positive result	82	31
Screening tool negative result	27	212

Options available

A 82/113
B 82/109
C 31/113
D 31/243
E 27/109
F 27/239
H 212/239
I 82
J 31
K 27
L 212
M 239
N 243

Select the appropriate option

☐ 25 specificity
☐ 26 positive predictive value
☐ 27 false positive
☐ 28 false negative
☐ 29 sensitivity
☐ 30 negative predictive value

Mental Health Act

The following are important sections of the Mental Health Act 1983 (England and Wales):

A Section 2
B Section 3
C Section 4
D Section 5
E Section 7
F Section 135
G Section 136

Match the appropriate section to the following statements:

☐ 31 allows for reception into guardianship
☐ 32 its purpose is compulsory admission of a patient with a mental disorder for treatment

☐ 33 the purpose of this section is compulsory admission for assessment in an emergency; the patient has no right of appeal
☐ 34 this allows removal of a patient by the police from a public place for medical examination
☐ 35 this allows in-patients to be detained on an emergency basis

Voluntary bodies

The following are well-known voluntary bodies:

A NSPCC
B Marie Curie Memorial Foundation
C Turning Point
D The Samaritans
E ASH
F Terrance Higgins Trust
G Relate
H Cruse

Which voluntary body would most appropriately deal with these problems?

☐ 36 marriage guidance
☐ 37 AIDS
☐ 38 smoking
☐ 39 child abuse
☐ 40 cancer
☐ 41 drug abuse
☐ 42 bereavement in the widowed

Literature

Consultations are discussed in literature which includes

A *Culture, Health and Illness* by C Helman
B *The Exceptional Potential in Each Primary Care Consultation* by Stott & Davies
C *The Inner Consultation* by R Neighbour
D *Effect of a General Practitioner's Style on Patients' Satisfaction: A Controlled Study* by Savage & Armstrong
E *Games People Play* by E Berne
F *Six Minutes for the Patient* by Balint & Novell
G *Doctors Talking to Patients* by Byrne & Long

Match the statements below with the most appropriate of the titles listed

☐ 43 coined the term 'safety netting'
☐ 44 noted severe time constraints of the consultation on audio tape
☐ 45 described the 'flash'
☐ 46 looked at complex transactions between people, described as pastimes
☐ 47 used the terms 'connecting' and 'summarising'
☐ 48 described a four-part framework of the consultation, one of which is 'opportunistic health promotion'

Infectious diseases

Infectious diseases, at some time of importance to general practitioners, include

A *Haemophilus influenzae* type B infections
B measles
C smallpox
D chickenpox
E influenza

Match the following with the appropriate disease:

☐ 49 immunisation against this was introduced in 1992 and is now given to children
☐ 50 antigenic shift occurs
☐ 51 90% of adults are immune to this infection despite no routine immunisation programme
☐ 52 antigenic drift occurs in this
☐ 53 subacute sclerosing panencephalitis is a rare late complication
☐ 54 this has been eradicated and vaccination is only indicated for a few laboratory workers

Drugs used in hypertension

The following drugs are used in hypertension:

A thiazide diuretics
B calcium antagonists
C beta-blockers
D ACE inhibitors
E vasodilators

Which class of drugs should not be used in the following patients:

☐ 55 patients with asthma
☐ 56 patients with gout
☐ 57 patients with chronic obstructive pulmonary disease
☐ 58 patients with glucose intolerance
☐ 59 patients with heart failure

Study types

Types of study include

A quantitative
B qualitative
C cross-sectional
D descriptive
E retrospective
F prospective
G case control
H longitudinal
I intervention

Using these types only once, match the following with the most appropriate study type:

☐ 60 used to explore attitudes or beliefs; its methodology comes from social sciences
☐ 61 involves a counting study and comes from epidemiology
☐ 62 a study looking at the consulting patterns of diabetic patients over the last 3 years
☐ 63 s study looking at patients with diabetes to see if they will develop ischaemic heart disease
☐ 64 a study of poorly controlled diabetics and well-controlled diabetics looking at the development of diabetic retinopathy
☐ 65 a study of patient satisfaction in diabetic patients
☐ 66 a study of drug use in weight control in diabetic patients

Minor surgery

In general practice, minor surgery procedures are usually

A injections
B aspirations
C excisions
D incisions
E curette or cryo-cautery

Match the following with the procedure in general practice:

☐ 67 thrombosed piles
☐ 68 haemorrhoids
☐ 69 lipomas
☐ 70 verruca
☐ 71 molluscum contagiosum
☐ 72 hydrocoele

Thrombolytic trials

Thrombolytic therapy trials include

A ISIS-2
B ASSET
C ISIS-3
D ISAM
E GREAT
F GISSI

For which trial is the following true:

☐ 73 compared side-effects and efficacy of thrombolytic agents and showed aspirin and streptokinase as probable treatments of choice
☐ 74 compared streptokinase against aspirin against both and against neither
☐ 75 compared alteplase versus placebo
☐ 76 compared streptokinase plus heparin versus placebo
☐ 77 compared streptokinase against placebo

Back pain

Causes of back pain seen in general practice include

A mechanical back pain
B disc prolapse at L4/L5 level
C disc prolapse at L5/S1 level
D depression
E ankylosing spondylitis
F neoplastic lesions

Choose the most appropriate of these causes for the following scenarios:

☐ 78 a 38-year-old labourer has recurrent back pain, worse on coughing and sneezing; he has reduced right-sided straight leg raising; further examination shows weakness of dorsiflexion of right foot and sensory disturbance at the dorsum of the foot

☐ 79 a 33-year-old mature student complains of low back pain especially worse in the morning when he feels stiff

☐ 80 a 41-year-old accountant describes pain worse on movement which came on after a weekend gardening; it has improved since going back to work

☐ 81 a 35-year-old roofer has back pain which prevents him working; he has noticed a strange feeling on the outside edge of his left foot; examination reveals that plantar flexion of his left foot is weak and the ankle jerk is absent on the left

Prostate problems

The following drugs are sometimes used in patients with benign prostatic hyperplasia:

A tamsulosin
B finasteride
C prazosin
D indoramin

Match the following statements with the most appropriate drug:

☐ 82 inhibits 5α-reductase resulting in shrinkage of prostatic glandular tissue

☐ 83 a selective alpha-blocker initially given in a dose of 500 micrograms twice daily

☐ 84 an agent which is more selective than other α1-blockers; said to act on α1A-receptors

Bowel disorders

Change in bowel habit may be caused by a variety of disorders other than carcinoma. These include

A irritable bowel syndrome
B diverticular disease
C Crohn's disease
D ulcerative colitis
E ischaemic colitis

Match the following clinical scenarios with the most appropriate bowel disorder from the above list:

☐ 85 a 32-year-old male presents with painless bloody diarrhoea; there is no abdominal tenderness and no masses are felt in the abdomen

☐ 86 a 60-year-old lady presents with abdominal pain and bloody diarrhoea; she is known to have angina; abdominal tenderness is noted at examination

☐ 87 a 43-year-old man has abdominal pain and diarrhoea; there is abdominal tenderness at examination; anal tags are also noted

☐ 88 a 33-year-old teacher complains of wind and diarrhoea with several loose motions passed in the morning and after meals; abdominal pain is often relieved by defaecation; examination reveals tenderness over the sigmoid colon

☐ 89 a 51-year-old laboratory technician complains of pain in the abdomen with alternating diarrhoea and constipation; examination reveals tenderness in the left iliac fossa

Hypertension trials

Some important trials in hypertension include

A Hypertension Optimal Treatment (HOT) Trial
B MRC Mild Hypertension Trial
C Veterans Administration Co-operative Study
D European Working Party on Hypertension in the Elderly
E MRC Trial for Hypertension in Older Adults

Link the following statements with one of these studies:

☐ 90 a randomised trial studying calcium channel blockers with other drugs
☐ 91 single-blind trial which recruited over 4000 patients, and used diuretic, beta-blocker and placebo
☐ 92 almost 400 men with hypertension took part in this double-blind trial, which had a particular impact on stroke reduction; the average age of participants was 50 years
☐ 93 a 15-year trial which involved about 86,000 patient years of observation of almost 200 GPs
☐ 94 a single-blind trial using bendrofluazide, propranolol and placebo, but using higher doses of bendrofluazide than used now; one CVA was saved for 850 patient years of treatment

Certificates

The following certificates are issued in general practice:

A Med 3
B Med 4
C Med 5
D Med 6
E DS1500

Which would be the appropriate certificate to issue in the following circumstances?

☐ 95 a patient is seen with a chest infection and he is advised to be off work for the next 2 weeks

☐ 96 a patient tells you that she is being assessed under the all work test and has been asked for a certificate from her GP

☐ 97 a patient is terminally ill and wants to claim Attendance Allowance

☐ 98 a patient brings you a hospital discharge letter after an admission of 3 weeks' stay, but he has not had a certificate from the hospital

☐ 99 you issue this certificate to give an accurate diagnosis, when the patient has been given a medical certificate for his employer with a vague diagnosis

☐ 100 a patient has had medical certificates to be off work for the last 9 months, and you are now giving a long term certificate to be off work

PRACTICE PAPER 1 — SECTION 1: MCQs ANSWERS AND TEACHING NOTES

1:True 2:False 3:False 4:True 5:True
The so-called 'Wilson Criteria' for screening are important to know. The condition must be important, there must be a recognisable latent stage of the disease (when effective treatment is possible) and there must be a policy about screening and treatment. Diagnosis must be by an acceptable method which might or might not involve clinical examination.

6:True 7:False 8:False 9:True 10:True
Eighty per cent of thyrotoxic patients have Graves' disease with positive thyroid antibodies. A raised TSH in a thyrotoxic patient would indicate a rare TSH-secreting tumour of the pituitary. Blocking all thyroid function with antithyroid drugs such as carbimazole and then replacing with thyroid hormone is the treatment of choice for Graves' disease. Thyroid adenoma is best treated surgically. Graves' ophthalmopathy is more common in smokers and people who have had recent radio-iodine treatment. Post-partum thyroiditis is common, occurring in 5% of pregnancies, and often requiring no treatment, as it is frequently a minor disturbance.

11:False 12:False 13:False 14:False 15:True
The regulations with regard to practice leaflets have to be carefully adhered to. The age does not have to be stated but the sex of the doctor does! The date of first registration of the practice nurse does not but that of the doctor needs to be stated. Fees charged are of no concern to the FHSA. Computerization is often stated on leaflets but is not a requirement. However, the facilities for the disabled must be stated as must the means by which people may comment on the service available.

16:True 17:True 18:True 19:True 20:True
Clomipramine tends to cause erectile dysfunction and delayed ejaculation, in low dosage it is used for the treatment of premature ejaculation. Beta-blockers are associated with reduced sexual interest and erectile dysfunction as is chlorpromazine. Indomethacin reduces sexual interest, corticosteroids also do this and additionally cause delay in ejaculation.

21:True 22:False 23:False 24:False 25:True
Basal cell carcinoma is the most common skin malignancy. Although due to exposure to ultra-violet light, it rarely appears on the bald scalp, ears, lower lips, or back of the hands. It typically starts as a small pink or pearly papule. Eventually the centre breaks down forming the ulcer which may

become crusted. It is more common in those with freckles, red hair and blue eyes.

26:False 27:False 28:True 29:True 30:False
The onset of jaundice in cirrhosis is variable, malaise and lethargy are common at the onset. Vague gastrointestinal symptoms and especially pain with tenderness over the liver are common. Spider naevi are frequent along with other symptoms of liver failure such as gynaecomastia, testicular atrophy and a loss of male hair distribution. The prognosis is poor but is dramatically improved if alcohol can be avoided.

31:False 32:False 33:True 34:False 35:False
Primary herpetic infection in the third trimester carries a 40% risk to the fetus. There is also a risk of premature labour. Post primary infection only carries an approximately 5% risk of fetal infection. Acyclovir is not licensed for use in pregnancy but it has been used extensively with no evidence of harm to the baby. If herpes lesions are apparent at the onset of labour a caesarean section is indicated. In pregnancy there is a decrease in cell mediated immunity and therefore the risk of infection is probably increased.

36:False 37:False 38:True 39:True
Most children will be pain free within 24 hours in acute otitis media whether given antibiotics or not. Antibiotics appear to have no effect on sinus pain. Antibiotic prescribing appears to increase patients' belief in antibiotics. Patient expectation is important in compliance.

40:True 41:False 42:False 43:False 44:True
In Henoch–Schönlein purpura there is usually a preceding upper respiratory tract infection in the two weeks prior to the onset of symptoms. Arthritis only usually lasts a few days, at the most a week. It most commonly affects the knees and ankles and is usually symmetrical in distribution. Gross or microscopic haematuria occurs in 40% with most cases recovering completely and only a few going on to renal failure or nephritis. Skin biopsy shows the characteristic changes of acute inflammatory reaction and eosinophilic infiltration.

45:False 46:False 47:True 48:True 49:False
No study has shown an improvement over placebo with diuretics or pyridoxine. Gamolenic acid produces improvement in over 50% of cases, tamoxifen 10 mg daily improves pain but this is not covered in the product licence. HRT and the combined oral contraceptive make pain worse because of the oestrogenic drive.

50:False 51:True 52:True 53:False 54:False
The only two of these that are so-called 'First Rank' symptoms are thought insertion and auditory hallucinations commenting on the patient's appearance or actions. Visual hallucinations and paranoid delusions may occur but are not diagnostic. Ideas of reference can occur in other disorders.

55:True 56:True 57:False 58:False 59:True
A fee is payable for notification of a variety of diseases but the rate of reporting still under-represents the true incidence of the diseases. AIDS is not notifiable but a central register is kept of all patients with the disease which relies on voluntary reporting.

60:True 61:True 62:True 63:True 64:True
Aphthous ulcers are small round ulcers with a red margin that heal within 10 days. Lichen planus typically lasts weeks or months, the base is indurated. A recent article has associated lichen planus with the use of NSAIDs. Primary syphilitic ulcers are painless, round and have an indurated base. Agranulocytosis may be the first manifestation of leukaemia or a side-effect of drug therapy. Behçet's disease is rare, usually affects young men and is associated with arthritis, iritis and recurrent oral and genital ulceration.

65:True 66:True 67:False 68:False 69:False
Section 47 of the National Assistance Act allows an application to be made by a community physician supported by another doctor to make an application to a magistrates court. The supporting doctor is usually the patient's GP. Once the section is approved the individual may be removed immediately, for an initial period of three weeks. The patient must not be treated without informed consent if the admission is to a hospital. Most patients are over 65 years of age and are usually women.

70:False 71:True 72:False 73:False 74:False
Eating disorders produce definite symptoms. There are certain features that would suggest an organic disorder. A loss of pubic hair would indicate hypopituitarism. LH levels are typically low in eating disorders. The ESR is normal and cortisol levels are usually high, normal or above normal, possibly related to an associated depression. If the eating disorder has started before puberty gonadotrophin release will be delayed and therefore amenorrhoea will be primary.

75:False 76:True 77:False 78:False 79:True
An IUCD is effective for five days after coitus. The morning after pill is only effective for 3 days. There is no teratogenic risk to the fetus and it is

not contraindicated when breast feeding. Mastalgia is in fact a side-effect in the non-pregnant woman. Because 50% of the female population is unaware of these methods they have failed to reduce unplanned pregnancies.

80:True 81:False 82:True 83:False 84:False

Pain is usually accompanied by vomiting. It is common to pass flatus or faeces after the onset of the pain. However, if the obstruction is in the descending or sigmoid colon, distension may be very marked before vomiting commences. Visible peristalsis is not reliable, it is a normal finding in thin individuals with lax muscles. Bowel sounds are characteristically tinkling.

85:False 86:True 87:False 88:False 89:False

It is possible for viral infections to behave in this way. Asthma is the most common missed diagnosis and a trial of bronchodilators is always worthwhile. Pertussis, after five weeks, will probably have started to resolve slowly. It will have been accompanied by malaise and probably vomiting accompanying the cough. Inhaled foreign bodies will produce signs in the chest and be accompanied by tachycardia and malaise by five weeks. Antibiotics are rarely justified, but often given on a 'blind' basis.

90:True 91:False 92:False 93:True 94:False 95:True

Balint observed how doctors' personalities influenced patient care. Pendleton defined communication tasks of defining problems and choosing appropriate action. Neighbour described safety-netting as anticipating what might happen next and planning; he described house-keeping as dealing with the feelings left over by one consultation. Byrne & Long looked at 'doctor-centred' and 'patient-centred' consultations; Berne looked at a transactional model. Longer consultations improve patient satisfaction especially if there is a major psychological component.

96:True 97:True 98:False 99:False 100:False

Of patients with osteoarthritis 40% have a first-degree relative affected. The knee is the most commonly affected joint and is made worse by obesity. There is little correlation between X-ray appearances and the clinical condition. Activities such as swimming should be encouraged, low impact sporting activities should be gradually increased.

101:False 102:False 103:True 104:False 105:False

A bilateral progressive sensorineural loss can be induced by noise exposure. Generally there is sparing of low frequencies and also very high frequency sounds. Excessive noise damages the hair cells of the Organ of Corti. Recruitment (sudden amplification of the sound) is common as it is in presbyacusis. Hearing aids are particularly effective. The hearing loss is typically insidious progressing over a long period of time.

106:False 107:False 108:False 109:True 110:False
Ten per cent of shiftworkers like nightwork, 20% hate it, and the rest tolerate it. There is no increased cardiovascular mortality but peptic ulceration is much more common due to irregular diet, poor meals, chronic fatigue, excessive smoking and alcohol. Mental symptoms are not increased and the rate of industrial accidents is not increased.

111:True 112:True 113:True 114:True 115:False
Solvent abuse is usually a group activity of boys between 11 and 16 years of age. Surveys show that it is a transient form of experimentation with 75% stopping abuse within 6 months. Acute effects include visual hallucinations, impaired judgement, slurred speech and dizziness. Chronic effects are cerebellar signs with cerebral ventricular enlargement and sometimes peripheral neuropathy. Death is not due to toluene but is due to freons.

116:True 117:True 118:True 119:True 120:True
Seventy-five per cent of children will be dry by the time they reach 3 years of age. Daytime wetting is associated with the various causes of detrusor instability, neurological disorders or anatomical abnormalities. Pad and buzzer alarms have been shown to be most effective in those patients who have insight into their problems and actively want to have an aid to help keep them dry. Lifting the child at night repeatedly although very effective can be very wearing on the parents. Restricting fluids has not been shown to be of any value.

121:False 122:True 123:False 124:False 125:True
The confusing range of what is and is not available on prescription is illustrated by this range of items for just one condition — diabetes.

126:True 127:False 128:True 129:False 130:True
Too rapid a reduction in steroid treatment can lead to severe symptoms such as hypotension, acute adrenal insufficiency and death. More minor symptoms such as conjunctivitis, rhinitis, malaise, arthralgia but not arthritis, loss of weight and painful itchy skin nodules are more common and their true cause may go unrecognised.

131:True 132:False 133:True 134:False 135:True
Night visit fees are complex! Higher rates are paid for visits done by non-commercial rotas between GPs. Requests for visits must be received and the visit made between the hours of 22.00 and 08.00. Patients can be seen at home, in the surgery, or in a community hospital. In the case of the latter the fee is only payable if the doctor makes the arrangements with the patient and the hospital does not call the doctor out at night.

136:True 137:True 138:True 139:True
Although the incidence of chronic bronchitis is falling in men it is rising in women. Great Britain still has the highest incidence in the world reflecting high smoking rates, poor management of industrial waste and a readiness of doctors in this country to make the diagnosis. It accounts for more days away from work than any other illness including back pain and is associated with living in an urban industrial environment.

140:False 141:False 142:True 143:False 144:True
Tinnitus is typically associated with sensorineural deafness but conductive deafness can lead to an awareness of sounds generated within the body, such as from a carotid bruit. Treatment is often unrewarding, but treatment for depression by drugs or psychotherapy helps a proportion of patients. Surgical treatment is rarely used and the patient must be aware that the condition can be made worse by the operation.

145:False 146:False 147:False 148:True 149:False
Closed questions are easy to quantify and analyse, but may give limited information. A combination may be needed. Validity indicates it measures what it was meant to measure. Reliability indicates patients would give the same answers on another occasion. Comprehensibility shows that patients understood the questionnaire. In a Likert scale, a score is given to a preferred response on a continuum of possible responses.

150:True 151:False 152:True 153:True 154:False
It is virtually impossible to distinguish clinically between gastric and duodenal ulceration. They have many features in common, 10% of gastric and 15% of duodenal ulcers bleed. Night pain is present in both but is more common with duodenal ulcers. *Helicobacter pylori* is found in 90% of duodenal ulcers but the significance of this is controversial at present. A familial tendency is common to both and both have a blood group association. Patients over 40 years of age presenting for the first time with dyspepsia should be investigated because this presentation accounts for about 26% of the total number of cancers detected.

155:True 156:True 157:True 158:False 159:False

Eighty-five per cent of carcinomas of the bladder present with an episode of haematuria. It is associated with exposure to various industrial carcinogens, the use of phenacetin and cyclophosphamide, and of course cigarette smoking. It is probably because of the latter that the incidence is rising in women. About half the superficial lesions treated with cystodiathermy will reoccur within 2 years.

160:False 161:True 162:True 163:False 164:False

Haemorrhages, especially the more minor ones are often misdiagnosed as infarcts. This has important implications if aspirin is to be given. A cerebral haemorrhage typically has an abrupt onset with headache, vomiting and possible neck stiffness. The patient will often remain unconscious after 24 hours and will have a raised diastolic blood pressure at this time.

165:False 166:True 167:True 168:True 169:False

Ten per cent of all new entrants to the blind register are directly due to chronic glaucoma, they are usually over 65 years of age. Myopic patients are at a greater risk than long sighted patients, who are at a greater risk of acute glaucoma. There is a very strong familial tendency and first-degree relatives of those patients with glaucoma get free eye tests.

170:True 171:False 172:True 173:False 174:False

Idiopathic thrombocytopenia would be the most common cause. Inadequate mixing can cause platelet aggregation and a falsely low count. Polyarteritis nodosa tends to cause an eosinophilia, whereas SLE may present with a low platelet count. Viral infections are the usual cause of a neutropenia and do not typically affect platelet count. Dipyridamole is an anti-platelet drug but there is no significant association with thrombocytopenia.

175:True 176:True 177:True 178:False 179:True

Chest infection is common, the prognosis is worsened by co-existing heart disease. A very high or a very low white cell count is an adverse indicator of prognosis. Confusion is often the presenting feature of an underlying pneumonic process in an elderly patient who may appear otherwise well and have a minimum of chest signs.

180:True 181:True 182:True 183:True 184:False

Cholestyramine, a bile acid sequestrant is allowed in pregnancy, breast feeding and for use in children. Fenofibrate is allowed for the latter group, experience with all the other agents is limited. Sleep disturbances with simvastatin are typically minimal. The flushing with nicotinic acid may be severe and is also associated with dermatitis. Fibrates and HMG CoA reductase inhibitors adversely affect liver enzymes.

185:True 186:True 187:True 188:True 189:False
General Practitioner contracts state that the individual doctor is responsible for care at all times, even if this care is delegated to a deputising service or practice nurse. The GP is also responsible for all staff including when their family answers the telephone. If a GP perceives the need for a drug and it is available on a NHS prescription it must be provided. A private prescription cannot be used even if the drug is cheaper to the patient privately. Of course if it is available 'over the counter' without a prescription the patient can be advised of this. The most common reason for a complaint against a GP is failure to visit.

190:True 191:False 192:True 193:False 194:True
Surveys have shown that 50% of women who complain that their menstrual loss is heavy have an average loss by normal criteria. Dysfunctional uterine bleeding is diagnosed when there is absence of other factors such as fibroids. D&C is usually employed to detect an underlying endometrial carcinoma, the incidence of which in those under 40 years is 1:100,000. Younger patients would probably be better given a vabra curettage or a hysteroscopy. Mefenamic acid has been shown to decrease blood loss by 25% and also to decrease associated pain.

195:True 196:True 197:True 198:True 199:True
Retinal detachment has a reasonable prognosis for sight if detected early. If central vision is spared, visual acuity will be normal. Black spots and floaters probably are the presenting symptom that cause the most worry to GPs as they are often associated with disturbances within the vitreous which are of little importance.

200:False 201:False 202:False 203:False 204:True
About one-third of all subarachnoid haemorrhages occur in those over 65 years. The majority are due to a ruptured cerebral aneurysm, pre-existing hypertension worsens the prognosis. The most common presentation in the elderly is with confusion or coma. The mortality in this age group is greater than 50%.

205:True 206:True 207:False 208:False 209:True
The drugs quoted here join a growing list, the most important of which appears to be aspirin.

210:True 211:False 212:False 213:True 214:True
Emergency care is free to all visitors to the UK no matter which country they come from. So is any domiciliary nursing care that is needed. For other care, reciprocal arrangements exist with many countries and their nationals can be treated under the NHS; Australia is one such country. A fee can be charged by the first doctor who attends any person involved in a road traffic accident. The bill is usually paid by the insurance company of the vehicle involved without detriment to the driver's 'no claims bonus'.

215:True 216:False 217:False 218:True
Constitutional delay is the most common reason and is defined as puberty delayed beyond 16 years in girls and beyond 18 years in boys. It can be regarded as a variation of normal. The bone age corresponds to the stage of development not chronological age. A raised gonadotrophin level would be indicative of perhaps Turner's syndrome, Klinefelter's or primary gonadal failure. There is typically a family history of late puberty, so it is always worth asking the parents.

219:False 220:False 221:True 222:True 223:True 224:False
Breast feeding fails because of inadequate support and poor, inconsistent and antiquated advice from health care workers. Practices that were shown to be incorrect 30 years ago are still being taught. Initial feeds should not be time restricted, they should be for as long as mother and baby feel comfortable. If sore breasts occur it is usually poor positioning of the baby, not excessive sucking. Just feeding from one breast at a particular feed is justifiable. The fat content of the milk has been shown to increase as the feed progresses. The subsequent incidence of breast cancer in breast feeding women is not increased, various studies have shown a decrease.

225:True 226:True 227:True 228:False 229:True 230:True
When sampling populations it is essential to decrease bias. Retrospective studies are prone to bias as are subjective studies because the results are based on opinion rather than fact. Standardization is essential between the control group and the group under investigation. Stratified sampling compartmentalises the groups within a sample allowing less variation. It is better to use random numbers than sampling at regular intervals. The regularity could coincide by chance with some other unforeseen regularity in the material under study.

231:True 232:True 233:True 234:False 235:False
Suicide in alcoholics is especially prevalent during relapses after a period of abstinence. If episodes of aggression are directed towards themselves they are particularly at risk. The social and psychological isolation engendered by physical illness leaves patients at an immense risk. An urban environment is more associated with suicide than a rural one. The most vulnerable people are male, older age and single, but there has been an increase recently in the incidence in younger males.

236:False 237:False 238:False 239:True 240:True 241:True
There is no specific diagnosis in about 80% of presentations. More than 50% will have recurrent problems, and about 50 million working days are lost each year. About one in five of all new orthopaedic referrals are for back problems.

242:True 243:False 244:True 245:True 246:False
Hair loss of a diffuse nature is associated with iron deficiency in the elderly. Conversely scalp ringworm only causes localised loss in children. Warfarin has hair loss as a reported side-effect. Alopecia areata, with the typical exclamation mark hairs typically causes patchy loss but diffuse loss is known. Trichotillomania, in which the patient deliberately pulls the hair out, produces a well defined area of hair loss. The hairs are very short rather than absent.

247:True 248:True 249:False 250:False 251:False
Ectopic pregnancy has increased by 30% in the last 20 years, possibly due to the increase in pelvic inflammatory disease. The death rate has fallen but it still accounts for 10% of maternal mortality. If the pregnancy test is positive with low levels of HCG and the uterus is empty at 6 weeks' gestation then ectopic pregnancy is likely. Ultrasound on its own is unreliable with 5–10% showing an adnexal mass with a gestational sac. Neither the IUCD or progestogen only pill are associated with ectopic pregnancy.

252:False 253:True 254:True 255:False 256:True
It is always worth knowing a few drugs that are safe and checking any others in the BNF.

257:False 258:True 259:False 260:False 261:True
Pompholyx is an extremely itchy variant of eczema, typically affecting the soles of the feet and the palms of the hands. The epidermal fluid of the eczematous condition is trapped in the thickened stratum and produces a

'sago' like appearance. Strong steroids are often needed in resistant cases. It is not associated with atopy or eczema elsewhere. Mycology should be checked before starting treatment if the condition is severe.

262:False 263:True 264:False 265:False 266:True
Ovarian cancer is much more common in nulliparous women, even a single early spontaneous abortion seems to afford some degree of protection. One year of treatment on the combined pill produces the same protection as a full term pregnancy. If a first degree relative has had the condition the risk is increased by 2–3-fold. The overall survival is 30% rising to 65% if detected at stage 1. Unfortunately, the presentation is often silent, only 15–20% have abnormal bleeding The most common presentation is abdominal pain either with or without abdominal swelling.

267:True 268:True 269:True 270:True 271:False
Cognitive behaviour therapy is in vogue at the moment, it assumes that how people perceive and structure their experiences determines how they feel and behave. Negative aspects and unadaptive patterns of thinking are concentrated on, in a number of sessions which may need to be as many as 15 at weekly intervals. It is suitable for a wide variety of psychological conditions.

272:True 273:True 274:False 275:False 276:False
Ethosuximide is used in the treatment of absence seizures, peak serum levels occur 1–4 hours after administration and the control is highly correlated with the plasma levels. Primidone is converted to phenobarbitone at a steady rate in the ratio 1:2.5. Sodium valproate is completely absorbed from the gut after oral administration. It is highly protein bound and this makes interpretation of blood levels difficult. Vigabatrin increases brain levels of GABA (gamma amino butyric acid) which is a powerful inhibitor of neural transmission. Plasma monitoring at present does not appear to correlate well with efficiency. Clonazepam tolerance develops and drug levels are therefore of no value.

277:False 278:True 279:False 280:False 281:True
Faecal occult blood testing is unacceptable to a lot of people. It has a high false positive rate of approximately 54% in one trial. Sensitivity is of the order of 75% for a three-day test rising to 90% for a five-day test. It is more sensitive for distal tumours. In caecal tumours, haematin released may be broken down in its passage through the remaining colon. Certain foods such as banana, radish, broccoli, parsnip, turnip and cauliflower have peroxidase activity which can lead to false positives.

282:False 283:True 284:True 285:True 286:False
Proliferative retinopathy is seen on the optic disc but background retinopathy is first seen on the temporal side of the macula. The earliest visible changes are micro-aneurysms and haemorrhages. In the UK, diabetes is the most common cause of blind registration between the ages of 20 and 65 years of age.

287:True 288:True 289:False 290:True 291:True
Breath holding attacks tend to occur in children who are easily frustrated. Recovery from an attack is rapid and there are no after effects such as drowsiness which would occur after a fit. Cyanosis is transient and extended tonic posture and shaking or twitching might make the parents think that the child has had a convulsion.

292:False 293:True 294:False 295:True 296:True
If the femoral stretch test is positive this localises the lesion to an L2–L3 level. Pain is felt in the muscles innervated by the damaged nerve. The spinal cord ends at L1 therefore an extensor plantar response suggests that there is some other pathology. A large central disc prolapse may compress the sacral roots in the cauda equina and cause a loss of bladder function.

297:True 298:False 299:True 300:False 301:False
Many antibiotics have been implicated in causing pseudomembranous colitis but systemic clindamycin, amoxycillin, ampicillin and the cephalosporins are the most common. The toxin of the organism *Clostridium difficile* is the causative factor. Vancomycin and metronidazole have been shown to be effective in a patient who is toxic. Blood in the stools is a rare finding usually only with the severe type of infection. The peripheral blood film shows a polymorph leucocytosis and there are leucocytes in the stools.

302:True 303:False 304:True 305:True 306:False
Alzheimer's disease is often missed in the early stages because early symptoms such as preference for routine and mild spatial disorientation are associated with 'forgetfulness' of age. Memory loss is characteristically short term for recent events. In the later stages loss of speech, *grand mal* seizures and spasticity of limbs add to the worsening mental problems.

307:False 308:True 309:False 310:False 311:True
Sulphonylureas are associated with an increase in weight, metformin is the drug of choice in the overweight diabetic if dietary measures fail. This

increase in weight and the loss of effect the longer they are used is the greatest limitation to the use of sulphonylureas. In the elderly there are probably more important problems than strict control, such as good foot care, associated hypertension and control of eye symptoms. Clinically 20–30% will show retinopathy at the time of diagnosis, however fluorescein angiography shows that the majority have started with retinopathy. The current view on diet is that it should be kept simple with a restriction of fat and encouragement to eat complex carbohydrates.

312:False 313:True 314:True 315:False 316:True
Care needs to be taken with prescribing for hay fever in children. Terfenadine has had its product licence modified so that it can now be used from 3 years of age upwards. Xylometazoline can be given at a dose of 1–2 drops every 8–12 hours. Sodium cromoglycate drops are given at a dose of 1–2 drops, 4 times daily.

317:False 318:True 319:False 320:True 321:False
Resting ECGs are of little value, ST segment and T wave changes could reflect LVH, or in inferior leads they can appear with changes in respiration and posture. The amount of ST depression at a given workload and the time this persists after exercise is highly relevant. The normal physiological response to exercise is an increase in heart rate and a rise in systolic blood pressure. If the BP falls this indicates impaired left ventricular function due to myocardial ischaemia. Ambulatory monitoring indicates how easy it is to underestimate the problem of ischaemia. The morbidity of coronary angiography is 1:300 with a mortality rate of 1:2000.

322:False 323:True 324:True 325:True 326:False
Dupuytren's contracture is progressive fibrosis of the palmar fascia causing painless flexion. More than one finger is often affected with 65% ring, 55% little, 25% middle, 5% index and 3% thumb. There is also a high incidence in patients with liver disease especially alcoholics. It is said to affect the white race only and is eight times more common in men than women.

327:False 328:True 329:False 330:True 331:True
Risk factors for congenital dislocation of the hip include female sex, breech delivery, being first born, a family history and oligohydramnios. The left hip is more likely to be affected.

332:True 333:True 334:True 335:True 336:True
Placebos have a high response rate of the order of 30–40% in many conditions. Studies have also shown that factors such as colour and shape of the pills are important in promulgating the depth of the placebo response.

337:True 338:False 339:False 340:False 341:True
Currently in vogue is the term 'heartsink patient', they are difficult to define and are not always frequent attenders. GPs usually contain such patients within the practice and do not refer elsewhere. The average doctor has 20–30 such patients and examining their medical record folders reveals a variety of different diagnoses at each consultation. They also have significantly more psychological, social and family problems.

342:False 343:False 344:True 345:True
At birth about 4% of foreskins are retractable, at 6 months it is 20%, at one year 50%, and by 3 years it is 90%. If left untreated phimosis may ultimately lead to problems with micturition and sexual function. Inability to clean under the foreskin is associated with stones in the preputial sac and the development of cancer of the penis. Circumcision has a low rate of complications and is reported to be the safest surgical procedure in childhood.

346:True 347:True 348:True
Health inequalities reflect social inequalities and the risks from each of these conditions are enhanced in the lower social classes: motor vehicle accidents 2.3:1.0 pneumonia 4.8:1.0 lung cancer 3.0:1.0.

349:False 350:True 351:True 352:True 353:True
The management of glue ear is one of the main controversies in general practice/ENT. Early referral leads to unnecessary intervention and subsequent damage to eardrums which would have remained healthy. Conservative management, especially decreasing passive smoking, and possibly treatment with antibiotics has much to recommend it.

354:True 355:False 356:True 357:True 358:False
One hundred babies with sickle cell disease are born in the UK each year. 6000 people in Great Britain have the disease. Priapism can occur in any male after 5 years of age, most commonly in sexually active men and if prolonged can lead to impotence. Fertility is normal in women but pregnancy is associated with potential serious medical and obstetric complications. Stroke occurs in about 7% of patients and can affect any age

group from 18 months onwards. It is often precipitated by dehydration or infection. Gallstones occur in 70% of adults. Hypersplenism occurs in infancy and is gradually replaced by a state of hyposplenism as the patient's spleen becomes more damaged, eventually leading to a state of 'autosplenectomy'.

359:True 360:False 361:False 362:False 363:False
Seventy-five per cent of patients have a preceding history of psoriasis, in 15% the onset of the rash is synchronous and in 10% the arthritis precedes the rash. Distal interphalangeal joint involvement is common and is associated with psoriatic nail changes. About 20% develop conjunctivitis and 7% iritis. Only 7% of patients with psoriasis will develop evidence of arthropathy.

364:True 365:True 366:True 367:False
Non-A–non-B hepatitis has an incubation period of 6–8 weeks and is transmitted by blood transfusion, coagulation products and by contaminated water. It is associated with a carrier state unlike hepatitis A in which carrier states do not occur. Acute cholangitis is a medical emergency with a high mortality rate. 5–10% of people fail to eliminate the virus in hepatitis B, it has a poorer prognosis especially if associated with the presence of virus D.

368:False 369:False 370:True 371:True
Hypokalaemia results from induced vomiting and diarrhoea. Lanugo, a downy hair, is found on the extremities. Women experience amenorrhoea and men may experience loss of libido.

372:False 373:True 374:True 375:False 376:True
The range of laboratory normal results must be treated with some degree of circumspection in the elderly patient. It is always important to look at the patient's clinical condition and if necessary to repeat a result.

377:False 378:True 379:True 380:False 381:True
AIDS is a rapidly increasing problem world-wide. France has the greatest number of cases in Europe, with the UK lying 5th in the European league table. The majority of cases are in homosexual/bisexual men with intravenous drug users accounting for 3% of the UK total. However, in Scotland the problem of i.v. drug abuse has led to a greater proportion with HIV positivity.

382:True 383:False 384:True 385:False 386:True
The symptoms and signs of colorectal cancer vary depending upon the site of the tumour. Right-sided lesions typically are painful with a palpable mass in 70%, rectal bleeding only occurs in 20%. In the left colon pain occurs less frequently but 60% have a change in bowel habit. 40% have a palpable mass. In the rectum, change in bowel habit is the most common symptom, bleeding occurs in 60% and pain in only 5%.

387:False 388:False 389:False 390:True
Dithranol has been used for many years and is the mainstay of treatment for psoriasis. Contraindications include rapidly spreading lesions, pustular psoriasis, or the use of potent steroids in the recent past. Prolonged use is not associated with skin malignancy and it can be used in patients with hepatic and renal problems. Short contact therapy of 30 minutes per day is as effective as conventional overnight treatment.

391:False 392:True 393:True 394:False 395:True
Bereavement is prolonged if it lasts more than six months. Men are affected by post-bereavement mortality more than women, with 20% of widowers dying in the first year of bereavement. Blunted emotion is a common initial reaction.

396:True 397:False 398:False 399:False 400:True
Febrile convulsions are associated with temperatures in the 6 month to 6 year age group and 90% of the fevers are caused by viral infections. The prevalence in one recent study was 2.4%. The fits typically last less than 10 minutes and autonomic behaviour and transient neurological sequelae are not usual. Diazepam can safely be repeated within 20 minutes of the first dose if the fit does not respond or recurs. There is a 50% chance that a first-degree relative has had a febrile convulsion; with idiopathic epilepsy there is only a 10% chance of a family history.

PRACTICE PAPER 1 — SECTION 2: EMQs ANSWERS

Visual loss
1:B 2:C 3:E 4:D 5:A
Depression
6:E 7:B 8:F 9:A 10:D 11:C 12:C
Social class
13:B 14:F 15:C 16:D 17:C 18:A
Mental Health Act
19:A 20:B 21:B 22:D 23:C 24:E
Child development
25:D 26:E 27:A 28:C 29:D 30:E
Benefits
31:C 32:C 33:B 34:A 35:C
Paraesthesia and weakness
36:B 37:D 38:F 39:G 40:A 41:E
Dermatology
42:G 43:D 44:F 45:E 46:C 47:B
Hypertension
48:B 49:E 50:C 51:A 52:A
Literature
53:D 54:F 55:E 56:A 57:C 58:C
Dyspepsia
59:D 60:C 61:E 62:G 63:B 64:A
Normal distribution
65:B 66:A 67:C 68:C
Studies
69:C 70:D 71:B 72:A 73:E
Screening
74:A 75:G 76:H 77:B 78:J
Infectious diseases
79:E 80:A 81:B 82:C 83:D
Anaemia
84:A 85:C 86:B 87:B 88:A 89:C
Lipid-lowering drugs
90:B 91:A 92:E 93:B 94:D 95:A
Lesions in the mouth
96:A 97:C 98:G 99:E 100:B

PRACTICE PAPER 2 — SECTION 1: MCQs ANSWERS AND TEACHING NOTES

1:False 2:True 3:True 4:True 5: False 6:True

Kawasaki's disease is seen mainly in children under five. There is an acute febrile illness with a cluster of symptoms; these may include fever, conjunctivitis, swelling of cervical lymph nodes, rash on trunk and extremities, reddening of the palms and soles and changes to the lips and oral cavity.

7:False 8:True 9:True 10:False 11:False

Approximately 60% of patients die in hospital. Most patients with pain have two or more different pains so a careful history needs to be taken as different pains need different methods of control. About 95% of chronic pain can be controlled with drugs. If the patient is able to swallow, intramuscular drugs have no advantage over oral. If they cannot swallow a syringe driver will last 24 hours before the syringe has to be changed.

12:True 13:True 14:True 15:True 16:False

Intraventricular haemorrhage is more common in premature babies than small for gestational age babies. There is a definite association with convulsions in later life and remaining small. 50% will have mental handicap and learning difficulties. Diabetes tends to be familial and the babies of diabetic mothers tend to be larger than average rather than smaller.

17:True 18:False 19:True 20:False 21:False

Patients with Korsakoff's syndrome have no awareness of their problem. They are disorientated for time, they make up stories to cover gaps in their memory and typically confabulate. Ritualistic behaviour is associated with obsessional disorders. Echopraxia is the imitation of another person's movements and is associated with catatonia.

22:True 23:False 24:True 25:False 26:True

Bacterial pneumonia may complicate measles infection, however measles virus itself may cause a bronchopneumonia. Chickenpox, especially in adults, can cause a pneumonia which may be severe. Cytomegalovirus, like glandular fever, may produce an infection which may be sub clinical, but especially in the newborn and the immunocompromised it may produce a severe infection.

27:True 28:False 29:True 30:False 31:False

Seventy-five per cent of patients with Bell's palsy will recover within 3 weeks. Although controversial the use of steroids has been shown to be effective in some trials. Neither taste nor lacrimation is affected in a brainstem lesion. Loss of lacrimation would indicate a lesion between brainstem and geniculate ganglion. Repeat attacks typically are less likely to resolve than the initial attack.

32:True 33:False 34:False 35:False 36:False
It is now generally accepted that episiotomy has been overused. It does not protect against subsequent prolapse or rectocele. The babies have no decreased incidence of immediate problems after birth. A significant proportion of those who have an episiotomy performed have a double wound due to an associated tear. GPs and community midwives have known for a long time that it is rarely necessary and that the relaxed atmosphere of a well-controlled home delivery reduces the need.

37:True 38:True 39:False 40:False 41:False
The pain of a tension headache is typically bilateral, occipital, biparietal or diffuse, either being described as a weight on top of the head or a band. Tender spots occur because of irritation of the cervical nerve roots. Flushing and pallor are features of vasomotor instability and would suggest migraine. A watery eye is a feature of cluster headache and unilateral pain of migraine.

42:True 43:False 44:False 45:True 46:False
There is also an association of pyloric stenosis with Turner's syndrome and phenylketonuria. It usually presents between 2 and 4 weeks and rarely beyond 2 months of age. The ratio of males to females is 4:1. The vomiting is not bile stained but 20% contains blood. Persistent vomiting leads to loss of acid, the consequence of this is a hypochloraemic alkalosis.

47:True 48:True 49:True 50:False 51:True
By lowering BP by 6 mm the stroke incidence of a population would decrease by 30%. Some studies have shown that regular walking decreases cardiovascular mortality. Oily fish such as herring or mackerel contain high levels of unsaturated fats. Decreasing sodium levels would decrease blood pressure and fluid retention. However decreasing calcium levels would increase the incidence of osteoporosis.

52:True 53:False 54:True 55:False 56:True
Acute pancreatitis is a severe and often fatal disease. In the UK it is typically associated with gall stones or alcoholism. Hypocalcaemia occurs in 30% of patients and has an adverse prognostic significance. There is an association with raised triglyceride levels. First episodes tend to be the

worst and subsequent attacks have a lower chance of death than the initial attack.

57:True 58:False 59:True 60:True
In people over 65 years the most common causes of accidents are falls, road traffic accidents and fire.

61:True 62:True 63:False 64:False 65:True
Surveys have shown that 65% of patients develop immunity to the wart virus and they will disappear within 2 years. Salicylic acid preparations are effective if the patient is able to persist with treatment for longer than 3 months. Podophyllum is irritating and it is teratogenic, it works quickly. It is usually washed off after 6 hours. Liquid nitrogen gives a rapid cure with little or no scarring, it can be painful.

66:True 67:True 68:True 69:True 70:False
By 6 months of age children should have settled into a regular day/night pattern of behaviour. Hypnotics should be avoided except in extreme circumstances. Strict adherence to a regular bed time routine followed by leaving the child in bed will usually rapidly bring about an improvement in the problem. If allowed to continue there is an increased incidence of behavioural problems and an increase in family stress.

71:True 72:False 73:True 74:False 75:True
The dermatitis following gold injections can be avoided by careful management and good patient co-operation. Azoospermia is a complication of sulphasalazine treatment, which is also associated with thrombocytopenia. Chloroquine produces retinal damage and patients on long term treatment should have regular ophthalmoscopic examination. Methotrexate has been implicated in hepatic fibrosis.

76:True 77:False 78:False 79:False 80:False
A sore throat is usually an early feature of hand, foot and mouth disease and it is often the main symptom of the illness. Ulcers are painful in the mouth and tender on the limbs, they do not usually itch. Spots on the buttocks are very typical. It has an incubation period of 2–10 days and is caused by an enterovirus usually Coxsackie.

81:True 82:True 83:False 84:False 85:False
Down's syndrome is the most common cause of moderate or severe subnormality. Only 20% have heart disease at birth. Death in early or middle life is still usual. Aggressive and disruptive behaviour is less common than

in other disorders. Hypothyroidism is much more common than in the general population but not that common!

86:True 87:True 88:True 89:True 90:True
In Reiter's disease the aspirate typically shows inflammatory cells only and it is clear. The ESR is raised and in the acute stages can be as high as 100 mm/h. Mouth ulcers and stomatitis are common, the lesions on the soles of the feet known as keratoderma blennorrhagica occur in 15% and are unique to Reiter's disease. Conjunctivitis is one of the classic symptoms and may be accompanied by iritis or keratitis.

91:False 92:True 93:False 94:False 95:True
The most common presentation of motor neurone disease is with weakness and wasting in the muscles of one hand. Cramps occur particularly in the muscles of the forearm. The intellect is typically spared and dementia rarely develops. Sphincter function is often spared. The mean duration of the disease is 2–4 years with only 20% surviving more than 5 years.

96:False 97:False 98:True 99:False 100:True
Subarachnoid haemorrhage is typically due to rupture of an intracranial saccular aneurysm. Ten per cent die without warning, 45–50% of all patients will die within 3 months. Only 30% of patients will survive without disability and of those coming to surgery about 45% will achieve their previous quality of life. Surgery has an operational mortality of approximately 2% in major centres. Peak age range is 55–60 years of age and there is a familial tendency.

101:True 102:True 103:False 104:True 105:True
In the second trimester of pregnancy cardiac output increases dramatically so that by 20 weeks it reaches a peak output of 40% more than in the non-pregnant state. Enhanced utilisation of dietary iron is one of the arguments used against routine iron supplementation in normal pregnancy. Gastric acid secretion is decreased but there is delay in gastric emptying leading to increased reflux and 'heartburn'. Introversion increases throughout the second trimester and can lead to marital problems.

106:True 107:True 108:False 109:True 110:True
Phenytoin and carbamazepine both potentiate the effect of alcohol, also an epileptic taking these drugs who drinks alcohol will be at a greater risk of having a fit. Although indomethacin does potentiate alcohol, salicylates do not have this effect. Atenolol does not cross the blood–brain barrier

and therefore does not interact, however propranolol has been shown to cause drowsiness, presumably because of its lipid solubility. In susceptible individuals even the newer non-sedating antihistamines can cause some sedation with alcohol. Nearly all antidepressants potentiate alcohol and affect psychomotor performance.

111:False 112:False 113:False 114:True 115:False
Section 3 is for up to 6 months, and is renewable after that. The patient must have been seen within the last 24 hours when signing a Section 4 recommendation. Detention under Section must be in the interest of the patient's health or safety or for the safety of others. The appropriate forms can be completed in any reasonable location.

116:False 117:True 118:True 119:True 120:True
Lasers are being used with greater frequency in the treatment of many conditions. Acute glaucoma is treated either by iridectomy or trabeculoplasty. The distortion of senile macular degeneration caused by leaking areas on the retina is amenable to laser treatment. Radial keratotomy is used for the treatment of myopia and surgical treatment is now being replaced by laser.

121:True 122:False 123:True 124:True 125:False
One in 10 mothers get a depressive illness which can be differentiated from 'maternity blues'. It may need no more than support and counselling. Various studies have shown various associations. Obvious things such as hormonal state, social class, parity and legitimacy are NOT associated. Housing needs have been shown to be a factor in one survey. Maternal deprivation as a child, previous psychiatric illness and ambivalence or anxiety about the pregnancy have all appeared as risk factors.

126:True 127:True 128:True 129:False 130:True
Cancer of the cervix can occur at any age from 20 to 90, the majority of cases occur in the 40–55 age group. Risk factors also include high parity, early pregnancy and lack of participation in screening. Fifty-five per cent of patients will survive more than 5 years and 47% more than 10 years.

131:True 132:False 133:True 134:True 135:False
Although this is the accepted definition the response of patients is very individual. Catecholamines, such as adrenaline, increase blood sugars and the outpouring of adrenaline at the onset of a hypoglycaemic episode accounts for symptoms such as pallor, feeling of hunger, tachycardia,

trembling and sweating. The main causes of hypoglycaemia in a previously stable diabetic are diet, exercise, infection and alcohol ingestion.

136:False 137:False 138:False 139:False 140:False

Squamous cell carcinoma appears on the helix, rodent ulcers on the skin behind and below the ear. Tophi appear on the antihelix. Psoriasis affects the external auditory meatus and the skin behind and below the ear. Atopic eczema affects the whole ear. Kerato-acanthoma appear as rapidly growing lesions on the helix. Chilblains of the ear are common, painful and itchy.

141:True 142:False 143:True 144:True 145:True

A rare complication but if pulmonary fibrosis occurs it is worth looking at drug therapy as a cause.

146:True 147:True 148:False 149:True 150:False

Flat feet are common especially in children, usually they are asymptomatic. Although more than 50% of 2 year olds have the condition by the time they reach 10 years it occurs in less than 10%. Surgery is a last resort, physiotherapy and orthotic devices are the treatment of choice.

151:True 152:False 153:False 154:False 155:False

The expenses of running a practice are divided into three main groups. Those directly reimbursed by the FHSA. Those partly reimbursed by the FHSA, e.g. staff salaries. Those which are included in the expenses element of the GP reimbursement and increased annually in line with the Review Body recommendations.

156:True 157:False 158:True 159:True 160:False

These two conditions have a lot of similarities, sharing the same histology and the same age and sex distribution. They occur in the 60–70 age group with a male:female ratio of 1:2. They are more common in Caucasians, especially those of Scandinavian origin. There are no typical plasma protein changes.

161:True 162:False 163:True 164:False

Attico-antral perforations are the dangerous ones and they produce a foul smelling discharge. The perforation is marginal and cholesteatoma may be produced. Even a large central perforation may be repaired after the otorrhoea has resolved. A marginal perforation should be referred without delay.

165:False 166:False 167:False 168:True 169:True
Normal BMI is 20–24.9. BMI is calculated by dividing the weight in kilograms by the square of the height in metres. Weight-watching groups can be successful but there is no evidence that GPs are more successful than other groups. The basal metabolic rate remains elevated for several hours after exercise. Exercise has probably been under-used as a method of weight reduction.

170:False 171:False 172:True 173:True 174:True 175:True
Aluminium salts cause constipation, magnesium salts diarrhoea. Cisapride does not have dopamine receptor antagonist properties and therefore does not cause the dystonic reactions of metoclopramide. Intermenstrual bleeding with misoprostol occurs because it is a prostaglandin analogue, it can result in menorrhagia, intermenstrual bleeding and postmenopausal bleeding. The raised prolactin induced by metoclopramide can lead to galactorrhoea and gynaecomastia. The confusion induced by H_2 receptor antagonists is reversible on stopping the drug, it can also occur in a younger age group. Omeprazole is also associated with severe skin reactions in the absence of photophobia.

176:True 177:True 178:False 179:True 180:False
Avascular necrosis is a consequence of the interruption of the blood supply to the femoral head. Precipitating factors include a fall on the hip even without a fracture, dislocation of the hip, vasculitis, SLE, and being on NSAIDs. Deep sea divers are particularly at risk because of nitrogen bubbles causing emboli or compression of vascular channels. Onset may be insidious but often there is a dramatic onset of pain. X-ray changes take time to develop, bone scans show early changes.

181:False 182:True 183:True 184:False 185:True
Amiodarone does not impair left ventricular function to any significant extent and can be used safely in failure. The majority of patients develop corneal deposits but they do not interfere with vision. Thyroid function tests may show a hypo or a hyperthyroid picture but clinical symptoms rarely develop. Photosensitivity is very common but does respond to total sunblock creams.

186:True 187:False 188:False 189:False 190:True
Air travel is being undertaken by an increasing proportion of the population. Dehydration occurs which thickens secretions and therefore vital capacity can be reduced still further. Epileptics are vulnerable to a mixture of hypoxia, fatigue and stress which will all increase fit frequency.

Diabetics on oral agents should take their drugs as per local times. Diabetics on insulin do need to change their dosage regimes and this depends whether the flight is eastbound or westbound. Motion sickness on aircraft decreases with age and with flying experience. Gas trapped in the eye or any internal cavity will expand on increasing altitude therefore patients should not fly until all the gas is absorbed, possibly 6–12 weeks.

191:False 192:False 193:False 194:True 195:False

Fundholders have their prescribing costs included in their general fund. Savings on the indicative budgets cannot be carried forward. Formularies are not compulsory they are to be 'encouraged'. If drug spending is found to be excessive without clinical justification the GP can be called before a hearing in front of three doctors and a withholding of remuneration can result from this. If the FHSA is aware of patients whose drug therapy is expensive this can be allowed for in the calculation of the budget.

196:False 197:True 198:True 199:False 200:True

Nocturnal diarrhoea is rare in irritable bowel syndrome. One painless variety of the syndrome is profuse diarrhoea on waking in the morning. Pain is often related to menstrual disorder and the patient may have a lot of gynaecological investigations prior to recognition of the problem. If painful the pain is typically relieved by defaecation.

201:True 202:True 203:False 204:False 205:False

Antenatal care is done in a blind routine fashion by some health care workers. Concepts of care have been handed down from hospital obstetric practice in an unquestioning manner. In one survey only 44% of small for gestational age babies were detected antenatally. Also for every one born with a correct diagnosis 2.5 were given the diagnosis incorrectly.

206:False 207:False 208:False 209:False 210:True

Breast lumps occurring in those under 30 years of age are usually fibroadenomata. In those over 30 years they are either a cyst or a carcinoma. Aspiration is an easy technique for a GP, if the lesion is solid or the aspirate blood stained, referral is indicated. There is a 30% chance of a cyst recurring or further cysts developing. Cyclical mastalgia rarely requires treatment, oil of evening primrose is effective, but is expensive.

211:True 212:True 213:False 214:False 215:True

Diabetics of any age are exempt. Pregnant women and the elderly are not exempt. First-degree relatives of those with glaucoma can get a free test. People on income support but not those receiving a rent rebate can also get a free test.

216:True 217:True 218:True 219:False 220:True
Charges can be made for ear piercing because it is a treatment not usually provided by a General Practitioner. Housing letter payments are often dealt with on a local basis. Payment is often made by the local council or housing association.

221:True 222:False 223:True 224:False 225:False
Those persons at high risk of developing diabetes include patients with a positive family history, those with gestational diabetes, obese patients and those who have given birth to large babies weighing more than 4.5 kg.

226:False 227:False 228:True 229:True 230:False
Rheumatic fever does not present with atrial fibrillation but rheumatic heart disease does. Thyrotoxicosis and alcoholic causes are relatively common, even American presidents are not exempt.

231:True 232:False 233:False 234:False 235:False
Normal pressure hydrocephalus is a reversible cause of the symptoms of dementia. The usual progression of the triad of symptoms is of gait disturbance of which apraxia (forgetting how to walk) is the most common. Following this most cognitive impairment occurs and then urinary incontinence develops. The symptoms are temporarily reversed by lumbar puncture. Approximately 50% of patients are improved by shunts, but the operative procedure has a high incidence of complications.

236:False 237:False 238:False 239:False 240:False
Following admission for an act of deliberate self-harm 20% of patients will require admission to a psychiatric unit. Twenty-five per cent of all patients will repeat the episode at least once in the next year. No amount of psychiatric or social help seems to reduce the incidence. 'Help' lines are useful in individual cases but have not reduced the overall incidence. About 2% will successfully commit suicide within the next year.

241:True 242:True 243:False 244:True 245:False
Polycythaemia vera may well present with a vascular incident secondary to haemodynamic changes. Increased turnover of cells leads to hyperuricaemia and gout may be a presentation. Itching is a common presentation. Approximately 30% terminate as acute leukaemia and the incidence of this is increased by radiotherapy or chlorambucil therapy.

246:True 247:True 248:False 249:False 250:False

Sudden loss of vision in a migrainous episode is associated with complete recovery. Central retinal vein occlusion can lead to an extensive haemorrhage visible at the fundus. The visual loss typically develops over a period of a few hours. Senile macular degeneration produces a gradually progressive loss of central vision with preservation of peripheral vision. Optic neuritis presents with gradual loss in the 20–45 age group with intact peripheral vision. Toxic optic neuropathy may be due to heavy cigarette smoking or alcohol intake, again peripheral vision remains intact.

251:True 252:False 253:False 254:False 255:False

The inclusion of child surveillance as a part of general practice was one of the more positive aspects of the 1990 contract. A GP must either undergo further training or have had special experience in order to be included on the list of approved doctors. The child must register separately for inclusion on the child surveillance list. Child clinics are not eligible for a payment as a health promotion clinic and immunisations are subject to target payment regulations. Any suitably trained doctor within the practice can perform the check and some of the tests still remain more the responsibility of the health visitors.

256:True 257:True 258:False 259:False 260:True

SLE is the most common autoimmune disease in childbearing women. The rate of miscarriage is 70%, some people who miscarry repeatedly develop SLE in later life. High follicular levels of LH correlate with failure to conceive and recurrent miscarriage. An abnormal parental karyotype is present in 5% of those couples who have recurrent miscarriages.

261:True 262:True 263:False 264:True 265:False

Neonates and older children are little affected by RSV. Stridor is indicative of croup not bronchiolitis. In the UK it has a strict seasonal pattern occurring between December and May. Examination of the throat is a problem in acute epiglotitis which is caused by *Haemophilus influenzae* infection.

266:True 267:True 268:True 269:True 270:True

Head injury is often followed by a variety of symptoms, hypochondriasis, fatigue and irritability are the most common. They can occur even when there is no definite evidence of brain damage. Depressive and schizophrenic-like psychoses are more common. The reason why suicide is more common is not known. Personality disorders are more common especially after frontal lobe damage.

271:True 272:False 273:True 274:False 275:True
Topical steroid absorption is enhanced by urea and by occlusion. This includes nappies and plastic pants. It takes about 4 g of steroid for a single application to the trunk, 1 g to the arm, 2 g to the leg, 1 g to the hand and foot. Local side-effects of prolonged steroid use are thinning of the skin, acne, mild depigmentation and increased hair growth. Ointments are indicated for dry conditions and creams for moist conditions.

276:False 277:True 278:True 279:True 280:False
Notifiable deaths, that should be reported to the coroner, include cases when a doctor has not attended within the preceding 14 days, when accidents, injuries or industrial diseases are involved, and deaths in prisoners. Chronic alcoholism is no longer notifiable unless death is associated with accident or injury or there is some other reason for reporting the death.

281:True 282:False 283:False 284:True 285:True
Ischaemic ulcers are typically painful presenting for the first time in those over 70 years of age. They are punched out, necrotic and found anywhere on the lower leg or foot. Venous ulcers tend to be painless, pigmented with marked induration and oedema. The surrounding skin may be eczematous.

286:False 287:True 288:False 289:True 290:True
The average age of menarche in the UK is 13 years of age. The periods stop at an average age of 50 years. There are a lot of 'old wives tales' about periods, it is often quoted but untrue that an early menarche begets a late menopause. Estimation of LH and FSH is the most reliable method of determining that symptoms are due to the menopause.

291:True 292:False 293:True 294:False 295:True
Epiphora often occurs because the irritant effect of having dry eyes causes an overflow of tears. It is associated with sarcoid and also autoimmune diseases such as rheumatoid arthritis. Schirmer's test is diagnostic. Sjögren's syndrome is an autoimmune disease in which dry eyes are but one feature. People with entropion often have epiphora.

296:False 297:True 298:True 299:True 300:True
Most malignant lesions have reached 1 cm in diameter before they are recognised. In the absence of other symptoms it is probably benign, if less than this size. Benign lesions are round or oval in shape, malignant ones have a scalloped or notched border. Malignant lesions can vary in colour from black to light brown. They may have a reddish tint due to inflamma-

tion. Benign lesions never have any evidence of erythema either within or around them. Crusting, oozing or bleeding all indicate a need for referral.

301:False 302:False 303:False 304:True 305:False

The main indication of lithium treatment is to prevent the relapses in bipolar affective disorders. It is only available as an oral preparation and is of no value in acute episodes of illness. It does not cause a chronic nephropathy and changes in urea and electrolytes are reversible on stopping the drug. Thyroid enlargement may occur and thyroid function tests should be monitored regularly.

306:True 307:True 308:False 309:True 310:True

The consent must also state whether the patient wishes to view the report. The patient has the right to provide a statement of his/her views to be attached to the report in the event of disagreement with the doctor over the content. The doctor should keep a copy for 6 months only and the patient has a right to view this. If the patient requests a copy the doctor can charge a reasonable fee for providing one. If there is a problem about divulging a patient's records it may well be prudent to consult your medical defence organisation.

311:True 312:True 313:False 314:False 315:True

Schizoid personalities are emotionally cold, introspective and self-sufficient to a fault. They are aloof and ill at ease in company, they lack warmth and it is difficult to discover their real problems. Self-dramatisation is a feature of hysterical personalities.

316:True 317:True 318:True 319:True 320:True

Measuring the middle is not a simple matter and it is important to be clear about the difference between the mode, mean and median.

321:True 322:True 323:True 324:True 325:True

The first three questions are the cardinal rules for the treatment of undescended testes. The only other point is that some people think that 2 years is the latest age by which a testes should be placed in the scrotum because this increases fertility even more. A hernial sac is present at most operations, but usually it is asymptomatic.

326:True 327:True 328:False 329:True 330:True

In differentiating between depression and dementia, the symptoms develop more rapidly in the former. Complaints of memory loss would suggest that insight is retained, depressive symptoms are worse in the morning. Rather than 'don't know' demented patients tend to reply with near miss or inappropriate replies.

331:True 332:True 333:True 334:True 335:False

Jet lag is due to an upset in the usual circadian rhythm. It is less marked if travel results in a longer day, i.e. when going towards the USA from the UK. The effects of jet lag on individual performance may last for several days.

336:False 337:True 338:False 339:False

Long term follow-up in hospital does not favour outcome and is probably an inappropriate use of resources. Psychological support is best effected by the primary health care team. Tamoxifen if given for 5 years has been shown to improve survival and decrease the risk of recurrence. Cancer in the opposite breast is six-fold greater in those already having a malignancy, it is especially greatest for those who develop their first tumour under 40 years of age. Hormone manipulation is often used first because of the decreased incidence of side-effects. However the response rate is only 30% compared to 60% for chemotherapy.

340:True 341:True 342:True

Although all the women were upset by the experience, just over 50% had lasting effects, usually involving negative feelings about themselves, about men and about sex. Their ability to form lasting relationships was severely hampered.

343:True 344:True 345:False 346:False 347:False

Only after employment for one month is a new employee eligible for a minimum period of notice based on the length of service. A written reason for dismissal must be given on request only after 2 years of service. Absence due to maternity is only payable after 26 weeks of employment but paid time off must be given for antenatal care.

348:False 349:False 350:True 351:True

Sumatriptan is a 5HT analogue which probably causes cranial blood vessels to constrict. It is administered via an sc injection or orally. About 40% of patients will get a recurrence of headache and of those 70% will obtain relief from a further dose. It is contraindicated in hemiplegic migraine, in those with unstable angina and uncontrolled hypertension. There has been an increasing incidence in the reports of ventricular arrhythmias occurring with the drug. It should not be given less than 12 hours after ergotamine and these preparations should not be given within 12 hours of sumatriptan administration.

352:False 353:False 354:True 355:True 356:False
The average practitioner will have 2–3 new patients with gout per year, 20% of patients will have a family history. It is six times more common in males than females. Chronic tophaceous gout is now rare, but that and renal gout with calculi are indications for allopurinol treatment. 25–40% of those with gout will have or will develop hypertension. Triglyceride levels are higher in gout sufferers.

357:True 358:True 359:True 360:True 361:True
Systemic gold therapy for rheumatoid arthritis may produce oral pigmentation similar to that of Addison's disease. Bulimia leads to parotid enlargement and erosion of the teeth due to regurgitation of acid. Erythema multiforme may cause extensive crusting of the lips or intra-oral vesicles and bullae. Intra-oral bullae are a prominent feature of pemphigus vulgaris, they are either yellow or haemorrhagic and burst to leave an area of ulceration. Lichen planus classically affects the mouth giving erosive lesions or producing 'cotton wool' patches.

362:False 363:True 364:True 365:True 366:True
Only residents of nursing homes, residential homes and other long stay institutions are recommended to have the vaccine. In non-pandemic years health care workers are not included. Patients vulnerable to acute infections because of a variety of chronic diseases should also be immunised.

367:False 368:True 369:False 370:False 371:False
Maternity medical fees are payable to all doctors, however those on the obstetric list receive a higher fee. The fees are payable for all pregnancies once the patient has signed the FP 24, if she subsequently decides that she wants a termination then a fee is payable. The GP does not need to attend the confinement. Post-natal visit fees are only payable for visits up to the 14th day.

372:False 373:False 374:True 375:True 376:False
About 90% of patients will stop bleeding spontaneously. However the mortality rate is still about 10% and is not reduced by urgent endoscopy. Drugs, such as ranitidine do not stop bleeding but some studies show that they prevent rebleeding. Gastric ulcers are more likely to rebleed than duodenal, also if blood vessels are visible at endoscopy a rebleed is more likely.

377:True 378:True 379:True 380:False 381:False
Terfenadine is an OTC antihistamine and there have been reports of serious cardiac arrhythmias if given with erythromycin or systemic

antifungal agents. Ciprofloxacin causes a potentiation of theophylline levels. Theophylline has a narrow therapeutic window and therefore toxic effects can occur. Cimetidine potentiates the effect of oral anticoagulants including warfarin. There is no significant interaction between allopurinol and captopril, it is included in the manufacturer's list of interactions because of the risk of renal damage in patients with gout.

382:True 383:False 384:True 385:False 386:True 387:False
Follow-up studies of opiate users show that after 7 years 25–33% are abstinent but 10–20% have died from drug-related causes. Methadone liquid is used as an aid to withdrawal because it cannot be used intravenously, unlike the tablets which can be crushed and injected. Cocaine and hallucinogens are 'recreational' drugs associated with the more privileged groups in society. Chronic amphetamine abuse is associated with a paranoid psychosis indistinguishable from paranoid schizophrenia.

388:False 389:True 390:True 391:True 392:True
Alcohol abuse can be detected by the use of simple questionnaires of which CAGE and MAST are good examples. Fishermen, along with publicans and barmaids, are at high risk of alcoholism. Single males over 40 years are also at high risk. The incidence of carcinoma of the oesophagus is increased three-fold in patients with alcohol problems.

393:True 394:False 395:True 396:False
Angular cheilitis is characterised by painful fissures at the angles of the mouth, *Candida* often combines with *S. aureus* to produce the infection. Denture stomatitis is usually found under a complete upper denture and the fitting surface is an important reservoir of the organism. A ranula is a mucus retention cyst and is caused by obstruction of the duct of a minor salivary gland. Sjögren's syndrome is a triad of dry mouth, dry eyes and a connective tissue disorder.

397:True 398:False 399:False 400:True
Symptoms most correlating with peptic ulcer disease are epigastric pain with a definite food association, night pain, periodicity of symptoms and prompt predictable antacid relief. A positive family history is also important.

PRACTICE PAPER 2 — SECTION 2: EMQs ANSWERS

Shoulder pain
1:H 2:F 3:I 4:E 5:C 6:A

Epilepsy
7:A 8:E 9:B 10:B 11:D

Mental Health Act
12:A 13:C 14:F 15:D 16:B 17:E

Statistics
18:B 19:C 20:D 21:B 22:A

Coronary heart disease
23:F 24:H 25:G 26:B 27:E 28:C 29:A

Prescribing
30:D 31:A 32:C 33:E 34:F

Professions
35:C 36:A 37:D 38:B

Lipid tests
39:C 40:A 41:D 42:B

Misuse of drugs
43:A 44:C 45:D 46:C 47:A

Benefits
48:C 49:A 50:D 51:E 52:B

Developmental milestones
53:C 54:D 55:E 56:A 57:B 58:C 59:D

Immunisations
60:E 61:A 62:B 63:C 64:D

Screening
65:H 66:C 67:D 68:G 69:J

Swellings in the neck area
70:C 71:E 72:D 73:B 74:A 75:D

Paraesthesia
76:A 77:C 78:D 79:E 80:B 81:F

Studies
82:A 83:B 84:A 85:A 86:B 87:B 88:A

Literature
89:E 90:F 91:A 92:D 93:C 94:B

Ear problems
95:F 96:E 97:D 98:C 99:B 100:A

PRACTICE PAPER 3 — SECTION 1: MCQs ANSWERS AND TEACHING NOTES

1:True 2:True 3:False 4:False 5:True

About 40% of all accidents in children under 14 years are due to road traffic accidents. In the over 65-year-old age group, falls account for about 50% of accidents. Seat belt legislation resulted in a substantial reduction in death or serious accidents in drivers. Drowning is another common cause of accidents in under 14 year olds, with alcohol being a significant factor in accidents in young people and the elderly.

6:True 7:True 8:True 9:False 10:True

Dopamine inhibits prolactin, therefore dopamine agonists such as bromocriptine inhibit prolactin release and are used to treat prolactinomas. Conversely dopamine blockers such as metoclopramide will stimulate prolactin release.

11:True 12:True 13:True 14:False 15:False

Ototoxicity induced by quinine is usually reversible on stopping the drug but if it is given in the first trimester of pregnancy it may cause hearing loss in the baby. The hearing loss induced by frusemide occurs if the drug is given rapidly intravenously, it is typically transient. However the loss may be permanent if aminoglycosides are given concurrently. Erythromycin is only ototoxic if given in high doses.

16:True 17:True 18:False 19:False 20:True

Post-menopausal bleeding is defined as any vaginal bleeding occurring 6 months after the last period. It should always be investigated. Exogenous oestrogens from whatever source can cause bleeding. Polyps can still occur in this age group and urethral caruncles do bleed. If the discharge is profuse and offensive, cervical cancer is a distinct possibility, but senile vaginitis also leads to vaginal infection.

21:False 22:False 23:True 24:False 25:True

Coronary artery bypass is highly successful with an operative mortality of less than 3% in the UK. Patients with improved lifespan after operation are those with triple vessel disease, unstable angina and blockage of the left main coronary artery. The results of grafting are better if an artery rather than a vein is used. Operative mortality is greater in females and in those with unstable angina. The recurrence of angina occurs at a steady rate of about 3–4% per annum.

26:True 27:False 28:False 29:False 30:True
Hysteria is a difficult and dangerous diagnosis to make, it is easy to miss genuine physical and psychiatric morbidity. Depression and anxiety are extremely common and a trial of drug therapy is often worthwhile. Hysteria is a diagnosis of younger life and should not be made in those over 40 years of age. 'Belle indifference' and amnesia are very rare.

31:True 32:True 33:False 34:True 35:True
By February 1991, 89% of all 2-year-old children had received MMR vaccine. The vaccine is not contraindicated in those who are HIV positive but it is in those who are immunocompromised, for example those receiving chemotherapy for leukaemia. The rates of laboratory confirmed rubella in pregnancy have fallen from 164 in 1987 to 20 in 1990. Although meningoencephalitis has been reported following exposure to the vaccine it is much less than the rate for mumps prior to introduction of the vaccine.

36:False 37:True 38:True 39:True 40:True
Thirty per cent of women and 33% of men smoke. However in the 11–15 age group 7% of boys and 9% of girls smoke and this is a decreasing incidence in both groups. Male smokers consume an average of 20 cigarettes daily and females 15 daily. Gastrointestinal and psychiatric problems plus accidents account for the increased consultation rate of those with alcohol problems. Heavy drinkers have an increased incidence of cancer of the oral cavity, larynx and oesophagus. There was an increased rate of breast cancer in one survey.

41:True 42:False 43:False 44:True 45:False
Post-viral fatigue syndrome is a complex subject. The overwhelming feature is fatigue and fatiguability that is both physical and mental. Approximately 75% of the patients have a significant psychiatric problem and over 50% have depression of such severity that a trial of antidepressants is worthwhile. Prolonged rest is not advised, patients need to regain control of their illness and need to be encouraged to increase activity.

46:False 47:True 48:True 49:False 50:True
Episcleritis causes slight or no pain with normal vision and usually settles without treatment. Conjunctival haemorrhage should be painless with normal vision. Keratitis causes impairment of vision if the ulcer or opacity is near the visual axis. Acute glaucoma causes severe pain with vomiting and severe visual impairment. Finally iritis could also cause an increase in floaters and the pupil would be small and distorted.

51:True 52:True 53:True 54:False 55:False
Infected eczema is usually an endogenous eczema with a secondary staphylococcal infection. With scabies look for burrows along the sides of the fingers. Pustular psoriasis will probably also occur on the soles of the feet as well. Ichthyosis causes a scaly dry skin and erythema multiforme has a characteristic rash of a large vesicle with a surrounding red halo.

56:True 57:False 58:False 59:True 60:True
The onset of schizophrenia is usually between 15 and 45 years with males having an earlier onset by about 5 years. Paranoid delusions are not themselves diagnostic. Negative symptoms of schizophrenia include apathy.

61:True 62:False 63:False 64:True 65:True
If the dehydration is significant the eyes are sunken and crying produces few tears, the skin is doughy and there is tachycardia and tachypnoea. The mouth is dry and the fontanelle if open, is sunken. Weight loss is not reliable; a child with diarrhoea who has been starved but is well hydrated may have lost a visible amount of weight.

66:False 67:True 68:True 69:False 70:True
Acute asthma is often under-diagnosed and under-estimated by both patient and the doctor, and undue reliance placed on bronchodilators. Peak flow levels at this age should be a good predictor of severity whereas the extent of expiratory wheeze is not related. Tachycardia greater than 120 and pulsus paradoxus are good indicators of a severe attack. Young men in their late teens and early twenties are vulnerable to the development of spontaneous pneumothorax.

71:True 72:True 73:True 74:True 75:True
In addition to the conditions listed obesity can also lead to a worsening of arthritis and an increase in ischaemic heart disease and stroke. However do remember that it can be secondary to drug therapy, e.g. steroids, pizotifen, and various medical conditions.

76:True 77:True 78:True 79:False 80:True
When intra-ocular pressure rises there is transient oedema of the cornea and this can give rise to haloes. An associated red eye may mean that there is acute glaucoma or inflammation of the iris or ciliary body. Amblyopia is usually long standing often due to untreated or badly treated squint. It does not give rise to headache. A pale optic disc may be due to a compressive lesion.

81:False 82:False 83:False 84:False 85:True
Some heavy drinkers are not physically dependent but conversely some moderate drinkers develop severe symptoms of withdrawal. Seizures typically occur within 10–60 hours of the last drink. The mortality of delirium tremens is about 10%. Many psychiatric symptoms including confusion, disorientation, paranoia, auditory or visual hallucinations may occur 72 hours or more after the last drink. The typical early withdrawal symptoms are tremor, sweating, anorexia, nausea, insomnia and anxiety.

86:False 87:True 88:False 89:True 90:True
SIDS shows no association with the mode or type of delivery. The risk increases with the parity especially if the pregnancies are closer together. If the mother is addicted to narcotic agents there is a 30-fold increase in risk. Twins are at risk and if one twin suffers a sudden infant death or a 'near miss' the other twin should be monitored very closely. Children are best placed on their side or supine at night.

91:False 92:True 93:False 94:True 95:False
Hot baths cause vasodilatation enhancing penetration of the drug and increasing the risk of CNS toxicity. This toxicity is why the drug is contraindicated in pregnant women. A single application is usually sufficient to eradicate the mite and it decreases the chances of toxicity. Scabies typically does not affect the face, except in one variety that occurs in mentally handicapped patients and is known as Norwegian scabies. Itching may take 4 weeks to resolve after successful eradication of all the mites.

96:False 97:True 98:False 99:False 100:True
Hodgkin's disease typically presents with lymphadenopathy and in over half this is a cervical gland enlargement. Hepatomegaly is an indication of advanced disease and has a poor prognostic significance. Early localised disease has been treated successfully with radiotherapy whereas generalised disease is treated with chemotherapy. 'Cure' rates of between 70% and 80% are usual.

101:True 102:False 103:True 104:False 105:False
Agoraphobia is a disease which typically affects women. Although they are often highly dependent on their husbands there is no increase in the rate of divorce or separation. Thoughts tend to focus on a fear of losing control e.g. fainting. Depersonalisation (feeling that one's body is unreal or remote) is a very typical symptom but this can also occur in depression. Programmed behaviour therapy is the psychological treatment that produces the best results.

106:True 107:False 108:True 109:False 110:True
The most common drugs to cause fixed drug eruptions are NSAIDs, sulphonamides, tetracyclines and quinine. They may take up to 2 hours to develop, a brown discoloration of the skin may last for several months. The acute reaction of an oval inflammatory patch may or may not contain blisters.

111:False 112:True 113:True 114:True 115:False
Type A personalities show impatience and are competitive; they have twice the risk of heart disease compared to Type B.

116:False 117:False 118:True 119:True 120:False
Improvement grants are usually available to help GPs to improve existing premises and can be one-third of the cost of approved work. Separate rooms for a trainee are desirable but not compulsory. The cost rent scheme is highly advantageous but does strictly limit the number of rooms and the maximum sizes possible. It is possible to change from cost rent to notional rent schemes but only after a district valuer assessment which can only be done every 3 years.

121:True 122:False 123:True 124:True 125:False
The mortality of paracetamol overdosage is not falling, the reason being due to late presentation and that the antidote treatment with acetylcysteine is ineffective if given over 15 hours after the ingestion of the drug. Although chronic alcohol ingestion worsens the outlook, acute alcohol ingestion appears to be protective. Carbamazepine, phenytoin, and phenobarbitone, if taken as well, worsen the prognosis.

126:False 127:False 128:True 129:True 130:True
Following on from the provisions of the Data Protection Act this provides access to handwritten notes. It applies to all 'employed by the health service body'. Only notes made after November 1991 are included. As in the Data Protection Act the GP has 21 days to comply with request for access and can make a charge to the patient and can also charge for any copies provided.

131:True 132:False 133:True 134:False 135:True
Aortic stenosis is now the most common valvular lesion in all adults, usually due to degenerative calcific disease. A soft murmur does not exclude severe aortic stenosis especially if the patient has low output cardiac failure. In contrast mitral stenosis is invariably due to rheumatic heart disease. Mitral regurgitation is most commonly due to the same

factors as aortic stenosis. A prolapsing mitral valve is the next most common cause. Seventy per cent of patients over 70 will have a murmur.

136:True 137:True 138:True 139:False 140:False
Risk factors for osteoporosis can be divided into high, medium and low. Alcoholism is a medium risk factor and cigarette smoking, although a risk factor, carries a lower risk. The others quoted are high risk factors.

141:False 142:True 143:True 144:True 145:True
Fragile X is so-called because there is a gap in the long arm of the X chromosome which can be seen on examination of the amniotic fluid antenatally. Carrier females are usually of normal intelligence but 10% have mild mental retardation. It is the commonest form of X linked mental retardation and the children typically have bat ears a large jaw and maxillary hypoplasia.

146:True 147:False 148:True 149:False 150:True
Doctors must be available for 26 hours per week spread over five days with a possibility of four days if the doctor is undertaking health-related activity elsewhere within the public service. They have to be available for 42 weeks per year. Times and places of availability must be approved. An allowance for travelling is included in the 26 hours of availability. Job-sharing GPs must have a combined availability of 5 days but each doctor is not expected to be available on each of these days.

151:True 152:False 153:True 154:False 155:False
Drugs that undergo significant first-pass metabolism by the liver must be given with caution to those patients with liver disease, for instance coma may be precipitated in the cirrhotic by the use of analgesics containing opiates. Acyclovir along with many antibiotics is excreted unchanged by the kidney.

156:False 157:True 158:True 159:False 160:False
Before ovulation the cervix is closed and firm. During ovulation it is fully open admitting a finger tip and is wet due to the production of stringy mucus. Within 48 hours of ovulation the cervix closes and becomes firm again, the mucus becomes rubbery and thick forming a plug. Tests that predict ovulation measure LH secretion. Basal temperature rises during ovulation and stays raised in the luteal phase.

161:False 162:False 163:True 164:False 165:False
Parkinson's disease has an incidence of 1:1000 in middle life rising to 1:200 in the elderly. In the latter it typically presents with rigidity. Levodopa is effective in reducing symptoms but its effect lasts for 5–8 years. Selegiline is effective both early and late after levodopa has failed to be effective and may delay progression of the disease. Dementia is a common feature of late disease.

166:False 167:False 168:False 169:True 170:False 171:False
After a heart attack, patients are now told to avoid driving for one month. If a pacemaker is fitted, driving is allowed from one month after insertion, provided the pacemaker is checked regularly. Driving is to be avoided for one week following coronary angioplasty. An epileptic can drive when he has been fit free for one year. Patients with migraine should not drive from the onset of the warning period. Patients should not drive for 24–48 hours after a minor operation requiring general anaesthetic.

172:True 173:True 174:True 175:True 176:True
Fibroids are often asymptomatic, surgery is usually indicated if the bleeding is heavy or the fibroid is above 14–16 weeks in size. GnRH analogues are not licensed for use but certain centres are now using them to shrink fibroids prior to the menopause or surgery. HRT causes fibroids to increase in size if not monitored closely.

177:False 178:True 179:True 180:True 181:True
Anxiety may be triggered by a multitude of factors including physical illness, caffeine ingestion, alcohol withdrawal or the use of drugs such as sympathomimetics or antihistamines. Treatment is directed to both the somatic and psychological aspects. MAOIs are very effective in anxiety especially when there is a phobic element.

182:True 183:True 184:False 185:True 186:False
Congenital abnormalities occur in 7% of babies born to epileptic mothers. Sodium valproate increases the risk of spina bifida to 1–2% (normally 0.023% of all births). The incidence of congenital heart disease in the babies of mothers taking phenytoin is 8%, it is also associated with orofacial cleft deformities. Carbamazepine appears to be relatively safe, it is chloramphenicol which causes bone marrow suppression. Warfarin is associated with CNS defects, heparin is not implicated.

187:False 188:True 189:True 190:False 191:False
The peak incidence of acute suppurative otitis media is at 4–8 years of age. The majority of infections are mild and only 10% of these are bacterial. About 90% of severe cases are bacterial. Only 1% develop chronic suppurative otitis media and of these only a few will get mastoiditis.

192:False 193:False 194:True 195:True 196:True
Pulmonary embolism is the most common cause of death in the UK associated with pregnancy. Two-thirds occur post-natally. Increasing age and increasing parity are risk factors. Complicated delivery also increases the risk. Women who have had thromboembolism in the past have a 1:10 to 1:20 risk of a further episode and anticoagulation throughout the pregnancy with heparin is usually advised.

197:True 198:True 199:True 200:True 201:False
Appendicitis is still missed, especially in the young and the old. The incidence in a population is inversely proportional to the amount of dietary fibre consumed by that population. Therefore the incidence in the UK is decreasing. Retrocaecal appendices are associated with atypical symptoms and a high retrocaecal appendicitis may mimic the symptoms of renal tract infection.

202:False 203:False 204:False 205:True 206:True
The American criteria for consent are much stricter than the British. In Great Britain the doctor need only give the patient enough information to make a rational choice rather than provide details of every rare complication. Under the Gillick judgement, patients under 16 years of age can give consent if they are thought mature enough to understand the implications. Oral consent is as valid as written consent, the problem is proving that it was given. Under the Police and Criminal Evidence Act, intimate samples need the consent of patients over 17, of the patient and parent between 14 and 17, and of parent alone under 14 years of age.

207:False 208:False 209:True 210:True 211:True
The inclusion of certain items and the exclusion of others from the minor surgical list fails to make a lot of sense to doctors who have been doing surgical procedures for a long time before the 'new contract'. Intra-articular, periarticular and injections of varicose veins are included in the minor surgery list. Curettage, cautery or cryocautery to warts and verrucae and other skin lesions are also allowed.

212:False 213:False 214:True 215:True 216:True
Acute lymphoblastic leukaemia is the commonest 85% with 14% acute myeloblastic. The average age of onset of the former is 3–5 years and of the latter neonates. The best prognosis is for ALL in boys aged 1–8 years. The overall survival of the disease after completion of 5 years' treatment is 65%. Maintenance cytotoxics are usually continued for 3 years once remission has been achieved.

217:False 218:False 219:False 220:False 221:True
There are relatively few absolute contraindications to HRT. The main one quoted is oestrogen-dependent tumours, however recent evidence has cast some doubt on this. Diabetes is only a relative contraindication. All routes of treatment are helpful with the symptoms of atrophic vaginitis. Lipid levels are favourably affected by unopposed oestrogen, it is the progestogenic component which appears to cause problems with elevation of lipid levels. If given for 10 years it has been estimated that the incidence of osteoporotic fractures would be halved.

222:True 223:True 224:True 225:False 226:False
Familial adenomatous polyposis coli is uncommon. It is inherited as an autosomal dominant gene but accounts for only about 1% of all colonic cancer. Hereditary non-polyposis coli is relatively more common. Familial adenomatous polyposis coli is asymptomatic in teenage years but later causes a change in bowel habit with rectal bleeding and passage of mucus. Faecal occult blood testing is a sensitive test for blood but not sensitive or specific for colonic cancer.

227:False 228:True 229:False 230:False 231:False
Impotence due to an organic cause is usually of insidious onset. It is more common in patients with vascular diseases and various neurological abnormalities, e.g. diabetic neuropathy, multiple sclerosis. Papaverine is given by intracavernosal injection and an erection should last for 3 hours maximum. It is usually limited to twice-weekly use. Vacuum condoms are not available on NHS prescriptions.

232:False 233:True 234:True 235:False 236:True
This condition of extreme self-neglect usually affects people who live alone. The incidence is 0.5 per 1000 population so most GPs will have one patient on their list. Fifty per cent have a normal mental state but the rest have significant psychopathology. Physical illness is very common and often severe leading to a mortality of 50%. Admission to hospital worsens the condition with apathy developing. Patients tend to be of above average intelligence.

237:True 238:False 239:False 240:False 241:True

This is a common condition usually occurring in young children under 3 years of age. The mechanism of injury is typically that of a traction injury to the child's arm when it is held in an extended position, such as being pulled onto the feet by the hands or being 'bounced' with the arms above the head. It is more common on the left side. The annular ligament probably slips or has a small tear which allows subluxation of the radial head. X-ray shows no abnormality. Reduction is simply done by forced supination, anaesthesia not being necessary.

242:False 243:True 244:False 245:True 246:True

Crohn's disease is characterised by pain and diarrhoea but rarely blood. Rectal involvement is rare in Crohn's disease unlike ulcerative colitis where 95% will have rectal involvement. Annular strictures are common in Crohn's but in ulcerative colitis they are an indication that malignant change may have occurred.

247:True 248:False 249:False 250:True 251:False

If retinoblastoma is a cause of squint, instead of a red reflex there is the typical white reflex. The majority of squints in children are non-paralytic. If treatment is left until 8 years the eye will be amblyopic and surgery will only be cosmetic. If patching of the good eye is excessive, cases have been reported of it becoming amblyopic. To maximise sight, referral should be made before 6 months of age.

252:False 253:True 254:True 255:True 256:False

Cervical erosion is twice as common in pill users than in a matched population who have not taken the pill. Benign breast diseases are suppressed in long term users of combined oral contraceptives. Endometrial cancer and ovarian cancer rates appear to be reduced by about 50% in those who have had two years or more of continual ovulation suppression with oral contraceptives. Cervical cancer rates are not reduced, some data would suggest an increased incidence but because cervical cancer is so related to sexual activity, it is difficult to work out a relationship.

257:True 258:True 259:False 260:False 261:False

Addison's disease may present insidiously with episodic vomiting and diarrhoea accompanied by weight loss. Abdominal pain is often severe and colicky. Eventually symptoms may lead to an Addisonian crisis with a shocked, hypotensive patient. Chronic insufficiency is marked by postural hypotension. The typical blood picture is hyponatraemia, hyperkalaemia and a raised blood urea.

262:False 263:False 264:False 265:True 266:False
Dementia is not preventable by social support but depression is reduced. A well-balanced diet helps general health and may reduce cardiovascular disease but does not reduce dementia. Eating beef has not as yet been shown to cause a transmittable form of dementia. Treatment of hypertension over the years decreases atherosclerosis and therefore the incidence of multi-infarct dementia. Over 75 screening by GPs has not yet been shown to decrease dementia or related problems.

267:True 268:True 269:False 270:False 271:False
Restless legs syndrome has been described for over 100 years. It has been associated with many factors most of them disproved, however, it may be the presenting complaint in uraemia. It typically is worse in the evening and at night causing insomnia. Benzodiazepines are said to help. There is no association with coffee or tea ingestion.

272:True 273:True 274:False 275:False 276:True 277:True
At 6 weeks most children are smiling and it is a worrying sign if they are not. At 9 months most children stand with support, and walk with support at 12 months. Also at 12 months they can use about 2–3 words with meaning. By age 3, children are usually dry by day and can go both up and down stairs.

278:False 279:False 280:False 281:False 282:False
Audit is now a contractual obligation on behalf of General Practitioners. There are lots of ways and viewpoints as to how it should be practised. Audit is a process of education through experience, not looking for mistakes. It must be free from blame or guilt if it is to be successful. It should be dynamic with the aim of helping people to do their jobs better. It can illuminate problem areas but it is not solely concerned with problem solving. The boundaries between audit and research are often blurred.

283:True 284:True 285:True 286:True 287:True
All are available from pharmacists without an NHS prescription and all cost less than the current price of such a prescription.

288:False 289:True 290:True 291:True 292:False
Pyelonephritis is the most common medical emergency in pregnancy occurring in 1% of pregnancies. It typically presents in the second and third trimesters and in about one quarter of cases reoccurs throughout the rest of the pregnancy. There is an increased association with pre-term labour, fetal growth retardation and perinatal death. 4-quinolone antibiotics are

contraindicated in pregnancy because experimental work has shown an association with arthropathy in the fetus.

293:True 294:True 295:True 296:True 297:True
Ankylosing spondylitis is usually of gradual onset with low backache and morning stillness. Fifteen per cent present with a peripheral arthritis. Iritis occurs in 25% of cases, the ESR is raised in 80%.Six per cent have it as a familial trait and it is associated with specific histocompatibility antigens.

298:False 299:True 300:True 301:False 302:True
Dermatitis artefacta is the term given to self-induced lesions which characteristically have straight sides. Polymorphic eruption of pregnancy occurs in 1:150 pregnancies usually primigravidae occurring in the second and third trimesters and clearing within 2–3 weeks of delivery. Nodular prurigo often occur on the hands and heal to leave white scars with follicular openings in them. Dermatitis herpetiformis typically occurs in young adults, it has an intensely itchy vesicular rash with a psoriatic distribution. Lichen simplex needs to be treated by interrupting the itch/scratch cycle, then the lichenified rash disappears.

303:True 304:True 305:True 306:False 307:True
Severe puerperal psychosis presents in the early puerperium. It may present as psychotic depression or hypomania. Those with hypomania often become depressed at the end of a spell of being 'high'. Some show a fluctuating pattern. ECT has been shown to be of benefit and often produces a rapid remission. With treatment it tends to run a course of about 2–3 months of illness, the risk of infanticide during this time is increased.

308:True 309:True 310:False 311:True 312:False
Campylobacter often starts as a febrile illness after an incubation period of 3–5 days. If bleeding is present in a *Shigella* infection this is an indication that antibiotic treatment may be necessary. In *Giardia*, pain is not a feature but watery diarrhoea is. *Salmonella* without blood stream invasion is often a relatively mild diarrhoeal episode only lasting a few days.

313:False 314:False 315:False 316:False 317:True
Streptokinase is given via an infusion and is therefore unsuitable for community use. Anistreplase is given by i.v. bolus. Aspirin given as a concomitant has been shown to decrease mortality further. Age alone is no reason for limitation of use of these drugs. Streptokinase cannot be repeated within the next 12 months. Anything that may bleed such as a recent surgical procedure or a recently diagnosed ulcer is a contraindication to the use of these drugs.

318:True 319:True 320:True 321:False 322:True
At 7 months 90% can stand with support and 70% can sit without support. 75% can say three words at 12 months. At 30 months the majority will be dry in the day but not at night. At 54 months 75% of girls and 60% of boys can dress themselves.

323:True 324:False 325:True 326:True 327:True
Hypertrophic obstructive cardiomyopathy is important because it is the most common cause of sudden death in apparently healthy young adults especially athletes. It was found in half of athletes who died during participation in a sporting activity. It is an inherited condition and it occurs at any age from neonate to old age. All family members should be investigated preferably by echocardiography. The commonest presentation is with shortness of breath often accompanied by syncope and angina. The electrocardiograph typically shows changes of left ventricular hypertrophy.

328:True 329:True 330:False 331:False 332:True 333:True 334:False
Poor predictive factors include early and insidious onset, low socio-economic status, a schizoid personality trait, history of perinatal trauma, a family history of schizophrenia, and being in a developed country.

335:True 336:False 337:False 338:True 339:False
Neck pain is very common, women are more prone than men in a ratio of 2:1. It is usually a benign transitory condition with 85% of patients symptom free within 1–4 weeks. About 18–20% relapse within 2 years. Soft collars are of no proven benefit and they are not prescribable on an FP10. NSAIDs have a role in reducing the severity of symptoms and in selected patients manipulation is of definite benefit.

340:False 341:True 342:False 343:False 344:True 345:False
Herpes simplex infection usually heals within 6–10 days with topical acyclovir. Recurrence rate is less than 5% if treatment is commenced promptly. Visual acuity is not affected with peripheral lesions, but is more likely if the central cornea is affected. Referral is indicated because of the potential threat to vision.

346:False 347:True 348:False 349:False 350:True
In women *Chlamydia* is usually asymptomatic and causes a cervicitis rather than a vaginitis. A negative MSU with dysuria in a sexually active woman should lead to a search for the organism. If present in pregnancy there is a 50% transmission rate to the neonate with the risk of conjunctivitis, and pneumonitis, treatment should begin before delivery. In men the

common presentation is with non-specific urethritis or epididymitis, it is not associated with prostatitis.

351:True 352:False 353:True 354:True 355:True
There are about one million new cases of back pain per year and the average General Practitioner sees about 50 acute backs per year. Many people do not consult, however 10–15 million working days are lost per year because of back pain. Eighty per cent recover in 3–4 weeks, however in 50% of patients there is a recurrence within the next 5 years. About one- third of patients are referred for specialist opinion but only 1:200 of the original sufferers and 1:60 of those referred undergo surgery. Several studies have shown that rest, in the early stages, reduces the overall time away from work.

356:True 357:True 358:True 359:False 360:True
Irritable bowel syndrome has been treated by increasing dietary fibre, however some patients find that excess bran makes the symptoms worse. In one study, 70% of patients improved on a bland diet free of wheat and milk. Increased fermentation in the gut is directly implicated as a trigger for the condition. Metronidazole substantially alters the aerobic/anaerobic balance within the bowel and can increase the fermentation rate. Nystatin has been shown to decrease fermentation and improve symptoms. Stress is a well-known trigger factor and hypnosis and relaxation techniques decrease the symptoms and the relapse rate of IBS.

361:True 362:False 363:False 364:True 365:True
Cramps, especially occurring during the night, are common. However there are a large number of causes which should be excluded. Drug therapy, especially diuretics and sympathomimetics, even if the latter are inhaled, are frequent causes. Peripheral vascular disease and venous obstruction do not cause cramps, but cramps may coexist. About 80% of those with cirrhosis have nocturnal cramps. Lumbar spine dysfunction especially nerve involvement at the L5/S1 level is a potent cause of nocturnal cramps.

366:True 367:False 368:True 369:False 370:False
At present less than 50% of mothers breast feed their babies successfully. Whether this government target can be met is a matter of considerable doubt. Mastitis is typically caused by *Staphylococcus*. Breast feeding does take considerably longer than bottle feeding and this point should be emphasised to reassure mothers. Obesity is rare in breast fed infants but more common in bottle fed infants. Introduction of cows' milk should not take place until one year of age. The solute load is too great for children until this age. Full cream milk and not semi-skimmed should be used.

371:False 372:False 373:False 374:False 375:True
Spacer devices decrease the incidence of oral candidiasis by preventing the deposition in the mouth. Salmeterol is a long-acting beta-antagonist, its action is slow in onset and therefore it should be given regularly rather than p.r.n. The Committee on Safety of Medicines has reported that salbuterol and terbutaline have not been shown to lead to a worsening of mild asthma. In adults an inhaled dosage of steroid of 1500 micrograms daily is associated with adrenal suppression. Sodium cromoglycate is of no value in an acute attack and is only indicated for prophylaxis.

376:False 377:False 378:False 379:True
Basic practice allowance is paid to principals whether they are full time or part time, for part time doctors it is rated proportionately. It is also down-rated for patient numbers less than 1200 for an individual doctor. However in partnerships the total list size is pooled.

380:True 381:True 382:True 383:True 384:True
Trials comparing active and physiological management of the third stage of labour have shown that it is reduced from an average of 15 minutes to 5 minutes and that the incidence of primary post-partum haemorrhage is decreased from 18% to 6%. However one study has shown that there is an increased rate of retained placenta and all studies have shown an increase in maternal vomiting and hypertension.

385:True 386:False 387:True 388:True 389:False 390:False
Hypercalcaemia can result from malignancy, thyrotoxicosis, thiazide diuretics, immobilisation, vitamin D excess and renal failure.

391:True 392:False 393:True 394:True 395:True
Clinical trials have shown the benefits of using antidepressants in many conditions.

396:True 397:True 398:True 399:False 400:False
Closure of the ductus arteriosus usually takes place within 48 hours of birth and is brought about by muscular contraction initially and then fibrosis. Delay is associated with maternal rubella and prematurity. Indomethacin therapy does close the duct but in some cases it reopens and surgery is necessary. If untreated, 20% of patients will have died by 30 years of age and 60% by 60 years of age. Bacterial endocarditis is especially common in patients with this condition.

PRACTICE PAPER 3 — SECTION 2: EMQs ANSWERS

Chest pain
1:D 2:E 3:A 4:F 5:G 6:B 7:H
Headaches
8:B 9:D 10:A 11:F 12:C 13:C
Stroke management
14:B 15:A 16:C 17:D 18:A 19:B
Childhood milestones
20:D 21:E 22:A 23:B 24:F 25:E
Breast cancer screening
26:D 27:A 28:B 29:E 30:C
Diabetes
31:D 32:B 33:A 34:B & C
Income
35:B 36:B 37:D 38:E 39:F 40:C 41:B
Thrombolytic trials
42:D 43:A 44:C 45:B
Mental Health Act
46:D 47:C 48:A 49:B 50:E
Benefits
51:C 52:E 53:A 54:B 55:C 56:D
Infectious diseases
57:E 58:D 59:B 60:C 61:A
Statistics
62:B 63:E 64:A 65:C 66:D
Screening
67:F 68:K 69:E 70:L 71:C
Scrotal swellings
72:C 73:A 74:B 75:D
Rheumatoid arthritis
76:C 77:B 78:A 79:C 80:A 81:B 82:E 83:D
Mouth ulcers
84:A 85:B 86:E 87:D 88:F 89:A
Diabetes
90:D 91:B 92:C 93:C 94:A 95:C
Bodies allied to general practice
96:A 97:D 98:C 99:E 100:B

PRACTICE PAPER 4 — SECTION 1: MCQs ANSWERS AND TEACHING NOTES

1:False 2:False 3:False 4:True 5:False 6:False
Cancer of the cervix accounts for less than 5% of all female cancer deaths. A large number of cervical smears are taken each year but there is an increasing death rate in young women from cervical cancer. High-risk groups include those with early age of first pregnancy and those in low socio-economic classes. HPV types 16 and 18 have been found in invasive cervical cancer, and HPV types 6 and 8 have been found in benign lesions. The time taken to progress from CIN I to invasive cancer is uncertain; many women with CIN I and II have treatment and many women with invasive cancer have never had a smear.

7:True 8:True 9:True 10:True 11:True
Prospective studies have shown an association with all the factors quoted. However the most important factor associated with increased mortality after a stoke is the level of consciousness.

12:True 13:True 14:True 15:True 16:True
Amenorrhoea or oligomenorrhoea accompanied by hirsutism is almost certainly due to Stein–Leventhal syndrome. Fertility is reduced and early miscarriage is common in those who do conceive. LH is raised and FSH is depressed but the significance of this is not fully understood. Ultrasound will detect polycystic ovaries.

17:True 18:False 19:False 20:False 21:True 22:False
Because of the availability of efficient pediculicides the overall incidence of head lice is falling. Resistance does emerge and because of this most health authorities operate a three-year rotational policy. Malathion confers a residual protective effect against reinfection which lasts up to 6 weeks. However frequent washing of the hair or swimming in chlorinated water destroys the effect. Lotions are the treatment of choice as they are more effective. Nit combing is not medically necessary but may be needed for cosmetic reasons.

23:True 24:True 25:True 26:True 27:True
Two separate studies on weight loss in the elderly have produced similar results. Weight loss of 5% in 6 months should not be ignored, 75–80% will have some pathology to account for the loss. Malignancy accounts for 20%, depression 10%, GI tract disease 15%. The reason is usually obvious at the initial examination or with simple tests. If not immediately apparent extensive tests are not helpful. Of those without an obvious

reason for the loss 80% will regain some or all of the lost weight within one year.

28:False 29:False 30:False 31:True 32:False

If the diagnosis of vitamin B12 deficiency is in doubt it is still possible to confirm the diagnosis by using the Schilling test even after replacement therapy has been established. Dietary deficiency is very uncommon except in very strict vegetarians. Vitamin B12 is now given every 3 months by injection and this appears to be adequate. However patients may become psychologically dependent and demand it more frequently. It is cheap and excess is excreted in the urine once stores are saturated. There are no clinical problems associated with more frequent injections.

33:False 34:False 35:True 36:True 37:False

Wood's light is a source of ultraviolet light from which visible light has been excluded. It does not fluoresce eczematous skin.

38:True 39:True 40:False 41:True 42:True

Depressive delusions often centre on poverty or physical illness. Initially depression may present with symptoms of dementia but these symptoms disappear with treatment of the depression. Bereavement is less likely to provoke a depressive illness than in younger age groups. Both agitation and retardation occur in significant numbers of elderly patients.

43:False 44:False 45:False 46:False 47:False

Usually cryotherapy cannot be tolerated until 7 years of age. Basal cell carcinomas are often suitable for cryotherapy but one must be sure of the histology. The usual pattern of response is a triple response followed by tissue swelling. Liquid nitrogen does not destroy virus effectively, therefore instruments should be disposable or be sterilized between treatments.

48:False 49:False 50:False 51:True 52:False

There are still patients who miss out on their free prescriptions and it is up to doctors to advise those so entitled.

53:True 54:False 55:True 56:True 57:True

Accidents are preventable, measures such as wearing seat belts decrease death and injury. One-third of all childhood deaths in the UK are due to accidents. Given that 10% of children attend their doctor each year with an accident the scope for opportunistic education is enormous. 40,000 children attend casualty departments annually with suspected poisoning, yet only 20 die, usually aged 1–5 years.

58:False 59:True 60:True 61:True
After blind registration, a reduced TV licence is payable, SDA is available along with parking concessions and free postage on certain items.

62:True 63:False 64:False 65:False 66:True
Cotton wool spots are retinal infarcts in the nerve fibre layer and are of serious prognostic significance. Once early changes of retinopathy develop they rarely respond to treatment. Retinal haemorrhages only interfere with vision if the macula is involved. Papilloedema due to hypertension is usually accompanied by other signs of hypertensive retinopathy and elevation of the optic disc. In the elderly hypertensive arterio-venous changes are the first discernible retinal change.

67:False 68:False 69:True 70:False 71:True
The majority of pacemakers are inserted for sick sinus syndrome. Activity is not restricted by the pacemaker, more by the underlying condition. Primary pacemaker failure is an uncommon cause of death. The average pacemaker lasts over 5 years with some lasting 20 years. If there is a myocardial infarct, ST and T wave changes may not be typical.

72:True 73:False 74:True 75:True 76:False
Grief reactions show an initial stage of non-reaction for a few hours or days, up to 2 weeks. Delay until 4 weeks is pathological. Hostility to somebody or something is normal, only if it is extreme does it become pathological. Some degree of social isolation may occur but if extreme and prolonged may indicate atypical grief. Most patients return to work within 2 weeks. Suicidal ideas are common, they are atypical when they are strong and well formulated.

77:False 78:False 79:False 80:True 81:True
Cystic fibrosis is the most common lethal genetic disorder in Caucasians. It varies in severity and milder cases are often detected later in life. If a child is affected there is a probability of 1:4 of subsequent children having the disorder. Survival now occurs into the third and fourth decade of life. Boys will be azoospermic but girls have reduced fertility and conception is possible. Fifty per cent of adolescents will develop a degree of glucose intolerance.

82:False 83:True 84:False 85:True 86:False
So-called 'brachial neuritis' is often caused by carpal tunnel syndrome especially if the pain is at night. If bilateral, carpal tunnel is usually worse

in the dominant hand. Local injections and immobilisation are often curative. It is also associated with acromegaly, amyloid, multiple myeloma, rheumatoid arthritis and pregnancy. Thenar wasting is a late feature and is rarely seen.

87:True 88:False 89:True 90:True 91:True

Ten per cent of myeloma are detected as an incidental finding whilst the patient is being investigated for something else. The classic features are of bone pain with osteolytic lesions on X-ray, and renal involvement with eosinophilic hyaline casts and slowly progressive renal failure. Bleeding may occur due to renal failure or thrombocytopenia. Peripheral neuropathy can occur especially if amyloid is associated.

92:True 93:False 94:False 95:False 96:False

Endometriosis is common and ectopic endometrium is very common. It is found in 10% of all gynaecological operations and has been reported as present in 60% of laparoscopies done for infertility. Cyclical pain, dyspareunia and a pelvic mass with lack of uterine mobility are typical signs and symptoms. Medical treatment produces improvement within 2 months both histologically and clinically. However it fails to produce an improvement if fertility has been affected.

97:True 98:False 99:True 100:False 101:True

Females are affected more than males and the first attack is on average at 30 years of age with a steep fall in incidence after 45 years of age. Eighty per cent of patients will remit after the first attack, with relapses occurring about twice per year. In the 20% that have the progressive form of the disease they usually present at over 40 years of age. In 25% it is relatively benign with no evidence of disability after 10 years. There are no specific tests available, MRI scanning is abnormal in many patients.

102:True 103:False 104:False 105:True 106:False

The Children's Act 1989 came into effect in October 1991. The main feature is making the wishes of the child paramount. Emergency protection orders replace Place of Safety orders, they last for 8 days and any person can apply to a court for the order. Parental access is not precluded. Police protection provisions provide for police protection for up to 72 hours if a child would otherwise suffer harm. Parental responsibility is not transferred to the police. Care orders place the child in the care of the local authority, whereas supervision orders place the child under the supervision of a local authority or probation officer. They cannot exist together.

107:False 108:False 109:False 110:False 111:False
Acute torticollis is a common condition occurring in the 15–30 age group. It starts acutely with a sudden pain and inability to move the head. Active and passive movements are restricted and the head is typically held in a position flexed away from the pain. It is not associated with significant arthritis and there are no neurological symptoms.

112:False 113:False 114:True 115:False
Seat belt legislation has resulted in an increased use of seat belts and a substantial reduction in deaths and serious injuries for drivers. People can be exempted when carrying out manoeuvres like reversing, and if they have a medical exemption certificate. Few conditions justify exemption and would not include pregnancy or recent surgery. If these patients cannot wear a seat belt they may need to consider if they are fit to drive at that time.

116:False 117:False 118:False 119:True
Metered-dose inhalers are the most effective way of giving inhaled steroids, nebulisers are very inefficient. Dry powder inhalers are slightly less inefficient than aerosol devices but are more user friendly and are also ozone friendly. Large volume spacer devices increase the intrapulmonary deposition and they are recommended for all patients on more than 1000 micrograms daily. A regular dose of 1500 micrograms in adults has been associated with adrenal suppression. Growth inhibition in children has been reported with doses of 200–800 micrograms daily.

120:True 121:False 122:True 123:True 124:True
Urinary tract infection is under-diagnosed in young children, approximately 3% of girls and 1% of boys will have an infection by 10 years of age. About 60% have no structural abnormality with 35% having vesico-ureteric reflux. Scarring occurs with missed or inadequately treated infection. A high index of suspicion is needed especially under 2 years of age. It may present with non-specific symptoms such as convulsions, dehydration, diarrhoea, vomiting, failure to thrive, pyrexia of unknown origin or abdominal pain.

125:True 126:False 127:False 128:True 129:True
Infective endocarditis occurs on valves that are deformed such as a bicuspid aortic valve or a prolapsed mitral valve. Only 25% of patients have an obvious source of the infection. Even if treated the mortality is of the order of 20%. Plasma viscosity is replacing ESR in most laboratories.

130:True 131:True 132:False 133:True 134:False
Penicillamine stains nails yellow and chloroquine blue-grey. White nail streaks are due to minor trauma and occur in most people. Familial leuconychia stains the whole of the nail white and is inherited as an autosomal dominant trait. Tinea causes white or yellow areas and thickening of the nail. It also slows the rate of growth. Yellow nail syndrome is due to disturbance of lymphatics, the nail becomes curved longitudinally and transversely and the rate of growth slows. It is associated with lymphoedema.

135:True 136:False 137:True 138:False 139:False
Research protocols need to be carefully written and need to adhere to a strict format. If there are excessive financial inducements to a researcher an ethical committee may withhold consent. When involving patients it is very important that a very detailed explanation is given. Retrospective studies do not usually require consent from the patient. The advantage of structured interviews is that they are standardised and they do not need specialised interviewers to conduct them.

140:False 141:False 142:True 143:False 144:False
Meningococcal vaccine is not available against group B strains. The prevalence is increasing because of recent changes in the cycle of the various strains. Despite the fact that there is decreasing sensitivity to penicillin emerging, benzylpenicillin is still the treatment of choice if the disease is suspected. Rifampicin is the treatment of choice for contacts, resistance to chloramphenicol has emerged. The increased risks for household contacts is over 1000-fold.

145:False 146:True 147:True 148:True 149:True
The majority of people with bulimia are of normal weight. Fluoxetine in particular seems to have a short term beneficial effect but not as much as psychological interventions. If they become pregnant there is an increased risk of cleft lip and palate. One-third of the patients have a history of anorexia nervosa and some have the two diseases together; if this is so the overall prognosis is worse than for bulimia alone. Diuretic abuse, purgative abuse and excessive exercise are all associated.

150:True 151:True 152:True 153:False 154:False
For years iron supplements have been given routinely in pregnancy. Selecting those that need them is a problem. Estimating the patient's haemoglobin is not an accurate reflection of the iron stores. Serum ferritin

is an expensive investigation to employ routinely in all pregnant women but it does reflect accurately the iron stores available. Demands for iron are greatest in the third trimester and maternal iron stores will be at their lowest at this stage of the pregnancy. The fetal iron stores are laid during this trimester.

155:True 156:True 157:True 158:True 159:True

Opiate analgesics cause delay in the absorption of paracetamol due to the delay in gastric emptying. Chlorpromazine and other phenothiazines increase the toxic metabolites of opiates especially pethidine, hence there is a significant increase in symptoms such as drowsiness, lightheadedness and dry mouth. Cimetidine reduces the loss of opiates from the body as it inhibits the hepatic enzymes responsible for metabolism of the opiates. Ranitidine does not appear to have the same effects. Methadone levels have been shown to be reduced by up to 60% if given with phenytoin. Lactulose does not interact and a laxative is usually necessary with opiates.

160:True 161:False 162:True 163:False 164:False

Contraceptive fees are only payable for services to female patients. A GP cannot claim for contraceptive advice or procedures on males. A procedure or appliance does not have to be performed, the fee can be claimed for advice only. Practice nurses can perform contraceptive services on behalf of a doctor.

165:False 166:True 167:False 168:True 169:True 170:False

Second-born children appear at greatest risk of SIDS. Most cases occur at less than 6 months with 70% occurring between October and March. The incidence has been reduced by the 'Back to Bed' campaign. There does not appear to be a relationship with type of delivery.

171:True 172:True 173:True 174:False 175:False

The average list size in England fell below 2000 in October 1988. In Scotland and Wales it is considerably lower than this level. Eleven per cent of GPs are single-handed, 15% are in a partnership of two, 19% in a partnership of three, the remaining 55% are in practices with four or more doctors. Only 30% practice from health centres. Workload surveys suggest that the average GP sees 138 patients per week in the surgery.

176:True 177:False 178:False 179:False 180:False

Gilbert's syndrome is a benign familial unconjugated hyperbilirubinaemia which is suffered by 2–5% of the population. The histology of the liver is typically normal. The incidence of gallstones is no greater and the jaundice is typically worsened by fasting.

181:False 182:True 183:True 184:True 185:False
Classic symptoms of moderately severe depression are early morning waking, a diurnal mood variation feeling worse in the morning and decreased libido. Delusions of poverty occur in psychotic depression. An abnormal dexamethasone suppression test occurs in some 30% of people with moderate to severe depression.

186:True 187:False 188:False 189:True 190:True
The changes at puberty are complex but show a similar pattern. The first sign in boys is testicular growth and in girls it is breast development. The major part of weight gain is due to muscle and bone increase not fat. Girls are ahead in all aspects of development. The final height is reached 4 years after the maximum growth spurt in both sexes.

191:False 192:False 193:True 194:False 195:False
Erythema chronicum migrans is a single lesion caused by the tick borne spirochaete. It has an area of expanding erythema. Erysipelas usually presents with a high fever and an unwell patient, there are large blisters with exudate. It is due to group A beta haemolytic streptococcal infection. Erythema nodosum is the most likely diagnosis, crops of lesions on the shins occur with individual ones lasting 7–10 days in crops over 3–6 weeks. Often it is associated with sarcoid, drugs or streptococcal infection. Acanthosis nigricans is increased pigmentation on the body associated with an internal malignancy such as the bowel or stomach. Kaposi's sarcoma are purple/red macules or papules usually on the trunk or back which grow quickly and become nodular or form plaques. It is classically associated with AIDS.

196:True 197:False 198:False 199:True 200:True
Immersion in water leads to hydrostatic pressure supporting the circulation in the lower body. Sudden removal from the water leads to a pooling of blood in the lower legs and a decreased venous return with the consequence of hypovolaemic shock. At 34°–35° C confusion and disorientation occur. Cardiac arrhythmias start at 33° C. The patient is usually semiconscious at 30°–33° C and loses consciousness below this temperature. Rewarming should never be rapid and the last statement is a practical 'rule of thumb'.

201:False 202:True 203:False 204:False 205:False
The density of a cataract does not affect the results of surgery. Retinal detachment incidence is increased but less so after extracapsular lens extraction. Thickening of the posterior capsule is a complication of extracapsular extraction, it can be dealt with by laser capsulectomy as an outpatient procedure. Modern surgical techniques mean that the patient is out of bed on the day of surgery. Intraocular implants are suitable for people with any type of visual defect.

206:False 207:True 208:True 209:False 210:False
Cough occurs in 1:8 patients on ACE inhibitors and only resolves if the drug is withdrawn, usually within one week. ACE inhibitors are both teratogenic and fetotoxic, they are also toxic to neonates. They inhibit the production of aldosterone and therefore cause hyponatraemia in the absence of diuretics. Skin rashes are common and occur in about 4% of patients.

211:True 212:False 213:True 214:True 215:False
Chondromalacia produces pain especially if the patella is pressed distally and the quadriceps muscle is tightened. The pain is worse on descending stairs and also after sitting. Although the X-ray is usually reported as normal it may show some thinning of the cartilage. Hyperextension of the knee joint above 10° suggests hypermobility syndrome.

216:True 217:False 218:False 219:True 220:True 221:True
Practice annual reports must contain the numbers not the names of those patients who refer themselves to casualty departments. Again the numbers not names of staff are required. The training undertaken by the staff needs to be recorded. All changes to the practice staff and buildings that have occurred during the last year and are planned for the next year need to be recorded. The numbers of people sent to all specialties needs to be included.

222:False 223:True 224:True 225:False 226:True
Even in women who have had three recurrent miscarriages, 60% will have a baby without any intervention. Bacterial vaginosis is associated with mid trimester miscarriage and warrants treatment. In first miscarriages 70–80% are due to chromosomal abnormalities.

227:False 228:False 229:False 230:True 231:True
Delusions, although they occur in schizophrenia also occur in a wide variety of other psychiatric disorders. They cannot be altered by reason or

demonstration of their falsity. An obsession is recognised by the person as being illogical and often causes them distress. Delusions are often defined as morbid false beliefs and they are often secondary to hallucinations.

232:True 233:False 234:True 235:True 236:True

Hypothyroidism is missed at some time by most doctors! Symptoms are diverse and the doctor needs to be on his guard.

237:True 238:True 239:False 240:False

Opiate addicts have now become a problem for many GPs. Very few practitioners are licensed by the Home Office. For them methadone or some other opiates are suitable for maintenance treatment or withdrawal regimes. Methadone takes about 36 hours after the last dose before the symptoms of restlessness, insomnia and diarrhoea occur. A withdrawal regime can practically and humanely get an addict free of the drug within 2–4 weeks. Convulsions are more associated with sedative addiction withdrawal.

241:False 242:False 243:False 244:False 245:False

Requests for home births seem to be increasing. A GP is under no obligation to respond positively to these requests. A doctor need not be present at the delivery but a midwife must be. Abnormal deliveries are more common in higher social classes and those who have had fetal monitoring. Only 6% of babies require any form of intervention after birth.

246:True 247:True 248:True 249:True 250:True

Any cause of upper airways obstruction can cause snoring, e.g. retrognathic jaw, polyps, deviated septum. Hypothyroidism does because of tissue swelling. One of the most common presentations of obstructive sleep apnoea syndrome is excessive daytime sleepiness leading to falling asleep at meetings and whilst driving. Less common than the above symptoms are morning headaches and memory problems. If severe, frequent oxygen desaturation leads to cardiovascular stress during the obstructive episodes this may be associated with systemic hypertension, cor pulmonale and cardiac arrhythmias.

251:False 252:True 253:True 254:False 255:True

Changing doctors was made much easier under the new contract. Once a patient has signed the registration form he is your responsibility. You have to offer a health check in writing and record the fact in the notes. Normally a health check fee is paid for examinations done within 3 months of registration but the time limit can be extended if a satisfactory explanation is appended to the form. New patient examinations are an ideal time to catch up with immunisations and these attract an additional item of service payment unless they are routine childhood immunisations.

256:True 257:True 258:False 259:True 260:False

The drug is poorly absorbed if given concurrently with both magnesium and aluminium antacids. It has a broad spectrum of activity and is effective against *Pseudomonas*. However it is less effective than doxycycline in chlamydial infections. If given to bronchitics it can cause potential serious theophylline toxicity because of microsomal enzyme inhibition.

261:False 262:True 263:True 264:False 265:True

In the last few years this has become the operation of choice for gall bladder disease in many centres. Ninety per cent of cases are suitable for laparoscopic surgery. In America, morbidity is low, day case surgery is common, and patients are up and about on the day of surgery. Operations take longer than conventional surgery. A nasogastric tube has to be passed to decompress the stomach to allow visualisation of the gall bladder.

266:False 267:True 268:True 269:False 270:True

The first feature to develop in pre-eclampsia is raised blood pressure, late features are proteinuria and a reversed circadian pattern of blood pressure, with it being elevated at night and lower in the day. Oedema is very common in pregnancy but in pre-eclampsia it is severe and generalised in the majority of women. There is no evidence that control of blood pressure arrests the progress of the disease.

271:False 272:False 273:True 274:False 275:False

Seborrhoeic eczema has a peak onset at 4–12 months, it usually involves the body, face, scalp and hands with erythema and scaliness but it is not itchy. It does resolve spontaneously in the vast majority of children. Emollients are the mainstay of treatment especially as soap substitutes. Atopic eczema involves the flexures, seborrhoeic does not.

276:False 277:False 278:False 279:False 280:False

Rubella has an incubation period of 14–21 days. It is an infectious disease but not transmitted by touching. Symptoms before the onset of the rash are often mild and fleeting, and the rash itself may be transient; the rash is erythematous. Clinical diagnosis is unreliable and the rash is certainly not diagnostic.

281:False 282:True 283:True 284:False 285:True
Swelling of the cheek is virtually never caused by maxillary sinusitis, it would indicate an infection in the root of a tooth. Once the exit to the maxillary sinus is blocked the pain can become severe and can be felt in the teeth. In acute sinusitis the discharge becomes yellow or green and may be bloodstained.

286:False 287:True 288:False 289:False 290:False
Health visitors usually have post basic training in midwifery and community nursing experience. Their statutory obligation is to continue visiting the baby once the midwife has stopped her visits, usually around the 10th day post-delivery. They are attached staff employed by the health authority but fund holding practices have been able to purchase their services directly since April 1993. Care of the elderly and over 75 visiting would seem to be a role suited to the skills and training of health visitors.

291:True 292:True 293:False 294:False 295:True
Chalazia are associated with blepharitis and acne rosacea. Blepharitis is more common in people with eczema and psoriasis. Correction of an entropion is usually a minor procedure done under local anaesthetic. Alkali is especially dangerous to the eye.

296:True 297:True 298:True 299:False 300:True
Drugs often produce changes in biochemical tests without producing any adverse effects on the patient. However, when an abnormal result is encountered it is important to know whether the patient's medication could be held responsible before subjecting the patient to further investigations.

301:False 302:False 303:True 304:False 305:False
In the elderly it is ill health or death of a partner that stops people from having intercourse. Atrophic vaginitis itself is itchy and causes pain and soreness, secondary *Candida* infection is common, but remember to exclude diabetes. The soreness induced by local oestrogens soon wears off with continued use.

306:True 307:True 308:True 309:False 310:False
Folic acid is found in liver, nuts and green vegetables. The daily requirement is 100–200 micrograms and it is absorbed in the duodenum and jejunum. Body stores last up to 4 months. The macrocytosis induced by alcoholism is not folic acid dependent and in fact beer contains some folate.

311:True 312:True 313:True 314:True 315:False
Psychological problems have been shown to constitute one-third of all consultations. Several surveys have shown that many of these problems are missed. Many factors within the patient and within the doctor either decrease or increase the number that are missed.

316:True 317:False 318:False 319:False 320:True
Absorption of drugs from the gut is influenced by many factors. If a drug is fat soluble the absorption will generally be enhanced in the presence of a fatty meal. Water soluble drugs such as digoxin and penicillin are best given with a drink of water one hour before a meal. The other three drugs in this question, are all gastric irritants and should be given with food.

321:True 322:True 323:True 324:False 325:True
All treatments for prostatic carcinoma whether surgical or medical seem to have the same prognosis. Current evidence suggests that microscopic asymptomatic disease is unlikely to spread within the patient's lifetime and can be ignored. Stilboestrol alters blood coagulation and therefore increases cardiovascular mortality. Androgen receptor blockers are often given during the initial stages of treatment with gonadotrophin releasing analogues in order to prevent the exacerbation of bony pain associated with treatment at the onset of therapy with the latter.

326:True 327:True 328:False 329:True 330:True
With early discharge from hospital GPs are having to contend with more of the problems of jaundice in babies. So called 'physiological' jaundice starts at the second day and peaks at the fourth day to disappear by the 10th day. 30–60% of all children will have discernible jaundice at some stage. Jaundice that persists or is intense should be investigated in a paediatric unit if possible. Infection and hypothyroidism are two of the most quoted causes for persisting jaundice.

331:False 332:False 333:True 334:False 335:True
Vitamin K deficiency is responsible for haemorrhagic disease of the newborn which is sometimes called vitamin K deficiency bleeding. Formula milks are supplemented with vitamin K. The risk of disease is increased if the mother takes anticonvulsants, anticoagulants, or is on medication for TB. If vitamin K is given orally, at least two doses are needed and three are suggested for breast-fed babies. Babies at particular risk are those born prematurely and those with delayed feeding.

336:True 337:False 338:True 339:False 340:True
Although the mean IQ is 80, it is often average or above. Specific learning difficulties are more common, but speech, language, hearing and visual difficulties are rarely a problem. If a diplegia is present, the early development of spasticity is associated with a better outcome.

341:False 342:False 343:False 344:True 345:True
Reactive or stress polycythaemia is a condition in which the red cell mass is normal but the PCV is raised, however, rarely above 0.55. There are strong associations with male sex, smoking, alcoholism and obesity. Alcohol decreases plasma volume by inhibiting the release of anti-diuretic hormone. Obesity leads to hypoventilation and oxygen desaturation.

346:True 347:True 348:True 349:False 350:False
Seventy-five per cent of couples will conceive within 12 months and a further 5% within the following year. The most common reason for failure is tubal abnormality (20–30%) with disordered spermatogenesis next (15–20%) and then ovulation problems (10–15%). Reconstructive surgery is associated with at least a 25% chance of a full term pregnancy but an increased risk of ectopic pregnancy. Clomiphene induces ovulation in 70% of women previously anovulatory, however only half of these conceive. *In vitro* techniques do not lead to an increase in the risk of abnormal babies.

351:True 352:False 353:True 354:False
Hyperventilation is typically associated with no history of relevant illness and absence of specific clinical findings. The peak expiratory flow rate is typically normal and there is no cyanosis. The overbreathing leads to a decrease in blood levels of carbon dioxide, producing alkalosis, this in turn leads to spontaneous discharge of peripheral nerves giving rise to paraesthesia, cramps and tetany.

355:False 356:True 357:True 358:False 359:False
The cost rent scheme is an extremely complex piece of legislation in which a practice may build new premises or substantially alter existing property. The interest on any loan is paid by the FHSA and the capital is paid by the partnership. The amount involved is generally independent of the district valuer's assessment of the worth of the premises at the end of the project.

360:True 361:True 362:True
The classic studies of Murray Parkes showed that bereavement has a definite and high mortality for the remaining partner. Over 55 years of age the death rate for men is 40% in the first year following death of a spouse. Overall the death rate is 20%. Even by the third year the death rate is still greater than for the normal population.

363:True 364:True 365:False 366:True 367:True
Unfavourable factors in depressive illness include an obsessional personality, previous significant depressive illness, loss of any parent but especially mother prior to the age of 12 years, bereavement in later life, no sympathetic close relationship, poor social circumstances, being housebound or tied to the house by an ill relative. Conversely, favourable factors include, a secure childhood, support from a friend or relative and an active social life with outside activities.

368:False 369:False 370:False 371:True 372:False
Progestogen-only pills cause little or no change in clotting mechanisms and do not affect lipid levels. They need not be stopped prior to surgery. They are not secreted in breast milk. If started on the first day of the cycle they provide immediate protection. If started after a combined oral contraceptive has been given they should be commenced immediately after the last combined pill has been taken and not at the end of the 7 pill free days.

373:True 374:False 375:False 376:False
Under the Children's Act the wishes of the child are paramount and the doctor must treat the child if he feels that the child is mature enough to make a decision about himself.

377:False 378:True 379:False 380:True
To claim PGEA 25 days of approved postgraduate education spread over the previous 5 years entitles a GP principal to make a claim for the full allowance. Unpaid clinical attachments under consultant supervision and distance learning courses can count. A recently trained GP principal must continue to attend 5 days of approved education per year after the first claim.

381:True 382:False 383:False 384:False 385:False
Forty per cent of throat swabs yield no growth, 30% are streptococcal, 20% viral and 10% other organisms including *Haemophilus*. The decrease in incidence of rheumatic fever and glomerulonephritis

predates the introduction of antibiotics and is ascribed to the raised standards of cleanliness and housing conditions. Tonsillar exudate in an under 15-year-old is more typical of *Streptococcus,* in an over 15-year-old of glandular fever. However the appearances and the presence of lymphadenopathy are not characteristic of any specific type of infection.

386:False 387:True 388:False 389:True 390:False

A highly sensitive test will have a low false-negative rate. The prevalence of a disease indicates the total number with that disease; the incidence is the number occurring in a period of time. The predictive value of a test depends on the prevalence when true positives will be higher if the prevalence is higher. The negative predictive value is the proportion of people who screen negative who do not have the disease.

391:False 392:True 393:True 394:False 395:False

The incidence of solar keratoses is increasing especially in fair skinned, fair haired people. About 10–25% of keratoses will develop into squamous cell carcinomas but it is usually a local tumour and they rarely metastasise. Basal cell carcinomas do metastasise but rarely (1:1000) and usually only to local lymph glands. Chronic sun exposure leads to loss of skin elasticity, an increase in telangiectasia and prominent sebaceous glands. Sunburn typically takes 4–8 hours to develop after exposure.

396:True 397:True 398:True 399:True 400:False

A study in the USA in 1980 showed that owning pets was associated with increased survival following myocardial infarction. An Australian study showed significant differences in blood pressure and lipid levels between pet owners and those without animals. A further study from Cambridge showed a 50% decrease in minor health problems within one month of cat or dog ownership. This reduction was maintained at 10 month follow-up.

PRACTICE PAPER 4 — SECTION 2: EMQs ANSWERS

Child development
1:E 2:F 3:G 4:F 5:C 6:C 7:B

Polyarthritis
8:A 9:D 10:B 11:G 12:C 13:E 14:F

Mental Health Act
15:F 16:E 17:C 18:D 19:B

Numbness and paraesthesia
20:G 21:E 22:B 23:A 24:F

Benefits
25:B 26:F 27:A 28:E 29:D

Acts
30:A 31:C 32:B 33:D

Hypertension trials
34:C 35:A 36:D 37:B 38:C

Immunisations
39:A 40:B 41:D 42:C 43:D

Statistics
44:D 45:C 46:E 47:H

Studies
48:C 49:B 50:A 51:D

Screening
52:H 53:K 54:E 55:I 56:B 57:C

Eye problems
58:C 59:D 60:A 61:B 62:A

Abdominal pain
63:B 64:E 65:C 66:A 67:D 68:F

Leg ulcers
69:A 70:B 71:A 72:A 73:B

Thyroid disease
74:A 75:B 76:C 77:B

Heart problems
78:F 79:D 80:A 81:E

Literature
82:A 83:E 84:C 85:B 86:H 87:A 88:C

Cancers
89:C 90:B 91:E 92:F 93:A 94:D

Social class
95:B 96:A 97:A 98:F 99:C 100:B

PRACTICE PAPER 5 — SECTION 1: MCQs ANSWERS AND TEACHING NOTES

1:False 2:False 3:True 4:True 5:True

An HGV driver should not drive for at least 3 months after a myocardial infarct and then, only if certain criteria are met, may he resume. The criteria for driving after fits are strict; an HGV driver needs to be fit-free for 10 years and off medication. He may then apply to hold an HGV licence. HGV driving has to be discontinued if the driver has insulin-dependent diabetes and an unrepaired aortic aneurysm. Any driver should avoid driving from the onset of a migraine attack.

6:False 7:False 8:False 9:True 10:False

Allergic conjunctivitis produces a discharge that is typically clear, mucopurulent discharge would indicate infection, visual acuity should not be affected and photophobia only occurs in very severe cases with involvement of the cornea. Epiphora and itching are the main symptoms. If the patient can tolerate contact lenses they are allowed.

11:True 12:False 13:False 14:True 15:False

Alcohol problems in women have increased over the last 20 years. Both cerebral and hepatic damage seems to be more prevalent in women. However, the incidence of cirrhosis has not yet reached the same level as for men. Women are far more likely to have an associated depressive illness than men. Alcohol intoxication is achieved with lower intake of alcohol during the premenstrual phase of the cycle. Women tend to start drinking at a later age than men and consequently become problem drinkers at a later age also.

16:True 17:False 18:False 19:True 20:False

Controlled drug prescriptions must be handwritten by the prescriber. The address of the doctor is pre-printed on all prescriptions. The drug is marked C.D. in the BNF to denote that it is a controlled drug. The prescription does not need to be marked with this.

21:True 22:True 23:False 24:True 25:True

Blood glucose levels have been shown to rise with age and 10% of the elderly are diabetic or have impaired glucose tolerance. Most people with glycosuria have diabetes but not all diabetics have glycosuria. Glucose tolerance testing is rarely needed and a raised fasting glucose is usually diagnostic. Fluorescein angiography shows the presence of early retinal changes in the majority of diabetics.

26:True 27:True 28:True 29:False 30:True
Pain due to cervical arthritic change is typically worse at night. Carcinoma of the pyriform fossa causes pain in the ear via referred pain along the Xth cranial nerve. The upper molar teeth, temperomandibular joint or the parotid gland can all cause referred pain. Trigeminal neuralgia does not cause otalgia, but glossopharyngeal neuralgia can produce a severe lancinating pain in the ear or throat. Tonsillitis causes pain from the oropharynx via the IXth cranial nerve.

31:True 32:True 33:False 34:True 35:True
Chronic schizophrenia is characterised by the negative aspects of the illness with social withdrawal being pre-eminent. Depressive features are often marked with delusions, hallucinations and disordered thinking, less prominent than in the acute stages of the illness. Complaints of physical symptoms are often the first evidence of schizophrenia.

36:True 37:False 38:True 39:True 40:False
There are many different models of the consultation, one of the most practical and easy to remember is the one quoted in this question which is a more doctor-centred approach. Four areas of the consultation are considered, the presenting problem, other problems, modifying health seeking behaviour and finally prevention. The candidate is also advised to compare this with other models such as the one proposed by Pendleton et al.

41:True 42:True 43:True 44:True 45:True
The differential diagnosis of chest pain is fraught with problems. The symptoms given here are considered to point more to the functional nature of the chest pain.

46:True 47:True 48:False 49:False 50:False
Dermatofibromata are hard raised lesions which typically occur on the legs of young women, 20% of the female population develop one or more. They are usually brown and grow slowly over many years, the edges are smooth and they do not ulcerate. An irregular edge would indicate a malignant growth and if ulcerated this would be more in keeping with a pigmented rodent ulcer.

51:True 52:False 53:False 54:False 55:False
Immunisation with both types of hepatitis B vaccine is specific for that virus. The preferred site of injection is the deltoid by deep i.m. route,

injection into the buttocks may lead to depositing the vaccine in fatty tissue and consequently low absorption. The level of sero-conversion in children is virtually 100% with a decreased level in older patients. Systemic reactions are few with hypersensitivity being rare. Local reactions have been reported in 15% of vaccinations.

56:False 57:True 58:True 59:True 60:True 61:False
The sensitivity of cervical smears is fairly high at about 80% and the specificity is very high at over 98%, hence false positives rarely occur. The false-negative rate will be about 20% and can be dependent on the smear taker. CIN is really a histological term; dysplasia and dyskaryosis are seen by cytologists.

62:True 63:False 64:False 65:False 66:True 67:True
Psoriasis has a world-wide incidence of 2%. It does not scar and the lesions are rarely itchy. It can occur at any age but the peak incidence is in young adults. The rash is typically symmetrical, red and scaly with clearly defined borders. Although dithranol is the treatment of choice for plaque psoriasis it cannot be used on the face.

68:False 69:False 70:False 71:False 72:False
The care of epileptics still leaves a lot to be desired. All patients should be referred for assessment after their first fit. Idiopathic epilepsy is a dangerous diagnosis in those having a first convulsion after 25 years of age. Epilepsy is not an inherited condition in the majority of cases. Most GPs do not know all their epileptic patients and they do not conduct annual checks on them as a matter of routine.

73:False 74:True 75:True 76:False 77:False
PACT data is automatically sent to all GPs at level 1. Level 3 is available on request and can be requested by individual therapeutic groups. The prescribing unit is based on the number of patients on the list with an additional allowance of 0.3 + the number of patients over 65 years of age, in order to compensate for increased prescribing in the elderly. The Prescription Pricing Authority is alleged to have a high level of accuracy of the order of 99%. Data is based on what the chemist dispenses, so if he has to split a pack, the PACT data will include the full pack price.

78:True 79:True 80:True 81:False 82:True
Listeria is present in soft cheeses, pre-packed salads, salad creams and mayonnaise, uncooked and undercooked meats, poultry, paté, and unpasteurised milk. *Toxoplasma* is excreted in cat faeces and anything that

could be potentially contaminated by cats. Exercise is to be encouraged, but care with starting exercise regimes in pregnancy should be taken if exercise was not undertaken in the pre-pregnant state.

83:True 84:True 85:True 86:False 87:False
A high index of suspicion is needed with anybody who has travelled further than Western Europe, especially if they have lived 'rough'. Diarrhoeal illness must be thoroughly investigated, as for instance treating 'ulcerative colitis' with steroids can be fatal if it is really amoebiasis. Lassa fever presents as a sore throat and fever, malaria with a non-specific 'flu-like' illness in the early stages.

88:True 89:False 90:True 91:True 92:False
In one survey 1% of the population had suffered symptoms of post-traumatic stress disorder. They occur soon after the event and can be helped by early expression of feelings with a professional care worker. Individuals respond in different ways with a mixture of fears of annihilation, emotional problems and reactions provoked by a challenge to control. About 20–25% of those involved in a major disaster go on to develop a chronic disorder.

93:False 94:True 95:False 96:True 97:False
Episcleritis is usually a localised area of inflammation and is a self-limiting condition. Visual disorder in ophthalmic herpes may indicate corneal scarring. Corneal ulcers need referral or sight may be lost. Corneal abrasions are usually dealt with in general practice. Blocked tear ducts in children can be left until 9 months of age and referral then is not urgent.

98:True 99:True 100:True 101:False 102:True
Reye's syndrome is rare but important as early diagnosis and treatment improves prognosis. It is associated with a previous infection which is probably showing signs of resolution. Vomiting is typically profuse and the child becomes overactive, combative and irritable before becoming lethargic and then comatose with signs of cerebral irritation. Liver function is always disturbed although jaundice is rare. The peak incidence is 2 years. The association with aspirin ingestion has led to a decrease in the paediatric use of this drug and a consequential fall in incidence of the syndrome.

103:False 104:True 105:False 106:True 107:True
Only 15% of GPs have direct access to community hospitals. The average age of patients within these hospitals has risen because of a decrease in

maternity work. Care is cheaper in community hospitals. The workload of doctors in these hospitals is greater but so is the job satisfaction.

108:True 109:False 110:True 111:True 112:True
Propranolol and nifedipine both have negative inotropic actions and therefore may precipitate heart failure. The hypoglycaemic effect of glibenclamide is antagonised by thiazide diuretics. Spironolactone is a potassium conserving diuretic and frusemide causes loss of potassium from the body. NSAIDs all reduce platelet adhesiveness and potentiate the anticoagulation achieved with warfarin. Alcohol and antihistamines are both CNS depressants.

113:False 114:False 115:False 116:False 117:False 118:True
Ten per cent of elderly people have a positive rheumatoid factor with no evidence of an inflammatory joint disease. Morning stiffness takes more than 30 minutes to wear off; the metacarpophalangeal joints are usually involved symmetrically. The feet are also involved. Many patients with early rheumatoid arthritis will have a negative rheumatoid factor. Regular use of NSAIDs has no effect on disease progression; this requires a disease modifying drug.

119:True 120:False 121:True 122:True 123:False
Now replacing hysterectomy in many centres, this procedure is suitable for most patients except for those with malignant or pre-malignant conditions of the endometrium or those with active pelvic infection. The endometrium needs to be thinned pre-operatively with danazol. Day case surgery is increasing and at the most it requires an overnight stay. The ideal result is to cause complete amenorrhoea but a scanty loss is deemed acceptable.

124:True 125:True 126:True 127:False 128:False
Achilles tendon problems are a common source of injuries in sports enthusiasts. Common factors precipitating tendonitis are a high heel tab, a low heel, running on a hard surface or a sudden change of running surface. Local steroid injections are traditionally associated with an increased incidence of rupture. Rupture is best treated by repair than by immobilisation. Tendonitis is best treated initially by a heel raise and ultrasound combined with rest from the precipitating activity.

129:False 130:False 131:True 132:False 133:False
HIV-positive patients run a variable period before symptoms of the disease manifest themselves. The earliest sign is generalised

lymphadenopathy which heralds the commencement of AIDS-related complex. This may produce weight loss, night sweats, diarrhoea and fatigue. The diagnosis of 'full blown' AIDS proper depends upon the presence of opportunistic infection or neoplasm such as non-Hodgkin's lymphoma, Kaposi's sarcoma or *Pneumocystis* infection.

134:False 135:False 136:True 137:True 138:True
Innocent murmurs are typically systolic, sitting or deep inspiration makes an innocent murmur quieter. An innocent murmur is soft and there is no thrill, the ECG and chest X-ray are normal.

139:False 140:True 141:False 142:True 143:False
Mania is characterised by elevated mood, increased activity and self-important ideas, insight is lost. It is associated with episodes of profound depression which make the consequences of previous hypomanic behaviour even more difficult to live with.

144:True 145:False 146:False 147:False 148:True
Exposure to asbestos leads to an increase in lung cancer in both non smokers and smokers, asbestosis does not have to be present. Compounds formed in the manufacture of aniline dyes are associated with bladder cancer. Exposure to radon gas in miners was the first described occupational association with lung cancer.

149:True 150:True 151:True 152:False 153:True
Tinnitus is often the first symptom of Ménière's disease and may occur episodically long before the first full attack. The feeling of fullness in the ear often accompanies tinnitus in the acute attack and may become intense. Hearing tends to decrease with each attack. Nystagmus only occurs during the acute attack. If Rombergism is present it would indicate either other pathology or an emotional overlay.

154:False 155:False 156:True 157:True 158:True
Splenomegaly occurs in glandular fever but the spleen is soft and friable and not easily palpable. Carcinomatosis rarely causes an enlarged spleen, a nodular, enlarged liver is a more common finding. Massive splenomegaly is most commonly due to chronic myeloid leukaemia or myelofibrosis.

159:False 160:False 161:True 162:True 163:True
Consent of the husband or father of the baby is not required prior to a therapeutic termination of pregnancy. If the mother is under 16 years of age, the consent of her parents is not necessarily required, however, the

doctor would be well advised to consult a medical defence organisation. Form HSA2 is for emergency situations where only one doctor is available. Form HSA3 is for notification that an operation has taken place and is sent to the Department of Health.

164:False 165:True 166:True 167:False
Pompholyx affecting the soles and palms will be very itchy. Keratoderma blenorrhagica is the specific lesion seen in Reiter's syndrome. Pustular psoriasis can affect the hands and feet. Lichen planus characteristically affects the mouth with erosive lesions or 'cotton wool' patches.

168:True 169:True 170:True 171:True 172:True
Anticoagulant therapy monitoring can suddenly produce results that fluctuate from an apparently stable situation. Often no reason can be found, however it is worth reviewing the intercurrent medication and if necessary looking for signs and symptoms of illness.

173:True 174:True 175:True 176:True 177:True
Smoking has an immunosuppressant effect and decreases the immune response. Therefore diseases such as farmer's lung and ulcerative colitis are reduced. Nicotine may affect dopaminergic activity in the brain and therefore the incidence of Parkinson's disease and Alzheimer's disease is reduced. Smoking reduces the incidence of circulating oestrogen levels and there is a lower incidence of dysmenorrhoea, uterine fibroids and endometriosis.

178:False 179:False 180:True 181:True 182:True
The incidence of carcinoma of the oesophagus is rising, possibly due to the increased ingestion of nitrosamines and alcohol. The prognosis is poor and especially worse for adenocarcinoma. The most common presenting symptoms are dysphagia for solids only and weight loss.

183:True 184:False 185:True 186:True
Psychological factors are of great importance in the management of chronic pain. It is important that the general practitioner appreciates that fear, anxiety and social and physical isolation increase the perception of pain. Also the patients personality type affects the overall comprehension of the pain. Placebo affects are great and this needs to be taken into account when gauging the response to therapy.

187:True 188:True 189:False 190:True 191:True
Beta-sympathomimetics, anticholinergics and sodium cromoglycate all have proven efficacy when given via a nebuliser. Beclomethasone is available but efficacy is not proven. Theophyllines are oral or injectable preparations.

192:True 193:True 194:False 195:False 196:True
Diverticular disease is common and often asymptomatic, Rectal bleeding is a frequent presentation and does not usually indicate underlying malignancy. The best treatment is non-fermentable fibre of which coarse wheat bran is the most effective. Fistula can occur and may cause pneumaturia if connecting with the bladder.

197:False 198:False 199:True 200:False 201:False
There is a 'pecking' order of relatives from husband or wife down to nephews and nieces. The majority of admissions are under Section 2. Section 4 should rarely be used except for extreme emergencies. Only a relative or an approved social worker can make an application for admission. Sexual deviancy, alcoholism and drug abuse are not in themselves grounds for admission. Section 139 protects doctors employing the act from legal retribution if they are over-enthusiastic.

202:False 203:False 204:False 205:False 206:False
There is no relationship between the tolerance to adverse and to therapeutic effects. Tolerance may develop in less than 48 hours after the initiation of treatment, but is rapidly abolished once there is a nitrate free period. There is no difference between the various preparations quoted in the question, what is important is the length of time above the therapeutic level likely to cause tolerance in any one particular patient.

207:False 208:False 209:False 210:True 211:True
Testicular torsion has a peak incidence at 12–18 years, not epididymitis. Iliac fossa pain is again typical of testicular torsion. In epididymitis the scrotal contents rapidly swell due to enlargement of epididymal structures. High-frequency B mode ultrasound is able to differentiate between torsion and epididymitis. Chlamydial infection is associated with non-specific urethritis.

212:True 213:False 214:True 215:True 216:True
The causes of agitation in the elderly are legion. The GP should be wary of all drug therapy especially if recently introduced but also if used for many years. Depressive illness may be the cause of agitation and it could

be worsened by benzodiazepines. Silent infarcts are common and vigilance is needed if they are to be detected. A withdrawn patient may not drink and in warm weather can soon become dehydrated leading to agitation.

217:False 218:False 219:False 220:False 221:True 222:True
Cholera immunisation is no longer indicated for travellers to any country. Yellow fever immunisation lasts for 10 years. Rabies vaccine is given into the deltoid muscle usually; the antibody response is reduced if given into the gluteal muscle. Gamma globulin interferes with responses to live vaccines and is normally given shortly before travel. Reactions to the typhoid vaccine are more common after the age of 35 years when it should be avoided if possible.

223:True 224:True 225:False 226:False 227:True
'Frozen shoulder' is a generic term encompassing a variety of conditions that are not always clinically distinguishable. It usually runs a chronic course of about 2 years then recovers completely. Local tenderness over the various muscles, e.g. supraspinatus, infraspinatus or biceps tendon reflects the site of the lesion accurately. Immobilisation may lead to permanent restriction of movement and exercise should be encouraged. The condition may be precipitated by unusual exertion such as home decorating and the pain is often worse at night.

228:False 229:True 230:True 231:True 232:False
In the UK, sarcoid is the most common cause of hilar lymphadenopathy in patients over 15 years of age. In lymphoma the glands may be mediastinal rather than hilar. Hilar glands due to tubercle are commoner in children but the incidence is increasing in adults especially in large cities.

233:False 234:False 235:True 236:False 237:False
Atypia is often due to human papilloma virus, however a single abnormal smear does not correlate well with the presence of CIN. However, if two or three smears show atypia, colposcopy should be performed. If there is evidence of genital warts a smear should be taken annually until negative smears have occurred on five successive occasions. Cervical erosions may bleed on touch during taking the smear but they do not show any typical abnormality. Carcinoma of the cervix is usually diagnosed on clinical history and appearance of the cervix.

238:True 239:False 240:False 241:False 242:True
Irritant contact dermatitis as contrasted with allergic contact dermatitis does not require the patient to have been exposed previously. The rash

typically develops within 24 hours as opposed to 2–4 days for allergy. The severity of the rash depends on the amount of irritant used, whereas in allergic conjunctivitis only a small quantity can produce a severe reaction. Reactivation at other sites does not occur in irritant conjunctivitis.

243:True 244:True 245:True 246:False 247:False
With prolonged use it is possible to develop anti-calcitonin antibodies. Pagetic bone is highly vascular and a 'steal' syndrome can occur leading to high output cardiac failure. Bone overgrowth can lead to deafness when foramina in the skull close. Ten per cent of patients with the disease will have a normal alkaline phosphatase prior to the commencement of treatment.

248:True 249:False 250:True 251:True 252:True
Toddler diarrhoea is common, the child passes several loose stools per day with undigested food (typically carrots and peas) in the stools. There is never failure to thrive unless other pathology is present. If it occurs, further investigation is necessary. Sometimes, it occurs after an acute infective illness and especially in these patients a milk free diet is helpful. Loperamide is of some use in cases which are proving to be intractable and in which there is no other cause.

253:False 254:True 255:True 256:False 257:True
Only about one-third of patients on benzodiazepines will become dependent on their drug. The first sign of dependency is often rebound sleep disturbance which has been shown to occur after one week in some people. The loss of appetite which occurs can often be severe enough to cause weight loss. More severe symptoms include auditory and visual hallucinations. Beta-blockers have been shown to help some patients who are having problems with stopping their drugs.

258:False 259:False 260:False 261:False 262:True
Scientific and medical papers quote a lot of statistics and it is a good idea to have a rudimentary knowledge of some of the concepts. The Null hypothesis is concerned with results that could occur by chance. The Student's '*t*' test is of use in small groups of data. Spearman's rank correlation is used when comparing rank correlated groups of data.

263:False 264:True 265:False 266:True 267:False
The cap, contraceptive diaphragm, should be left *in situ* for 6 hours after intercourse to be truly effective. Variations in size of the patient can make

it ineffective because of poor fitting, similarly if a prolapse is present the seal will not be adequate. The frequency of replacement depends upon usage, however they should be changed annually because the rubber may perish. All available caps quoted in the drug tariff are made from rubber.

268:True 269:False 270:True 271:True 272:False
Hyoscine (Scopoderm) is available as a transdermal patch, the effect of which lasts for 72 hours. Domperidone is available as syrup, tablets and suppositories; the injection was withdrawn because of an association with cardiac arrhthymias. Cinnarizine (Stugeron) is available over the counter from the pharmacist and is effective for travel sickness. Prochlorperazine is associated with parkinsonian side-effects, hypotension and occasionally acute dystonic reactions. Finally, chlorpromazine has a very weak anti-emetic effect and should not be used for this purpose.

273:False 274:True 275:True 276:True 277:False
DLA is not taxed or means-tested. It is a benefit given to people with care or mobility needs and paid at different rates depending on whether there are day and/or night time needs. The benefit is normally paid after a decision based on self-assessment which looks at functional requirements.

278:True 279:False 280:False 281:True 282:True
Febrile convulsions typically occur between 6 months and 6 years of age. There is no social class difference and there is no difference in the sex incidence. Prolonged fits are associated with residual neurological deficit. There is a 15% chance of a child having febrile convulsions if a first-degree relative has had them. In the normal population the risk is quoted as 7%.

283:True 284:False 285:False 286:False 287:False
Sclerotherapy gives good short term results but high saphenous ligation with multiple avulsions is the mainstay of treatment. After treatment, compression is only needed for about 1 week and walking should commence on the day of surgery. The majority of patients only need one week away from work.

288:True 289:False 290:False 291:False 292:True
In pregnancy about one-third of patients will show an increase in fit frequency. Seventy per cent of those with migraine have been shown to improve. Multiple sclerosis is rarely affected by the pregnancy but

relapses are common in the puerperium. Asthma appears to be unaffected. Sickle cell disease has a high mortality and needs skilled management.

293:True 294:False 295:True 296:False 297:True
Before replacing soft lenses in an eye which has been stained with fluorescein it must be thoroughly irrigated with saline. Pilocarpine characteristically causes tight constriction of the pupils. Oxybuprocaine is a local anaesthetic, tropicamide is a short acting drug which dilates the pupils and is useful in diabetic clinics. The local irritation caused by adrenaline is avoided by giving it as a pro-drug.

298:True 299:False 300:False 301:True 302:True
The syndrome of acute inflammatory polyneuropathy is an acute peripheral demyelinating condition which has a rapid onset. Motor symptoms predominate and paralysis may be profound requiring assisted ventilation. The majority of cases make a satisfactory recovery and usually remain free of problems.

303:True 304:True 305:True 306:True 307:True
Good control of diabetes pre-conceptually and during the first trimester will decrease the incidence of congenital abnormalities. Pre-term labour is more common and babies born early are at a greater risk of Respiratory Distress Syndrome than babies of equivalent gestation born to non-diabetic mothers. There is an unexplained incidence of fetal death after 40 weeks' gestation and pregnancies are usually induced no later than term.

308:True 309:True 310:False 311:True 312:True
Tuberculosis is possible but is more common at a younger age. Perthes' disease has a peak incidence at 6–8 years and is more common in boys than in girls. Slipped upper femoral epiphysis is typically pre-pubertal. Septic arthritis would be accompanied by pyrexia and malaise. Non-accidental injury is possible but is more common in those under 3 years old.

313:False 314:False 315:True 316:False 317:True
With erythema multiforme, there is usually a precipitating cause either a viral infection, bacterial infection or drug eruption. The rash is characteristic with round papules or blisters made up of rings of different colours (target or iris lesions). If mucous membranes are involved this is known as the Stevens–Johnson syndrome and carries a significant mortality. Recurrent episodes are common especially if it follows a *Herpes simplex* infection.

318:True 319:False 320:True 321:False 322:False
The MRFIT study in North America established that cholesterol was a risk factor and other studies have shown that decreasing serum cholesterol by 10% decreases cardiovascular mortality. However, no study has shown a decrease in overall mortality. One study showed that a very low cholesterol was associated with an increased risk of malignancy especially carcinoma of the colon. Good dietary control following counselling will decrease the level of cholesterol on average by 10–15%. The various risk factors are additive and therefore people who smoke and/or have a raised blood pressure are probably more in need of screening.

323:True 324:True 325:True 326:False 327:False
Low-dose aspirin is now very widely prescribed but it is not without side-effects both in the short term and the long term. After a myocardial infarction studies have shown a significant decrease in long term mortality if given at a dose of 150 mg for one month. In the treatment of venous thrombosis it does not appear to have a role, however it may have a place in prevention of thrombosis. It has no role in the primary prevention of cerebrovascular disease and may even increase the risk of cerebral haemorrhage.

328:True 329:False 330:True 331:True 332:False 333:True
Proton pump inhibitors can cause severe headache and diarrhoea. Gynaecomastia can result but is less common than after H_2-antagonist treatment. It is best to avoid proton pump inhibitors in pregnancy and breast feeding.

334:False 335:True 336:True 337:True
The diagnosis of child abuse is fraught with difficulties, however there are certain pointers, such as an implausible explanation for the injuries, previous abuse or abuse in siblings. The children are usually less than 3 years of age (contrasting with sexual abuse which may well continue into adolescence).

338:True 339:True 340:False 341:True 342:True
Baldness is usually physiological, however it may be associated with local disease of the scalp such as seborrhoeic eczema, tinea capitis, or simply hair pulling (trichotillomania). Minoxidil topically applied twice daily is effective in some people in treating male pattern baldness. However, hair regrowth stops and reverses within 3 months of cessation of therapy. Endocrine causes such as pituitary or adrenal tumours can cause hirsutism and hair loss. Hormone replacement treatment is associated with excessive hair loss in some patients.

343:False 344:False 345:True 346:False
Stress and urgency incontinence require different treatments and are often confused. Stress incontinence is typically associated with leaking of urine on coughing, sneezing or laughter, leaking on playing sport or sudden movement. Urgency incontinence or detrusor instability is more likely with a history of frequency of six or more times per day and three or more times at night, leaking at night and having to rush to the toilet. Dribbling is a symptom of overflow incontinence.

347:True 348:False 349:False
The statement of fees and allowances are negotiated by the GMSC and government, there needs to be no legislative change to amend these under the NHS regulations.

350:False 351:False 352:True 353:True
This allowance replaces and extends the benefits that were previously available as the attendance allowance and the mobility allowance. The disability should have arisen prior to the age of 65 years of age. It is paid after a qualifying period of 3 months (the attendance allowance previously was 6 months). It is a tax free allowance and is not means-tested.

354:False 355:False 356:False 357:False
There is no evidence that restriction of tea, coffee or cola decreases symptoms of PMS. An hourly starch diet may relieve symptoms in some patients. Fertility is not affected. About 20–40% of women consult their doctor at least once with symptoms of the condition. Approximately 150 different symptoms have been attributed to PMS. Suppression of ovulation by using either high dose oestrogen patches or the oral contraceptive does give a small reduction in symptoms in some patients but conversely some women report a worsening of symptoms.

358:False 359:False 360:True 361:False 362:False
The most likely effect of most of these is one of mild gastrointestinal upset. If in doubt always check with the local poisons information centre.

363:False 364:True 365:True 366:True 367:False 368:False
Grapefruit contains 0.5 g of fibre per 100 g, a banana has six times this amount. Spinach is always quoted as a good source of iron, it has 4 mg/100 g and cornflakes 7 mg/100 g. People on diets often stop eating bread and eat crispbread instead, 100 g of rye crispbread has 320 kcal, the equivalent of wholemeal bread 220 kcal. Green peppers are very rich in vitamin C with 100 mg/100 g (compare with oranges' 40 mg/100 g). There is no

significant difference between red and white wines each has 65–70 kcal/100 g. Beer contains a small amount of niacin (0.3 mg/100 g) but no other vitamin of the B complex.

369:True 370:True 371:True 372:True 373:False
Carbon monoxide poisoning accounts for about 1000 deaths per year in England and Wales. Faulty appliances and blocked vents are the usual cause. The initial symptom is often a dull pounding headache very like a hangover, mental apathy, nausea, and dizziness are also typical symptoms. If the exposure continues, convulsions, coma and respiratory distress follow. The skin typically becomes pink and cyanosis does not occur. The toxic effects are usually reversed within 12 hours of removal from the source of the carbon monoxide.

374:False 375:True 376:False 377:False 378:False
Azoospermia or oligospermia can be caused by the inadvertent use of spermicides but once simple causes have been excluded little hope can be given that a treatable cause will be found. If FSH levels are raised in a patient with small firm testicles further investigation is necessary especially to exclude a chromosomal abnormality such as Klinefelter's syndrome. By careful investigation a cause for the condition can be identified in about two-thirds of cases but only in a very few cases can a treatment be instituted which will lead to a successful outcome.

379:True 380:True 381:False 382:True 383:False
Oral decongestants are taken usually as over-the-counter remedies and may contain one or all of the following, paracetamol, phenylpropanolamine, phenylephrine, pseudoephedrine, antihistamine. They need to be used with caution in a variety of conditions. They can induce a hypertensive crisis especially in people taking non-selective beta-blockers. They stimulate the heart and cause an increase in oxygen demand and therefore should not be used in patients with ischaemic heart disease and hypertension. They can induce arrhythmias especially in hyperthyroidism and can induce a rise in blood glucose and should not be used in diabetics.

384:False 385:False 386:True 387:False 388:False 389:True 390:True
There is a decreased incidence of ischaemic heart disease in Down's syndrome; the syndrome is due to trisomy 21. Heart defects are commonly seen especially atrioventricular canal defects and patent ductus arteriosus. Hypothyroidism and glue ear with hearing impairment are more commonly seen than in the general population.

391:True 392:False 393:False 394:True 395:False
In 1992 notifications increased for the first time for many years, however there is still a significant under-reporting of the disease which has been estimated as about 25%. In the USA new cases have increased dramatically. Drug-resistant strains do occur but 95% of isolates are sensitive to all standard drugs (isoniazid, rifampicin, ethambutol, and streptomycin). Although trials in some parts of the world have shown BCG to be ineffective, in Great Britain there is overwhelming evidence for its efficacy. The homeless are significantly at risk as are patients with AIDS, however in Great Britain the number of such patients developing tuberculosis is approximately 5%.

396:True 397:True 398:True 399:False 400:True
In Great Britain and Scandinavia chronic low blood pressure has been dismissed as of no consequence. Conversely in the continental countries, especially France and Germany, it is often treated more seriously than raised blood pressure. Studies, some published in the BMJ have highlighted the fact that patients with the condition do have a significant morbidity and a perceived feeling of being unwell. The studies do not show if elevation of the blood pressure causes the symptoms described to disappear.

PRACTICE PAPER 5 — SECTION 2: EMQs ANSWERS

Income
1:C 2:D 3:F 4:F 5:D 6:F 7:B 8:B

Childhood development
9:I 10:E 11:C 12:B 13:F 14:G 15:E

Statistics
16:6 17:1 18:5

Benefits
19:D 20:H 21:B 22:A 23:C 24:E

Screening
25:G 26:A 27:J 28:K 29:B 30:H

Mental Health Act
31:E 32:B 33:C 34:G 35:D

Voluntary bodies
36:G 37:F 38:E 39:A 40:B 41:C 42:H

Literature
43:C 44:G 45:F 46:E 47:C 48:B

Infectious diseases
49:A 50:E 51:D 52:E 53:B 54:C

Drugs used in hypertension
55:C 56:A 57:C 58:A 59:C

Study types
60:B 61:A 62:E 63:F 64:G 65:D 66:I

Minor surgery
67:D 68:A 69:C 70:E 71:E 72:B

Thrombolytic trials
73:C 74:A 75:B 76:D 77:F

Back pain
78:B 79:E 80:A 81:C

Prostate problems
82:B 83:C 84:A

Bowel disorders
85:D 86:E 87:C 88:A 89:B

Hypertension trials
90:A 91:E 92:C 93:B 94:B

Certificates
95:A 96:B 97:E 98:C 99:D 100:A

REVISION INDEX